# A Humanistic Framework for Supporting Autistic Children and Young People



This book calls for a fundamental re-examination of how education, health, and care systems respond to autistic children and young people. Rather than focusing on how to manage behaviour or address perceived deficits, it shows how the practical application of acceptance can be a transformative way to support autistic children more effectively.

The act of acceptance is presented not as a passive attitude but as something you actively do. Something that reshapes environments, relationships, and expectations. When acceptance is applied deliberately and consistently, it reduces anxiety, builds psychological safety, and creates the conditions in which autistic children can engage, communicate, and learn without coercion.

Drawing from real-world practice and lived experience, this book offers a clear, unified framework for acceptance-based support that can be quickly applied in your work. This solution-focused guide includes detailed case studies, reflective insights, and clear strategies to help you move from theory to practice. It demonstrates how acceptance can be a purposeful, structured, and effective tool in mental health, education, at-home, and community settings. Yorke considers what happens when acceptance moves from an idea to an active practice, transforming environments, restoring psychological safety, and enabling autistic children to belong without feeling compelled to change themselves, revealing the wonder and the power of acceptance.

Written for educators, professionals, policymakers, service providers, and those with lived experience, this book offers a practical alternative to traditional autism support models.

**Aaron Yorke** is a qualified SEND teacher and autism specialist supporting schools, families, and educational settings. He is the founder of Accepting Behaviour Ltd, an independent organisation dedicated to supporting autistic children and young people who cannot access traditional education. Aaron is also the creator of the Accept Approach and the Acceptance-Based Curriculum. Through his work, he supports professionals and families to move towards acceptance-based, child-led approaches that prioritise psychological safety, autonomy, and meaningful engagement in learning.

To my beautiful wife, Jayne. Thank you for always believing in me, especially through all the times when I have struggled to believe in myself.

# A Humanistic Framework for Supporting Autistic Children and Young People

## An Introduction to the Accept Approach

Aaron Yorke

Routledge
Taylor & Francis Group
LONDON AND NEW YORK

Cover image: Amtitus via Getty Images

First published 2027
by Routledge
4 Park Square, Milton Park, Abingdon, Oxon OX14 4RN

and by Routledge
605 Third Avenue, New York, NY 10158

*Routledge is an imprint of the Taylor & Francis Group, an informa business*



*British Library Cataloguing-in-Publication Data*
A catalogue record for this book is available from the British Library

*Library of Congress Cataloging-in-Publication Data*
Names: Yorke, Aaron author
Title: A humanistic framework for supporting autistic children and young people : an introduction to the Accept Approach / Aaron Yorke.
Description: Abingdon, Oxon ; New York, NY : Routledge, 2026. | Includes bibliographical references and index.
Identifiers: LCCN 2026015151 (print) | LCCN 2026015152 (ebook) | ISBN 9781041167204 hardback | ISBN 9781041167136 paperback | ISBN 9781003686064 ebook
Subjects: LCSH: Autistic children | Autistic children—Services for | Autistic children—Care | Children with autism spectrum disorders | Autistic children—Education | Autistic children—Psychology
Classification: LCC RJ506.A9 Y65 2026 (print) | LCC RJ506.A9 (ebook)
LC record available at https://lccn.loc.gov/2026015151
LC ebook record available at https://lccn.loc.gov/2026015152

ISBN: 978-1-041-16720-4 (hbk)
ISBN: 978-1-041-16713-6 (pbk)
ISBN: 978-1-003-68606-4 (ebk)

DOI: 10.4324/9781003686064

Typeset in Times New Roman
by Apex CoVantage, LLC

Access the Support Material: www.routledge.com/9781041167136

**AI Declaration**

The research, interpretation, and writing in this book are the author's own work. During the research process, digital tools (OpenAI, GPT 5.3) helped with literature searches and assisted with drafting and editing. All academic sources cited were thoroughly reviewed and verified by the author, and all concepts, arguments, interpretations, and case studies are the author's original work. The ACCEPT Approach™ and the Acceptance-Based Curriculum™ are the author's original contributions, developed through professional practice, research, and previous publications.

# Contents

# Preface

Since the pioneering British psychiatrist, Lorna Wing,[1] raised her concerns about the lack of understanding and support for autistic children back in the 1960s,[2] not much has changed. Support is still lacking, still damaging, and still heading in the wrong direction. I experienced this firsthand when entering the world of education as a young psychology graduate. I was set on pursuing a career as a special educational needs teacher, and at the time, I genuinely believed I could make a difference. I aspired to be an inspirational teacher, breaking down barriers and supporting students who needed a different way of learning. Sadly, it did not take long to realise just how far that was from reality for many of the children I taught.

Around the time I qualified as a teacher, my first child was diagnosed autistic, and began struggling in school, requiring extra support and specialist provision. I quickly found myself on both sides of the battle. On one side, I was a parent fighting for support, and on the other, an educator trying to provide it. I quickly found myself struggling in both, realising that the support was just not there, at least, not the kind that truly met the needs of my child and the children I taught.

I grew up as a child in the '80s, and school did not work for me. I could never concentrate in class and would skip lessons whenever I could. I was often outside the head teacher's office in trouble for being disruptive or for not listening in lessons. At the age of 14, I was permanently expelled from school, losing all hope of ever making anything of my life. I just presumed I was one of those wasted individuals, so in the aftermath of being dropped from school, I developed specific skills to try to protect myself. I learned to act like I didn't care and focused as much as I could on hating myself and the world around me, accepting my fate as a lost cause who would never make anything of himself.

During my teenage years, my parents divorced, which, back then, was not as common as it is today. My whole world came crashing down on me, and my mental health deteriorated at a fast pace. I don't remember much from that time, just being passed from GPs to psychiatrists, to psychologists, to social workers, with no one knowing what was "wrong" with me, or how to help me. My panic attacks, my intrusive thoughts, and my obsessions dominated my daily life, and it felt like there was no escape. Eventually, the mental health system also wrote me off, just like education did. I was forgotten like so many kids, placed on the teenage delinquent pile of failed youth, with no plan or future ahead. I don't think I would have survived my teenage years if it weren't for the one person who never gave up on me. My mother.

When everyone wrote me off, she fought for me every step of the way. She was my place of safety, showing me that I had value *without* judgement. When everyone else had written me off, she accepted me no matter how I behaved or what I was going through. My mother taught me the importance of psychological safety and self-acceptance through her unconditional love. She stood by me, telling me that my struggles were "not my fault". She was the first person to demonstrate to me "unconditional positive regard".

I survived my teenage years and entered my 20s still much the same. My mental health struggles had a stronghold over me, and I presumed this was just *who I was*. Still, my life guided me to places I never would have expected, especially when I found out I was going to be a dad in my early 20s. This realisation transformed my outlook entirely. I finally found a purpose and meaning, committing myself to being the best father I could be. However, I was unsure how to achieve this, so I decided that securing a good job might be a good starting point, which led me back to the education system to find a way forward. I figured I was older, so maybe things would be different this time around.

The study of psychology seemed a good choice, as I had always been fascinated by the concept of human behaviour and why we act the way we do. I remember flipping through a university book and noticing a psychology degree course. I wondered whether studying human behaviour might help me understand what was actually "wrong" with me and, hopefully, land a good job in the process. So I completed an adult learning access course, paving the way for me to enrol in a degree programme, which, looking back, were some of the best days of my life. During this time, I found that I really enjoyed studying, especially when I discovered the peaceful freedom found in a quiet library, where I often got absorbed in reading old journals by great thinkers in psychology. I had discovered something about myself that had been overlooked during my school years: that I could learn about what interested me in my own way and at my own pace.

The concept of acceptance was first shown to me during a lecture on humanistic psychology. I remember a sense of connection. The ideas made complete sense. Up to that point, I had not managed to engage well with the other great thinkers in psychology. Freud confused me with his endless riddles and pathological views of human behaviour. B.F. Skinner comparing us to rats and pigeons never sat well with me. While those around seemed impressed by the cognitive and behaviouristic models that dominated our studies, I struggled to connect with many of the traditional psychological ideas.

Take, for example, the view that we can learn or unlearn behaviour. I could not see how my debilitating panic attacks were my choice, or how my obsessive thoughts were just wrong thinking I had picked up along the way. I did not choose to be different. I did not choose to have my "noisy brain". During some time in therapy, I recall being encouraged to pull on an elastic band whenever I had an obsessive thought, to teach my brain to *stop* thinking them. But I had too many thoughts, and trying to just "flick" them away only made my wrist bleed. I was also encouraged to use cognitive behavioural methods to "challenge" my thoughts, but again, they never went away; in fact, just like the elastic band, all these strategies did was increase my obsessions and made the thoughts worse.

Back then, I was searching for basic *needs* to be met, but I just didn't realise it. I did not want to be "fixed" or "cured" from a broken mind; I wanted to feel accepted, to belong to something, to feel safe and loved and to be able to offer all that to my own child. I was in a process that humanistic psychologist Abraham Maslow described as aiming for *self-actualisation*. I was striving to build a life of purpose, stability, and meaning, and to do so, I needed my basic needs met so I could reach the person I have always strived to be. That journey, I am still on today. Still searching for meaning and purpose, and for a place where I can truly accept myself *completely*.

When exploring humanistic psychology, I was instantly drawn to the idea that all people, when truly accepted for who they are, have an innate tendency towards growth, fulfilment, and self-actualisation, a concept Carl Rogers called *the actualising tendency*. It felt like he was speaking directly to me when he said,

> "*The curious paradox is that when I accept myself just as I am, then I can change*".[3]

That is precisely what I have always strived for: to accept myself, unconditionally. I have never desired worldly success, a lot of money, and loads of friends; I have only ever wanted to accept myself for who I am, *warts and all*. Back then, in my 20s, I was convinced that by learning how to accept myself, my mental health issues would fade away, and I could learn to be happy or at least content with who I was, flawed and imperfect, yet accepted just the way my mother accepted me. Maslow and Rogers emphasised that the most important thing we can do for a person is to help them experience self-acceptance, without judgement or conditions. Something that I do not see existing today, for many autistic children. I do not see that they have the option to discover their self-worth; acceptance only seems to exist in a conditional form.

As a young graduate, I was fascinated by the psychology and humanistic views on education, which led me to pursue a career as a teacher. I wanted to put the theories into practice. It made complete sense to me when Rogers said, "*The more the teacher tries to control, the more he undermines the student's ability to learn*".[4] That was the type of teacher I wanted to be: someone who understood that my role was not to be the all-knowing adult who controls the learning, but to facilitate it. I wanted to be a teacher who helped students explore their learning on their own terms and at their own pace.

During my early years as a special needs teacher, I was drawn to specialise in autism. So I took to studying again and completed an additional postgraduate certificate from the University of Sheffield, where I was fortunate to be taught by

Professor Luke Beardon. This course inspired me further to implement humanistic principles in my classroom and teaching role. However, I quickly learned that the curriculum lacked the capacity to engage my students with the idea of self-acceptance; instead, it focused more on encouraging children to conform. The idea that a child could *be*, without correction or control, seemed impossible.

Around about eight years into my career as a specialist teacher, I began to experience severe panic attacks that appeared out of nowhere, leading to a nervous breakdown. Again, I found myself in a psychiatrist's room, trying to find out what was *wrong* with me. Just like when I was a teenager, they couldn't find anything apart from the *usual* depression and anxiety. Until one psychiatrist requested that I be assessed for autism. During those years, adults were not commonly assessed by the NHS for autism, so they had to bring in a child paediatrician who was trained in diagnosing adults. I was finally assessed and diagnosed autistic with attention deficit hyperactivity disorder (ADHD).

I tried to return to teaching but was again held back by the constraints of the education system. So I chose to leave teaching completely and create a different route to helping autistic children. Using my teaching skills and the continued desire to support autistic children, I became a local authority autism advisor, supporting autistic children and young people in schools. I felt that by doing this, I could finally make a meaningful difference. My role was to work alongside educators and professionals to better support autistic children in school. I soon found myself supporting the children who couldn't sit still in lessons, who lashed out in the playground, who would run out of class, and who could no longer attend school. I was supporting children just like me, that anxious boy who could not cope, and who was misunderstood. During my time as an autism advisor, I met many children like me, and they, too, were lost in the education system, with no one knowing how to help them. I thought this was my chance to change *their* story.

Over the years, I trained hundreds of parents, families, teachers, and other professionals, showing them how to apply acceptance to support their autistic children and young people more effectively. I attempted to spread the message that it is not the children who need to change, but the environments they are in. I attempted to teach educators to identify unmet needs and then apply acceptance to support autistic children better, especially when nothing else had worked. Some embraced it. Others dismissed it.

Sadly, much like my time as a specialist teacher, I found that working as an autism advisor for a local authority was an uphill struggle, battling against a broader system that was also failing many autistic children. After many years as an autism advisor, I decided to leave and set up Accepting Behaviour Ltd.[5] Now, alongside my wife, Jayne, we lead a team of specialist tutors across the West Midlands, UK, supporting autistic children and young people through acceptance-based support.

In 2019, I began documenting our work and researching how acceptance-based support could help engage autistic children whom nobody else had been able to reach. I developed the ACCEPT Approach in 2021 and the Acceptance-Based Curriculum in 2023, as practical approaches to support autistic students, and I began publishing my research.

My life experiences, professional career, and research into acceptance-based support have led me to write *A Humanistic Framework for Supporting Autistic Children and Young People*, in which I further explore the impact of acceptance-based support within both mental health and education systems for autistic children and young people. Sharing real-life experiences, including my own, and my research, I show how acceptance can go beyond theory to become a practical support method that can significantly improve the lives of autistic children and young people.

This book highlights the significance of seeing every autistic child as a whole person. It encourages the humanistic principles of psychological safety, unconditional positive regard, and self-actualisation within environments that promote safety, belonging, trust, and growth. It is my hope that acceptance-based support will become more than just an optimistic idea. That it will be recognised as a new practical, evidence-based model that can effectively support autistic children and young people who need something different.

## Notes

1 Wing, L. (1976). *Autistic Children: A Guide for Parents*. London: Constable.
2 Gillberg, C. (2015). Lorna Wing OBE, MD, FRCPsych Formerly Psychiatrist and Physician, Social Psychiatry Unit, Institute of Psychiatry, King's College London, Co-Founder of the UK National Autistic Society. *BJPsych Bulletin*, February, 39(1), pp. 52–53. https://doi.org/10.1192/pb.bp.114.048900. PMCID: PMC4495836.
3 Rogers, C.R. (1961). *On Becoming a Person: A Therapist's View of Psychotherapy*. Boston, MA: Houghton Mifflin.
4 Rogers, C.R. (1959). A Theory of Therapy, Personality, and Interpersonal Relationships as Developed in the Client-Centered Framework. In S. Koch (Ed.), *Psychology: A Study of a Science. Vol. 3: Formulations of the Person and the Social Context* (pp. 184–256). New York: McGraw-Hill.
5 **Accepting Behaviour Ltd was set up Aaron and Jayne Yorke in 2019. We are an education alternative provider** that supports autistic students (who have disengaged from other educational settings) through acceptance-based support and **interest-led learning**. students. We are a growing team of specialist tutors, based in Worcestershire, UK, creating **meaningful learning** experiences tailored to each child's interests and needs. **For more info please www.acceptingbehaviour.com**.

# Introduction

"You are a lot like Marmite". Something a colleague once told me as we discussed my ideas on acceptance. I have only tried Marmite once. I didn't like it. I am more of a lime-flavoured marmalade kind of person. For over two decades, I have explored and researched how acceptance can support autistic children and young people in their everyday lives. Driven by the need for change, I set up a team of specialist educators and tutors supporting autistic children and young people in education.[1] Now, thousands of parents and professionals have joined our expanding online community, training programs, and webinars. With so many people embracing acceptance-based support, I was inspired to write this book, in the hope that it will reach a wider audience and help many more autistic children and their families thrive in education and in their broader lives.

This book is an encouragement for change. I have worked in education, supporting autistic children and young people for over 20 years, but I had to walk away. I was burnt out, not from supporting children, but from trying to survive a system that kept failing them. I left, unsure of what would happen. Thankfully, it was the right decision. Soon after leaving the council, I developed a fresh perspective on how we could better support autistic children and young people through *acceptance-based support.*

In the UK, concern is increasing that current support systems are insufficient for autistic children and young people. The economic cost in the UK of supporting autism treatment and care is astounding, estimated to be over £32 billion per year.[2] Despite these financial offerings, nothing has really changed. We are still seeing autistic children and their families failed by systems deemed unfit for purpose,[3] with autistic people bearing the brunt of these broken systems across UK society.[4] Even the United Nations have issued a stark warning to the UK, stating they are concerned that "*the situation of children with disabilities, including the lack of coordinated, age-appropriate services, particularly in education, health and rehabilitation*".[5]

Inspired by two decades of professional practice, shaped by my roles as a specialist teacher, a local authority autism advisor, and an independent autism consultant, I have developed a way to support autistic children, embedded in the principles of humanistic psychology, offering a practical alternative to traditional approaches,

DOI: 10.4324/9781003686064-1

challenging the outdated systems and deficit-based models of learning, providing professionals, parents, policymakers, and service providers with a clear framework to truly understanding and supporting autistic children and young people, not by changing who they are, but by meeting them where they are, empowering their voice, and building trust through the act of acceptance.

Autistic children and young people in the UK face many challenges because of a lack of understanding of their needs. Recognised as a lifelong neurodevelopmental disability, autism is now believed to impact 1 in 100 people living in the UK.[6] Although others suggest these numbers could be much higher, with one study suggesting 1 in 57 children is more likely.[7] Whatever the exact number is, it is clear that too many children are being let down. Despite all that has been done in an attempt to help over the past 25 years, there still exists a great divide between being aware of autism and actually understanding it to the level needed to make real change.

When I began supporting autistic children and young people two decades ago, I was confident that my training and strategies would work if I applied them in the classroom and in homes. I understood all the guidance frameworks and the standard support pathways required for children with SEND in schools, and I truly believed that, as a SEND teacher, I could make a difference. Sadly, it didn't take me long to realise it was not so simple.

I found I was working with autistic children and young people who did not respond to any of the strategies or guidance I had been trained in. The children I was working with became completely overwhelmed by even the simplest of activities. They would shut down whenever expectations or demands were placed on them. They would run out of class, hide under tables, or fall to the floor when something was asked of them. I was working with children and young people who would swear and throw chairs across rooms. They would stop going to school and hide in their rooms. Not eating and not washing. I was supporting children who were disengaged from a world that was just too much for them to cope with.

As an autism advisor for a local authority, I recognised that these children and young people did not fit into the standard education frameworks into which they were placed. Professionals would offer support and provide advice, but despite their efforts, the suggested strategies would often fail to produce *meaningful* change for these children. I also noticed two patterns would occur when support didn't work: first, the child would begin to withdraw further from school, unable to cope; second, nobody seemed to know what to do when that happened.

What I saw in my experience was that these autistic children, especially the demand-avoidant and anxious ones, do not fit *anywhere*. Traditional autism support approaches proved *ineffective* for them. Neither mainstream nor special needs settings work, and despite being offered various strategies, referred to multiple specialist teams, there was *no* improvement. In many cases, the situation just got worse. Mental health issues increased, parents had to leave their jobs to care for their children, and their education continued to falter, leaving them trapped in a void, remaining lost, without any support.

My decision to write this book was to support those autistic children and young people, the ones who are deemed as the misunderstood kids, the outcasts of society, the children whom nobody knows how to handle. I want to show mental health professionals, educators, policymakers, and service providers that there is another way to help. A way that takes them from the failing models of support into a world where they are in control, where they can experience psychological safety, hope, autonomy, and acceptance of who they are.

## How the Book Is Laid Out

This book is a mix of academic work and real-life experiences. I also share my own personal and professional experiences as an autistic person who has lived with mental health issues. Although not easy at times to share my experiences, this is a deliberate decision, grounded in the belief that personal insights are valuable qualitative evidence often overlooked in traditional research approaches.

**Part One** is a critical analysis of the current state of support systems for autistic children and young people, considering why so many are being failed. We examine why support systems are often ineffective for many, and why dominant models of education and mental health continue to misunderstand autistic children. The focus here is not just to reveal the state we are in, but to also explore why these failures persist.

I will demonstrate that these problems have persisted since the beginning of our education and mental health systems, and to illustrate this, I have identified a recognisable pattern of error that becomes evident when we take a step back and observe what is occurring. This error is the assumption that we need to fix autistic children and enable them to fit into existing systems. I will show why I believe this thinking is incorrect and reveal that the main problem is embedded in the systems we put these children in, which were never designed for them in the first place.

In Part One, we also examine the history of mental health and education systems. I cannot offer a comprehensive overview of our mental health and educational history, as this falls outside the scope of this book. Instead, I have carefully chosen key moments in history where we see the indifference and failings of autistic children and reveal where these indifferences still exist today. I highlight how disabled children were labelled as "mentally defective", "idiots", and "uneducable", removed from families, confined in asylums, and left with little hope for their future. I mention these historical facts because I believe, just like in the past, that we still *resist* accepting difference, focusing wrongly on trying to shape autistic children and young people to fit societal norms and agendas, instead of accepting them as they are, without conditions.

In **Part Two**, we shift from problems to solutions, introducing the principles of *humanistic psychology* to offer a new way to understand and support autistic children and young people. This approach emphasises that they do not need to be fixed, or to develop emotional resilience, confront their fears, modify their behaviours, or learn to conform to societal expectations. Instead, we learn how to see autistic children and young people as *whole human beings* to be accepted, exactly as they are, not as broken children in need of fixing.

In Part Two, we highlight Carl Rogers' groundbreaking ideas of unconditional positive regard and psychological freedom and consider how these can be used as effective methods of support. We will also consider Abraham Maslow's ideas on human motivation and why *safety* and *belonging* must be established before anything else. Taking both Rogers' and Maslow's ideas, I argue that autistic children who have withdrawn from life are in a *protective* state, and the only way we can effectively help them is to show that they can be accepted unconditionally, for exactly who they are, through creating spaces embedded in psychological safety and interest-led learning.

In **Part Three**, we continue with humanistic principles, introducing two new acceptance-based models of support: the Accept Approach and the Acceptance-Based Curriculum, both offering practical ways to support children and young people through acceptance. Whether you are a mental health practitioner, educator, parent, policy-maker, or service provider, you'll discover how these models can effectively support autistic children and young people, especially when other approaches have fallen short.

In Part Three, I also share real-life experiences of children and their families who have received acceptance-based support. They provide feedback on what happens when we *remove* anxiety from the child, when we *remind* them that it is not their fault they are struggling, and when we *reassure* them that things are going to be OK and *reaffirm* that we accept them unconditionally. I will also show how to apply the Accept Approach practically. It is surprisingly simple, offering a new perspective on how to support autistic children and young people wherever they are. Families don't need to be placed on waiting lists because they can apply the principles at home. Schools don't need to wait in line for external professionals; they can do it themselves. Teachers, dinner staff, pastoral care providers, GPs, and anyone supporting an autistic child and their family can use the Accept Approach in many situation they encounter.

## Terminology

This work reflects my personal views and insights, expressed as clearly as possible so the reader can understand. I don't aim to oversimplify complex ideas or terms; instead, I strive to explain things plainly because that's how I think, process, and understand the intricate worlds we are about to explore.

I also refer to "autistic person" rather than "person with autism", and when mentioning autistic children and young people, I occasionally use just "child" or "young person" because I find that saying "autistic children and young people" can sometimes be too wordy. However, whenever I use only one of these terms, I am still referring to both groups.

## Conclusion

*The Power of Acceptance* offers a new way forward, rooted in humanistic principles, for supporting autistic children and young people who have not been able to engage with conventional models of support. It may challenge your thinking and conflict with your current values or practices. If it does, I hope you read with an open mind and explore the possibility of acceptance. I also hope you see the real impact of acceptance throughout the book, as reflected in the real-life experiences shared, showing how lives have been transformed through the practical application of acceptance. One such story I want to share to end this introduction is an email I received from a family support worker who was supporting a foster family that had adopted an autistic child, and were thinking about giving him up because they could not cope with his behaviours.

Here is part of the email I was sent.

> *I was at a home visit recently supporting a young person who was going through a tough time with their foster parents. The journey has had ups and downs for the last year or so, and they mentioned it had gotten so bad that they had decided they were going to cease the placement as they felt they could no longer cope with the child's complex needs.*
>
> *However, they mentioned attending one of your training sessions and being so inspired by your words that they chose to continue the placement. They said that the message of acceptance offered them a new perspective they had never considered before. Even now, despite ongoing struggles, they are grateful to see things differently, gaining insight to work through their family difficulties using acceptance.*

I share this story because an approach that can genuinely change a foster parent's perspective so powerfully *needs to be heard.* Too many autistic children and families are being let down, and we cannot afford to continue this way. Schools and local authorities require more practical support, and mental health services need urgent change before another generation of autistic children is lost in systems designed to help but seldom do.

This introduction is the beginning of our journey. The rest of the book will be our guide through everything needed first to understand why autistic children and young people are being failed, and then how to effectively apply new acceptance-based support that can really make a lasting difference. Finally, I want you to consider that it is not the children who need to change. It is not the systems that need to improve. What is needed is something completely new, and acceptance-based support is one way to achieve it.

Let's begin our journey into the transformative world of *the power of acceptance.*

### Real-Life Experiences Disclaimer

All real-life experiences shared in this book have been carefully anonymised. No real names are used, and any potentially identifying details, such as age, location, or education settings, have been altered. All stories are shared to illustrate acceptance in practice, deepen understanding, and highlight the importance of acceptance-based support, true to the young people's journeys and the impact of the support provided.

## Notes

1 Accepting Behaviour Ltd was established in 2017. We are an established team of specialist tutors, based within the West Midlands, UK. We are an education alternative provide, supporting autistic children and young people who have not been able to engage in traditional education support. www.acceptingbehaviour.com

2 Knapp, M., Cyhlarova, E., Salehi, N., Stubbs, E., Walbaum, M., Jadoolal, S. & Shah, M.M. (2024). *The Economic Case for Prioritising Autism in Policy and Reform.* Care Policy and Evaluation Centre, London School of Economics and Political Science.

3 New analysis reveals autism assessment and support crisis with tens of thousands of children waiting months and years for help after demand rockets by over 300% since COVID-19

https://www.centreforyounglives.org.uk/news-centre/new-analysis-reveals-autism-assessment-and-support-crisis-with-tens-of-thousands-of-children-waiting-months-and-years-for-help-after-demand-rockets-by-over-300-since-covid

N8 Research Partnership (2024). *A Country That Works for All Children and Young People: An Evidence-Based Plan for Addressing the Autism Assessment and Support Crisis.* Child of the North and Centre for Young Lives. https://doi.org/10.48785/100/195

4 National Autistic Society (2025). A Constant Fight: The Reality of Autistic People's Struggle for Support Across Health and Social Care, Education, Employment and Mental Health. published 23 January 2025.

5 Committee on the Rights of the Child Concluding Observations on the Combined Sixth and Seventh Periodic Reports of the United Kingdom of Great Britain and Northern Ireland. https://docs.un.org/en/CRC/C/GBR/CO/6-7

6 The NHS Information Centre for health and social care. Autism Spectrum Disorders in adults living in households throughout England.

Report from the Adult Psychiatric Morbidity Survey. Published 2007.

7 Roman-Urrestarazu, A., van Kessel, R., Allison, C., Matthews, F.E., Brayne, C. & Baron-Cohen, S. (2021). *Association of Race/Ethnicity and Social Disadvantage with Autism Prevalence in 7 Million School Children in England.* JAMA Pediatrics. Published.

## Part One

# Addressing the Problems

No one has all the answers.
There is no blueprint for success.
The holy grail of autism support does not exist.

*However,*

acceptance comes close.
Closer than anything else,
to embrace the whole human being.

DOI: 10.4324/9781003686064-2

Chapter 1

# The Case for Acceptance

Imagine you have been invited by the Permanent Mission of the United Kingdom to attend a conference at the United Nations. Seated in the Human Rights and Alliance of Civilisations Room, also known as Room XX,[1] inside the Palais des Nations in Geneva, you look around at the multitude of country representatives, all seats filled, with not a single space left. You peer up at the magnificence of Miquel Barceló's ceiling, created to symbolise the diversity of cultures and the complexities of human rights, and scan the room full of leading experts from around the world, each representing their country's education and mental health services, today tasked with addressing a pressing global issue: *the failing of support for autistic children and young people in mental health and education systems*.[2] Over the next few hours, three speakers from education and psychology will share their ideas on addressing this growing issue. The lights go down. Everyone is poised with anticipation, headphones on, translators at the ready. The first speaker to take the podium is an expert in behaviourism.

## The Behaviourist

Looking around the room, a man stands poised, beginning with an opening statement,

> *I believe the best way to support autistic children in mental health and education is to stop focusing on what they "think" or "feel". Instead, our focus should be on supporting and impacting what they do, through their actions and behaviours. I believe we can better support autistic people by observing their behaviours and supporting them, rather than focusing on their "feelings". As the great Dr John B Watson said, emotions and feelings are much like "intangibles" and "unapproachables",[3] which cannot be scientifically tested or observed and therefore are not reliable sources of information.*

He goes on to explain,

> *What we need to do is focus our efforts on helping these children adapt to the world they live in and teaching them to learn the life skills they need and develop social understanding that will help them to exist with others, so that they*

DOI: 10.4324/9781003686064-3

> *can become valuable members of society. Now, I am not saying emotions are not real; it is important we recognise them for what they are. As B.F. Skinner said, emotions are excellent examples of the fictional causes to which we commonly attribute behaviour.*[4]

He then begins explaining the fundamentals of behaviourism and how we need to continue adapting and applying these approaches across both mental health and education services. He explains the work of Pavlov and B.F. Skinner,[5] and how behaviours can be shaped through positive reinforcement, repetition, and control,[6] whose research into understanding behaviour demonstrates how actions can be both predicted and modified.[7] He talks of the impact of positive rewards and consequences in schools,[8] stating that with the right structure and consistency, we can mould autistic children into what we know they can become.

He then reads out a quote from behaviourist Dr John B Watson,

> *John Watson famously said in his groundbreaking book* Behaviorism,[9] *"Give me a dozen healthy infants, well-formed, and my own specified world to bring them up in and I'll guarantee to take any one at random and train him to become any type of specialist I might select, doctor, lawyer, artist, merchant-chief and, yes, even beggar-man and thief, regardless of his talents, penchants, tendencies, abilities, vocations, and race of his ancestors".*

He then continues with the theme of education, as the next slide appears.

| The Benefits of Behaviour Strategies in School |
|---|

He goes on to describe the importance of behavioural targets, reward charts, and data collection, and shares some examples of "traffic light systems" in which teachers can be a little creative in showing how children benefit from being placed on red (for undesired behaviours) and green (for desired ones). He also discusses the importance of teaching rules to follow, because without them, the world would be a more challenging place for these children.

He briefly pauses and scans the room.

> *I now want to address the topic of discipline. It is so important that all educators here and around the world take note that discipline is vital. We need to teach all children the rules to follow and gently nudge them to do things they do not want to do. These are not negative strategies; they are effective for all children, whether autistic or not.*

He then mentions Dr Temple Grandin, a professor, author, animal behaviourist, and autism self-advocate.[10] He discusses how she openly describes that, as a child, her mother would often make her do things she "*didn't want to*", consistently pushing her even when she was reluctant.

> *Dr Temple Grandin's childhood, I would suggest, is a good example of how behaviourist approaches work for autistic children. When she was a child, her mother found her jobs, where she learned discipline and responsibility.*[11] *In school, she was taught basic social skills using methods that were similar to those at home.*[12]
>
> *Look at what she has accomplished by being given gentle nudges to do things at first, she didn't want to do. With support, she was able to overcome and reach her full potential as a professor, animal behaviourist, and best-selling author. Isn't that what we want for all our autistic children, to help them reach their full potential?*

You scan the room and see people nodding and taking notes. He then moves on to discussing the role of a professional in a wider context.

> *I want to speak directly now to all professionals in the room. I feel we have lost our way. We need to regain our focus on developing more positive behavioural strategies to shape, refine, and correct unwanted behaviours. As Dr Grandin's example highlights, the best support many autistic children can receive is a gentle but deliberate encouragement from professionals and parents to step outside their comfort zones. Autistic children need to be "taught" the appropriate behaviours they must adopt to become valued and productive members of their societies.*
>
> *Emotions are unreliable and impossible to measure. Behaviour is observable and measurable, therefore changeable. Autistic children need clear expectations and consistent consequences. They need to learn what behaviours and skills help a person become productive and successful. If we don't act now, we are only going to be letting down another generation of autistic children.*

The first speaker's session is drawing to a close, and he concludes with the following statement addressing the room.

> *We all need to raise our standards of structure and compliance. All children need clear expectations, consistent reinforcement, and accountability. Families, educators, and mental health teams need to see progress, and behavioural approaches can help achieve that. With every skill learned and every behaviour improved, we can help all children move closer to independence, and autistic children should not be exempt from this. The world cannot just adapt to autistic children; instead, we need to show how they must fit in alongside us.*
>
> *Finally, I just want to say, the solution to how we can support autistic children and young people is to remember this one fundamental thing: human behaviour at its core has been learned and therefore can be unlearned.*

As the first speaker departs the podium amid applause, you quietly reflect on what you've heard, feeling a little conflict. You want to help autistic children reach their potential and learn skills to handle their difficulties. You also agree that a gentle nudge of encouragement, such as Dr Temple Grandin's childhood experience, can be effective for some children. Still, you are unsure about relying primarily on behavioural approaches because, in your experience, some children don't respond to them, and you want to know what you can do to support *those* children.

## The Psychiatrist

The next speaker, a psychiatrist, steps up to the podium and adjusts the microphone. She begins with an opening statement:

> *I would like to thank our first speaker respectfully; however, I see behaviour as merely touching the surface. Yes, it is important to understand behaviour, but I believe it is more important to understand autism as a disability. There is so much more going on inside, and behaviours such as refusal, frustration, anger, or defiance are all signs of an underlying problem that needs intervention. We must not forget that children with autism are disabled and need constant medical care and intervention, not to be cured, but to be given support to live their lives.*

Behind her, you see the words "Medical Model of Disability" appear on a slide. You are familiar with this concept and are keen to hear her perspective.

| The Medical Model View of Disability |
|---|

She briefly discusses the medical model and its view of disability, sharing that we now have a better understanding of autism.

> *We now know for certain that a child with autism has a brain that functions differently. Without the medical breakthroughs in autism research, such as Kanner's autistic disturbances of affective contact,*[13] *Wing and Gould's triad of impairments,*[14] *Lovaas' normalising autistic behaviour,*[15] *or Baron-Cohen's theory of mind,*[16] *we would not be where we are today.*

She says,

> *I believe we're at a pivotal point in autism care. The medical model views autism as a diagnosable neurodevelopmental disorder with specific internal issues that we can "treat". To better support autistic children in mental health and education, professionals must take the lead. We are trained to understand, diagnose, treat, and manage autism. The individual with autism is, in essence, a patient;*

*it's our duty to guide them, and it's up to the patient to follow our guidance so they can receive the best support, as determined by us, the professionals.*[17]

She proceeds through her slides and presents a case of an autistic child who had difficulty making eye contact and socialising with others.

*I was introduced to a child who was very distressed when I first met them, and I could see the child was anxious, refused to talk, and during our consultation, was looking down at the floor for most of the time. I could see that there was much more to this behaviour, and knowing they had autism, helped me to find the right type of intervention. Taking a medical approach, we can identify where a child has a problem and can then access both medical intervention alongside behavioural approaches. I believe using both is a way that we can work more effectively to first identify underlying neurodevelopmental disorders and then treat them effectively.*

*To begin helping this child, we used one of our therapists, who is skilled in applied behaviour analysis, a model often regarded as an evidence-based approach to supporting autism and behavioural/educational needs.*[18] *The child's family felt it was important to address the child's lack of eye contact and social interaction because they were concerned this might present difficulties later in life.*

*Over a few months, with targeted, reinforcement-based intervention and the recommended hours of support, the child increased their eye contact and significantly improved their social skills. Parents were now hopeful about the child's future, believing there was a chance they would be able to get a job and attend job interviews when older. Without this approach, we would not have been successful. We were able to reduce impaired behaviours caused by autism and to help the child function more typically in society. This is where I see medical and behaviourist approaches working very well together.*

The psychiatrist then discussed disability as a concept and how best to define it. She suggests in her opinion, that the most plausible definition comes from Rhoda Olkin,[19] who said,

*Disability is seen as a medical problem that resides in the individual. It is a defect in or failure of a bodily system and, as such, is inherently abnormal and pathological. The goals of intervention are cure, amelioration of the physical condition to the greatest extent possible, and rehabilitation (i.e. the adjustment of the person with the disability to the condition and to the environment). Persons with disabilities are expected to avail themselves of the variety of services offered to them and to spend time in the role of the patient or learner being helped by trained professionals.*[20]

Sharing her views on disability, she discusses ways to further support autistic children and young people through a better understanding of the medical model view of autism. She explains that the model gives clarity and certainty for families and professionals. She talks about the importance of diagnosing and categorising, so that autistic children can be treated correctly. Her position is clear: autism needs to become something we can support through intervention, and the most effective approach is ensuring consistency across services by seeking support early and identifying issues promptly, allowing for effective treatment and support.

She concludes her session with the following statement:

> *We all owe it to the children and their families, and to all societies globally, to embrace the medical model and all the benefits it has to offer our autistic children and young people.*

The second session has ended, and a short break is underway. You grab yourself a coffee and reflect on what you have heard so far. You find yourself in conversations with other professionals, and many of you agree that this conference has so far been a little repetitive, offering no *real* solutions. You think to yourself, this is just like being in *Groundhog Day*, repeating the same failed and outdated ideas, polishing them up into new ways of presenting them.

You also overhear some permanent missions discussing their unhappiness, sharing the same frustrations of autistic children being let down at an alarming rate. Perhaps you are beginning to see that the ideas shared in these two sessions, once considered revolutionary, are much less effective now than they ever were for many of the autistic children you support. You wonder what we can do as professionals, if a behaviourist intervention does not work, or when a medical model view proves ineffective? What happens to those children and young people?

After the brief break, everyone is seated back in their places, and the room falls silent once more. There have been murmurs that the next keynote speaker is about to share something different, from a *humanistic perspective*, a view that is the polar opposite of what has been shared so far. Curiosity is spiked. The lights go down. Poised with anticipation, headphones back on, as you eagerly await the following case to be brought forward: *the case for acceptance.*

## The Humanistic Scholar

The speaker enters the hall and approaches the podium. Firstly, she thanks the special rapporteur on the rights of persons with disabilities and the special rapporteur on the right to education for inviting her to speak. Her presentation title appears on the screen.

**A Humanistic Approach to Supporting Autistic Children and Young People**

She opts not to start with an opening statement. Instead, beginning by reading out a recent warning from the World Health Organization:

> *I first want to address the reality that many autistic children and young people face today, as we read a recent warning from the World Health Organization: these children are being neglected, facing global barriers to accessing healthcare and inequalities in health and education outcomes.*[21]

She shares how autistic people are desperately struggling to find mental health support and therapy,[22] experiencing long waiting times, with services unavailable as a result of underfunding, and with widespread reports of a lack of specialised knowledge.[23] All citing the stark and harrowing truths that global failures are contributing to ongoing feelings of loneliness, hopelessness, and even suicide, with many autistic individuals feeling misunderstood or invalidated.[24]

Each slide reveals data on how disabled children are *still* excluded from education, facing higher rates of non-attendance and dropout due to persistent barriers, caused by stigma, untrained educators,[25] and limited learning resources,[26] with all of this compounded by continuing negative beliefs about what children with disabilities are capable of.[27]

She then pauses for a moment and addresses the room directly.

> *The message is clear: mental health and education systems all around the world are failing autistic children, and urgent action is needed. I am saddened to see that even in my own country, the UK, we are also at a point of no return unless we act now.*
>
> *Ofsted*[28] *is raising further concerns of the "widespread and systemic failings" in SEND. The National Audit Office is also declaring that England's SEND system is "not delivering better outcomes" and is "financially unsustainable", with tribunals on the rise and deep deficits projected.*[29] *Autistic children are viewed as too "complex", getting put on longer waiting lists, with their pleas for help being "heard but not understood".*[30]

She pauses again for a moment.

> *I believe we are failing autistic children because we are repeating the same mistakes, as we have done historically, and as we all know, if we change nothing, nothing changes. What I would like to suggest is that we move away from outdated approaches and consider applying a different perspective: the humanistic view of autism.*

Discussing the idea that, through humanistic psychological approaches, autistic children and young people are viewed as individuals with their own worth and capacity for growth, with support focused on psychological safety, empathy, autonomy, and self-acceptance.[31] She suggests that these perspectives differ from the dominant behaviourist approach, which emphasises external control of behaviour, and from the medical model view that considers autism a disorder needing treatment to be corrected.[32]

She then pauses for a moment and addresses the room

> *I want to take a moment and address the elephant in the room: you cannot pour new wine into old wineskins. The ideas I am about to share with you will not be effective if we try to place them within existing failing systems. What autistic children and young people need now are new ways of being supported, through new ways of thinking. Completely separate from the present models of education and mental health, which were not designed with autistic children in mind."*
>
> *Before I proceed, it is essential to acknowledge that what we have heard today is undoubtedly groundbreaking work. Behaviourism has laid the groundwork for modern psychology, transforming it into a more systematic and evidence-based discipline. It allowed us to observe and measure behaviour with precision, bringing scientific credibility to the study of the human mind.*[33]
>
> *The medical model also plays a vital role in advancing science. It has helped identify the biological causes of many conditions and has improved diagnosis and early detection. We have witnessed numerous lifesaving medical breakthroughs and expanded our understanding of neurology and genetics. Without the medical model, we would not have scientific foundations that inform modern healthcare and practice.*
>
> *But when considering autism, I argue that both fail to effectively support autistic children and young people. They treat autistic children through normative frameworks, prioritising change over understanding, both seeing autistic individuals with problems to be fixed instead of people who are different, not less.*[34]
>
> *To support autistic children and young people more effectively, we need to move away now from these outdated models because we can no longer expect change to work within the broken systems, unless we move towards new approaches away from the old ones. One such new way I want to share today is the Accept Approach,*[35] *a new acceptance-based support model developed in the UK.*

She explains that the Accept Approach is a new model of support grounded in the humanistic principles of psychological safety, unconditional positive regard, and acceptance. Influenced by Carl Rogers' ideas[36] and Maslow's hierarchy of needs,[37] which prioritise safety and a sense of belonging before learning, this new approach focuses on the child's voice and interests, encouraging self-expression.

She then explains the reasoning behind *the Four Foundations of Acceptance*, which are embedded in the approach.

| The Four Foundations of Acceptance<br>REMOVE, REMIND, REASSURE, REAFFIRM |
|---|

*The idea is simple and effective. Whenever an autistic child is struggling with an issue or a problem, the approach is to apply the Four Foundations of Acceptance. You first REMOVE whatever is causing the anxiety/stress. Then secondly, you REMIND the child that their struggles are not their fault. Then you REASSURE them that things are going to be OK, offering them unconditional support, and then finally REAFFIRM that you will stand by their side, accepting them unconditionally.*

You look around the room and see a mixed reaction. Some people seem to be fixed on the speaker, whereas others appear distracted. She begins to share a real-life experience from a family whose child was supported by the Accept Approach.

**Real-Life Experience 1**

She describes an autistic teenager who had reached the point of complete shutdown and had to leave his specialist school setting. He was exhausted and completely overwhelmed by the demands and expectations placed on him, leading to severe anxiety and self-harming. He lacked confidence and was housebound, unable to leave his room most days. He had no interest in engaging with the world around him and had developed severe mental health issues.

After a few months of this acceptance-based support, he rebuilt his confidence enough to attend community settings weekly and engage in learning again. Something that his mother never thought he would be able to do.

When asked for feedback, his mother reflected:

*He was in autistic burnout and unable to attend school. The school said they couldn't meet the need. He wasn't able to do any education and wasn't able to interact with people outside of the home, barely interacting with family members. He didn't leave the house for any social activities. Now, with this support, we can see a real change. He is no longer in autistic burnout and is even going out of the house a few days a week. This would never have happened if it weren't for him feeling accepted again.*

As the speaker read the parent feedback, people became more interested. What is it about acceptance that seemed to have made such a positive to this young person's life?

She continues to speak about the case.

*This young person was just one of many children who had been through both mainstream and special needs settings and were receiving acceptance-based support from a team of specialist educators in the UK,*[38] *using the Accept Approach to support autistic children who had not been able to engage with any other support from mental health or education.*

Sharing another slide that breaks down the components of the Accept Approach: the model is designed around self-acceptance, supporting each individual child in their own life and helping them find their own way at their own pace. She explains the approach represents a new development in the field of autism, offering a model that aligns with humanistic principles and extends this type of thought specifically to autistic children in mental health *and* education. She then sums up the model's definition:

> *The Accept Approach is an acceptance-based framework grounded in the principle that: whatever problem or issue a child/young person is experiencing, you accept them as a whole human being, exactly as they are, without condition or judgement.*
>
> *I believe it is time to move away from controlling behaviour or seeing these children as having problems that need to be fixed. Instead, I want to suggest that we can accept differences and view behaviours as a way of communicating unmet needs, specifically safety and belonging, remembering the child as a whole human being who needs support strategies that accept them for exactly who they are.*

The humanistic scholar concludes that, with this approach, professionals, therapists, teachers, parents, policymakers, and service providers can help autistic children feel free to be their *authentic* selves without conditions, expectations, or judgements.

The case for acceptance is at an end. She gives her closing statement.

> *I want to leave you with this final thought. Acceptance is not just a call for change; it's a blueprint for how acceptance-based support can help create inclusive and compassionate environments that enable autistic children and young people to unlock their full potential by being allowed to be themselves, completely without conditions. Whether you are a parent seeking answers to help your child, a teacher wanting to make a difference in the classroom, or a professional looking to deepen your understanding of the principles of acceptance, I believe that acceptance-based support is a new way for us to transform how we can support autistic children and young people who have struggled to engage not only in education, but also in wider aspects of life and society.*

As the speaker leaves the podium, you sit and consider what you have just heard. Maybe you are thinking about the children you support, those children who did not respond to strategies you have tried, those children who have withdrawn from education and are now just sitting at home doing nothing, those children labelled hard to reach or non-compliant. Have we got it all wrong? You leave the room without any clear answers, but maybe a shift in perspective. Maybe acceptance is a way forward. Maybe something different is what these children need, not to get them to adapt to what we already have, but to create something entirely new.

## The Final Session

It is now the end of the day, with one more session to go: a question-and-answer panel featuring all three keynote speakers discussing their final thoughts and answering questions from the remaining audience. The session's moderator begins by thanking everyone for coming and introducing the final session, then opens the floor for questions.

> *Would anybody like to ask a question to the panel?*

The first to take the microphone is a professional from education in the front row.

> *So, can you tell us then why autistic children, and their families, are still being failed by education and mental health systems?*

The behaviorist responds,

> *I would like to go first, if that's OK?" I believe because we have lost sight of what needs to be done. In schools, for example, there are no boundaries, and no one dares enforce effective discipline. For too long now, we have focused too much on emotions and feelings, which have diluted the fundamentals of human behaviour: that children learn through reinforcement. This is, of course, not a personal thing; it's just how learning works, and I believe we need to bring back rewarding desired behaviours and discouraging the unwanted ones.*

All of a sudden, there are more hands up. But before the microphone can be passed around, the psychiatrist speaks.

> *With respect to my colleague, as I have pointed out, behaviour is only a surface problem. Beneath all autistic children with mental health issues or school avoidance lie complex pathologies, such as trauma or attachment issues. These are the issues that must be addressed first; unwanted behaviours are a sign that something isn't right. This can manifest as defiance, dysregulation, masking, meltdowns, shutdowns, or a lack of eye contact; whatever we see on the surface is a direct result of something broken within. The most effective way to support, I believe, is through clinical assessments, structured interventions, and, as needed, medication. These children need restoring, not to be told off for unwanted behaviours!*

Sitting, listening to both sides, the humanistic scholar raises her hand and speaks.

> *Why do we keep discussing autistic children as if there is something wrong with them? As if they need fixing, adjusting, or improving? Why do we keep pathologising them? I believe the real solution is to shift our perspective from viewing autistic children and young people as problems and instead recognise*

> *that the systems meant to support them are where the real issues lie. If there's one problem that needs addressing, it is the broken systems we attempt to place these children into.*

The crowd's murmuring is now getting louder. The next person, a representative from a charity organisation supporting autistic children, is eager to question the panel. He is also a father of an autistic teenager who is not attending school.

> *My daughter has not been able to engage in school for two years. No help. The professionals told me it is a case of school refusal. But I keep telling them she is not refusing. She is terrified of school. I even tried to get her to the school gates to say hello to her teacher, but it just made things worse. Rewarding her attendance didn't work. Getting her to do a part-time timetable didn't work either. She has not been able to attend for two years, and we have since been left alone. She has had no support from anyone.*

The behaviourist responds,

> *I can only imagine how difficult your situation must be. However, I believe you can help your daughter by continuing to encourage her to return to school. We know that school is the best place for children, and there is devastating research that even shows children who do not go to school often end up as delinquents, unemployed,*[39] *or even end up in prison.*[40] *Avoiding school only strengthens her anxieties, which will take hold of her more. I can only insist that you continue to encourage her to attend, gradually and gently, remembering that every day she stays at home is another negative reinforcement. Keeping her at home will, in the long run, be worse.*

The humanistic scholar interjects,

> *Or, what if your daughter is staying home to protect herself, because she does not feel safe? I suggest that making your daughter go to school to overcome the very thing that is causing the anxiety will not work; in fact, that is what can make things worse. Let me give you an example of what I mean.*
>
> *I hate lifts because, as a child, I was once trapped in one. I feel extreme anxiety whenever going in lifts, and that feeling won't go away until the lift doors open. Now, I don't go in lifts. The point I want to get across here is that it would not help me overcome my anxiety of lifts by being encouraged to go back in until I no longer feel anxious. I have tried. Sometimes I feel OK, other times I don't. So now I just don't use lifts, and I don't get anxious about them anymore. I have removed the anxiety.*
>
> *The best thing that happened to me was the day I realised I did not have to use lifts, because there are always stairs nearby as a better option for me, and that is all I needed to feel safe: to be shown a different way.*

The humanistic scholar then addressed the father directly,

> *I believe your daughter has been let down because no one in school has provided any safety for her. You don't need to attend a parent group, and she doesn't need to keep attending school. My advice is to completely remove the expectation for her to go to school, so that she can be given the time to heal, and when she is ready, you will help find her own way, in her own time.*

The psychiatrist jumps back in, looking directly at the humanistic scholar.

> *But we must not forget that his daughter needs support; she cannot heal unless she is treated for her anxiety. I know there are waiting lists and delays but get her booked in to see someone. They can help her face her anxieties and get better.*

Then, turning to the father, the psychiatrist says,

> *My advice to you is that your daughter is more than her anxiety. It is her anxiety that is holding her back from achieving success in school, and the more time she spends there, the easier it will be for her. Have you tried medication? They may help to reduce her school-related fears. Then you can try gradual exposure to going back to school, which can be very effective for anxiety conditions, and help school refusers return to school. I have even seen teachers bring the school hamster to meet a child at the gates as an incentive for them to go in, or to encourage a child to sit in the reception area with a friend for 10-minute intervals. These interventions can help and will reduce her anxiety if she makes the effort to come to the building.*

The humanistic scholar responds again,

> *Yes, I agree exposure to fears and phobias works. I am aware of the research. I also know that medication can be effective for people, too. One thing you are failing to consider here is: what if her anxiety response is actually trying to protect her?*
>
> *If you fell into a lion's pit, would you stay there until you no longer feared the lions, or would you try desperately to scramble up the walls to escape? Sometimes the intervention itself can be traumatic and offer no relief. I believe we need to stop viewing children as broken and stop thinking they have to overcome their anxieties. Instead, maybe the best way to help is to learn to accept the anxiety, instead of exposing it.*

The hall goes very quiet. The parent attempts to sit back down, but then the behaviourist speaks.

> *What if your daughter is not anxious, but, excuse me for sounding a bit forward, just being a teenager? Have you considered teaching her more about emotional*

*resilience? The truth of life is that it is hard for all of us. We all have to do things and to go places we don't want to go. That is just part of life, isn't it?*

The psychiatrist adds,

*I actually agree. I think many of our teenagers nowadays lack emotional resilience. Not to downplay your daughter's struggles, but may I suggest you at least ask her school to offer some resilience support? Maybe she could attend a group in school? I would also ask the school to make some more reasonable adjustments, such as the idea of coming to school on a part-time basis or asking for a personal mentor.*

The father replies,

*My daughter is the most resilient person I know. She goes through these battles every day, only to receive no help or support from anyone. She wants to learn and build a life for herself. Our struggle is not with her; it is that there isn't a school that can meet her needs.*

The father sits down.

The moderator moves on swiftly.

*I think we have time for one more question.*

A young autistic man, invited to the conference as an advocate for the National Autistic Society, stands up in the audience and begins to speak. He does not wait for the microphone; he chooses to speak loudly instead.

*I AM NOT AN EXPERIMENT! There is nothing that needs to be fixed in me. I like who I am. I didn't like school, and as an adult, I find people very difficult to understand. My question is to you.*

He points to the humanistic scholar and asks her a question.

*Do you think acceptance can really help, or is it just another idea that sounds good on paper, but in reality, is impossible to implement?*

The scholar replies,

*Short answer, yes, absolutely. The long answer, acceptance is a choice that can only begin when we stop trying to change autistic children and start accepting them unconditionally, exactly as they are. The reality is that to achieve this, we need new systems, not by adjusting children to fit into existing ones. We need to create systems where children can fit in perfectly without conditions, just as they are.*

*I believe in a world where acceptance is the guide, autistic children will no longer be seen as problems to solve, but as children to understand. With new systems, there would be no need for reasonable adjustments, expectations, passive learning, or pathologising of conditions. With acceptance-based support, a child who can't cope with a busy school or cannot engage in maths or English subjects would be given the freedom to learn what they want to, in their way, and in their time.*

The scholar then addresses the autistic adult and looks over at the father who spoke previously.

*Support for children with anxiety would start with removing what is overwhelming, not by exposure or increasing demands. School avoidance should be supported, not by getting them back into school, but by doing everything to help a child feel safe again and to help them learn to find their own way of learning, not the system's way.*

The moderator now ends the session and draws the day to a close, thanking everyone who stayed behind to take part. As everyone is leaving the hall, the panel members shake hands with one another, and the behaviourist quietly turns to the others and whispers,

*See you at the next debate next year. I'm sure we'll find ourselves in the same mess then!*

## Notes

1 Description of the UN Meeting Room XX. https://www.ungeneva.org/en/meetings-events/rooms/room-xx
2 Cleary, M. (2024). When the Education System and Autism Collide: Evidence of School Exclusion and Psychological Impact. *Journal of Psychiatric & Mental Health Nursing*, 31(2), pp. 245–256; Li, Y., et al. (2025). Global Autism Prevalence and Exploring Montessori as a Novel Intervention for ASD. *Frontiers in Psychiatry*, 16, p. 1604937 and Nordin, V., et al. (2023). *School Absenteeism in Autistic Children and Adolescents: A Scoping Review*. Frontiers in Psychiatry.
3 Watson, J.B. (1913). Psychology as the Behaviourist Views It. *Psychological Review*, 20(2), pp. 158–177. https://doi.org/10.1037/h0074428
4 Skinner, B.F. (1953). *Science and Human Behaviour*. New York: Macmillan.
5 Skinner, B.F. (1938). *The Behaviour of Organisms: An Experimental Analysis*. New York: Appleton-Century-Crofts.
6 Pavlov, I.P. (1927). *Conditioned Reflexes: An Investigation of the Physiological Activity of the Cerebral Cortex*. Translated by G.V. Anrep. London: Oxford University Press.
7 Skinner, B.F. (1953). *Science and Human Behaviour*. New York: Macmillan.
8 Oliver, R.M., Wehby, J.H. & Reschly, D.J. (2011). Teacher Classroom Management Practices: Effects on Disruptive or Aggressive Behaviour in Elementary School Children. *Campbell Systematic Reviews*, 4(1).
9 Watson, J.B. (1925). *Behaviorism*. New York, NY: People's Institute Publishing Company (later revised editions, commonly cited 1930).

10 Website Description Temple Grandin Bio. https://www.cshl.edu/giving/double-helix-medals-dinner/past-dhmd/2011-2/temple-grandin/
11 Example Taken Directly from Temple Grandin's Website. https://templegrandin.com/temple_articles/work_skills.html
12 Example Taken Directly from Temple Grandin's Website. https://templegrandin.com/temple_articles/teaching_methods.html
13 Kanner, L. (1943). Autistic Disturbances of Affective Contact. *Nervous Child*, 2, pp. 217–250.
14 Wing, L. & Gould, J. (1979). Severe Impairments of Social Interaction and Associated Abnormalities in Children: Epidemiology and Classification. *Journal of Autism and Developmental Disorders*, 9(1), pp. 11–29.
15 Lovaas, O.I. (1987). Behavioural Treatment and Normal Educational and Intellectual Functioning in Young Autistic Children. *Journal of Consulting and Clinical Psychology*, 55(1), pp. 3–9.
16 Baron Cohen, S. (1995). *Mind Blindness: An Essay on Autism and Theory of Mind.* Cambridge MA: MIT Press.
17 Shakespeare, T. (2006). *Disability Rights and Wrongs*. London: Routledge.
18 Chung, K.M., Chung, E. & Lee, H. (2024). Behavioural Interventions for Autism Spectrum Disorder: A Brief Review and Guidelines with a Specific Focus on Applied Behaviour Analysis. *Journal of Korean Acad Child Adolesc Psychiatry*, January 1, 35(1), pp. 29–38. https://doi.org/10.5765/jkacap.230019. PMID: 38204739; PMCID: PMC10774556.
19 Olkin, R. (1999). *What Psychotherapists Should Know about Disability*. New York: Guilford Press.
20 Leone, C. (2020). Medical Approach to Disability: A History of a Multifaceted Relationship. *Medicina Historica*, 4(2), p. e2020002.
21 Executive Summary: Global Report on Children with Developmental Disabilities (15 September 2023). https://www.who.int/publications/i/item/9789240080539
22 Binte Mohd Ikhsan, S.N., Holt, R., Man, J., et al. (2025). Access to Services for Autistic People Across Europe. *Molecular Autism*, 16, p. 35. https://doi.org/10.1186/s13229-025-00664-2
23 Binte Mohd Ikhsan, S.N., Holt, R., Man, J., et al. (2025). Access to Services for Autistic People Across Europe. *Molecular Autism*, 16, p. 35. https://doi.org/10.1186/s13229-025-00664-2
24 Bournemouth University Article 'Cracks in the System' Drive High Suicide Rates for Autistic People in the UK, Says Study (5 September 2025). https://medicalxpress.com/news/2025-09-high-suicide-autistic-people-uk.html
25 Organisation for Economic Co-Operation and Development: Reinforce the Provision, Support and Training for Teaching Students with Special Education Needs (Accessed August 2025). https://www.oecd.org/en/topics/sub-issues/special-education-needs.html
26 UNICEF Children with Disabilities Data (Accessed February 2022). Education. https://data.unicef.org/topic/child-disability/education/
27 UNICEF Children with Disabilities Data (Accessed February 2022). Education. https://data.unicef.org/topic/child-disability/education/.
28 Government Statistics (Accessed November 2025). https://www.gov.uk/government/statistics/area-send-inspections-and-outcomes-in-england-as-at-31-december-2024/main-findings-area-send-inspections-and-outcomes-in-england-as-at-31-december-2024
29 https://www.nao.org.uk/wp-content/uploads/2024/10/support-for-children-and-young-people-with-special-educational-needs.pdf
30 Published Article from the National Autistic Society Highlighting Waiting Times for Support. https://www.autism.org.uk/what-we-do/news/a-constant-fight-report-launch
31 Rogers, C.R. (1951). *Client-Centred Therapy*. Boston: Houghton Mifflin.

32 Milton, D.E.M. (2012). On the Ontological Status of Autism: The "Double Empathy Problem". *Disability & Society*, 27(6), pp. 883–887.
33 Simply Psychology Introduction to Behaviourism (Accessed December 2025). https://www.simplypsychology.org/behaviorism.html
34 Milton, D.E.M. (2014). Autistic Expertise: A Critical Reflection on the Production of Knowledge in Autism Studies. *Autonomy, the Critical Journal of Interdisciplinary Autism Studies*, 1(2), pp. 1–11.
35 Yorke, A. (2021). A Case Study of Two Autistic Children Supported by the Accept Approach: A New Acceptance Based Strategy. *Good Autism Practice*, 22(2), pp. 34–45.
36 Rogers, C.R. (1957). The Necessary and Sufficient Conditions of Therapeutic Personality Change. *Journal of Consulting Psychology*, 21(2), pp. 95–103. https://doi.org/10.1037/h0045357
37 Maslow, A.H. (1943). A Theory of Human Motivation. *Psychological Review*, 50(4), pp. 370–396.
38 Accepting Behaviour was established in 2021 by Aaron Yorke and Jayne Yorke. It is an acceptance-based organisation comprising a growing team of specialist teachers working across the West Midlands. The organisation provides direct support to autistic children and young people and applies the Accept Approach as its foundational framework for practice, training, and decision-making. Accepting Behaviour. www.acceptingbehaviour.com
39 Klassen, J.A., Stewart, S.L. & Lapshina, N. (2021). School Disengagement and Mental Health Service Intensity Need Among Clinically Referred Students Utilizing the InterRAI Child & Youth Mental Health Assessment Instrument. *Frontiers in Psychiatry*, 12, p. 690917. https://doi.org/10.3389/fpsyt.2021.690917
40 Bacher-Hicks, A., Billings, S.B. & Deming, D.J. (2024). The School-to-Prison Pipeline: Long-Run Impacts of School Suspensions on Adult Crime. *American Economic Journal: Economic Policy*, 16(4), pp. 165–193. https://doi.org/10.1257/pol.20230052

Chapter 2

# An Introduction to Acceptance

Acceptance is a profound concept that can redefine our understanding of what it means to be human. It can change how we see ourselves and others, helping us accept both our limitations and achievements without trying to meet unrealistic standards. Acceptance gives us permission to *remove* anxieties, to *remind* us that some situations are not our fault, to *reassure* us that things can turn out OK, and to *reaffirm* that we are more than able to work through issues at our own pace and on our own terms. Acceptance is an empowering mindset that can free a person from doubt and blame, helping to stop seeing yourself as a problem and reassuring even the most insecure mind that "*you've got this; you are enough*".

## Defining Acceptance

When contemplating acceptance, terms such as self-acceptance, acceptance of others, self-compassion, empathy, validation, belonging, safety, and well-being come to mind. All describe an open, non-judgemental stance towards oneself and others. I define acceptance as:

> *the act of knowing I am enough, even with all my limitations and imperfections, I do not need to be fixed or corrected, and I choose to see other people through the same understanding.*

When Sir Peter Lely was commissioned to paint a portrait of Oliver Cromwell in 1653, the story goes that he was given specific instructions directly from Cromwell: "*Use all your skill to paint your picture truly like me, but remark all this roughness, pimples, warts, and everything as you see me. Otherwise, I will never pay a farthing for it!*"[1] At a time when portrait painting was often used to flatter faces by softening the skin and removing blemishes, Cromwell demanded that everything about him be painted, with nothing left out, perfectly capturing acceptance in its simplest form, true freedom to be yourself. Over time, despite some varying accounts of this conversation,[2] the command for Lely to include all of Cromwell's pimples and warts in the painting led to the phrase we now refer to as "*warts and all*".

DOI: 10.4324/9781003686064-4

The phrase "warts and all" conveys acceptance of a person exactly as they are, with all their character flaws and likeable traits. In psychological terms, this idea aligns with the process of developing a healthy self-acceptance and learning to view others the same way. Developing the skills to accept our own and others' imperfections means acknowledging that we all make mistakes, let people down, and let ourselves down, and it's all just a part of being human. With acceptance, we recognise that both our positive and negative traits are part of who we are, rather than trying to become someone who we are *not*.

## Skinner and Freud's Influence

The process of accepting oneself and others psychologically is not new; it is a well-established concept in humanistic psychology, gaining popularity in the '60s. Considered *the third force* in psychology,[3] humanistic ideas emerged to directly challenge the views of Sigmund Freud's psychoanalytic theory, and B.F. Skinner's behaviourism. Freud argued that human behaviour was largely driven by unconscious desires, motives, and conflicts stemming primarily from childhood experiences,[4] while Skinner believed that human behaviour is learned and, through conditioning, can be shaped and moulded by rewards and consequences.[5]

During this time, psychology began to narrow its focus to behaviours, rejecting the ideas of feelings, the soul, mind, and consciousness because these concepts were deemed not scientific, lacking evidence to explain behaviour effectively, and although quickly becoming the dominant view of human behaviour, many psychologists were fighting against these ideas. As Rolland H. Waters stated,

> *American psychology first lost its soul, then its mind, and finally its consciousness, but it still behaved.*[6]

### Reflection

Although Freud and Skinner are often believed to be opposites in psychology, this is actually far from the truth.[7] Both actually viewed human behaviour as driven by forces outside of conscious choice. Skinner himself had a strong interest in psychoanalysis and cited Freud more than any other author in his work. He also tried to be analysed himself but was rejected.[8]

In this book, I suggest that the influence of Freud and Skinner still remains today, and both contribute to the issues that autistic children and their families face, as both ideas focus exclusively on behaviour. Freud pathologised psychological distress, framing it as a disorder which should be diagnosed and treated as an internal problem to be fixed.[9] So, when professionals label an autistic child's issues as pathological or as a deficit caused by internal dysfunctions like anxiety or demand avoidance, they are influenced by Freud's ideas, even if they are not aware. Take, for example, his views here:

> *The moment a man questions the meaning and value of life, he is sick, since objectively neither has any existence; by asking this question, one is merely admitting to a store of unsatisfied libido to which something else must have happened, a kind of fermentation leading to sadness and depression.*[10]

Alongside pathologising ideas, we have Skinner's influence on autism around the development of strategies, specifically those designed to *modify behaviour*. His theory of *operant conditioning* focused on behaviours and how consequences shape them. For example, an autistic child is praised for sitting still on the carpet, reinforcing the desired behaviour. If the child doesn't sit still, they may be given warnings, e.g. three strikes and they have to leave the classroom, or their name will be placed in the "red" section of a behaviour chart for all to see. We discuss behaviourism more in Chapter 7.

## Humanistic Psychology

Led by many influential thinkers, such as Carl Rogers, Abraham Maslow, and Rollo May, humanistic principles were against the dominant views and argued that, instead, psychology should value human experiences, focusing on human growth through self-actualisation and emphasising the importance of unconditional positive regard, empathy, psychological safety, and belonging.

Humanistic principles hold that acceptance of self and others is one of the most important aspects of human development and growth.[11] Carl Rogers, in his work as a therapist, saw acceptance as both an act we give to others and one we give to ourselves. He believed that a person can be supported by experiencing acceptance from another person and, secondly, learn to accept oneself. Rogers argued that we can receive acceptance from others through *unconditional positive regard*, which is the experience of being accepted by another person regardless of our condition, behaviour, or feelings. The idea is that when we receive unconditional positive regard, we then begin to grow in this way of *being*, learning to accept ourselves and developing the ideal self. Then by accepting ourselves as we are, we develop the ability to reflect and grow.[12] Rogers said,

> *I have become more adequate in letting myself be what I am. It becomes easier for me to accept myself as a decidedly imperfect person, who by no means functions at all times in the way in which I would like to function.*[13]

Rogers believed the act of acceptance is *not* about thinking about how we can be better, do more, or improve the flawed parts of ourselves. He argued it is about acknowledging our self-worth, *regardless* of our accomplishments and flaws. We will discuss his ideas in more detail in Part Two.

**Reflection**

Humanistic psychology regards autistic children as complete individuals, without any conditions or expectations for them to be someone different from who they are in the present moment.

## The Curious Paradox

Having struggled with mental health issues most of my life, I spent years in therapy trying to move away from past traumas and improve myself, to fix what was broken, change my thinking, and become a *better person.* Despite my efforts, I often failed, unable to change my anxieties, thoughts, or reactions; no matter how hard I tried, I just couldn't *do it.* It wasn't until at 30, when I had a nervous breakdown, that I realised the best thing for me was to stop trying to fix myself. Instead, I started learning to accept my struggles, to accept my past, my intrusive thoughts, and my anxieties. Recognising the transformative power of acceptance was the turning point that changed everything for me and is what Rogers described in his book *On Becoming a Person*, emphasising here the importance of self-acceptance,

> *The curious paradox is that when I accept myself just as I am, then I can change.*[14]

In his work on client-centred therapy, Rogers also suggested that a person in therapy would only begin to receive help if he felt that he could be completely himself with the therapist. He stated,

> *I find that when I can accept another person . . . I am assisting him to become a person, and there seems to be great value in this.*[15]

When a person is accepted by someone else *without* conditions or judgement, allowing them to exist within a space where they feel safe, understood, and validated, they, in turn, begin to *believe in their worth*, learning that they are OK exactly as they are. Rogers inspired me to see that when an autistic child or young person receives acceptance from another, they can begin to develop meaning and purpose in who they are, learning to find their own answers in life, in their own way, and in their own time. This is something I actively do when supporting autistic children. I will now share one of those experiences.

**Real-Life Experience 2**

When Charlie was 12, he stopped going to school. Every attempt to help him re-engage failed. Despite being diagnosed autistic and receiving an education, health, and care plan (EHCP), he received no effective support, leaving his parents overwhelmed and desperate, not knowing how to help him. Charlie stopped leaving the house, unable to cope with even the simplest of demands. His mental health deteriorated as he struggled to engage with family and friends, masking his *true* feelings. The only way he could manage was to withdraw from the world, hiding under an old grey blanket when things got too much for him.

Professionals from various fields attempted to help Charlie. He was first assessed and diagnosed as autistic by the mental health team. He was also diagnosed with selective mutism from the speech and language team, sensory modulation disorder by occupational therapy, and specialist educators found strong signs of dyslexia and dyspraxia. Despite advice and guidance from these specialists, all support strategies failed, and professionals involved were then unsure what to do.

His anxiety increased to the point that he would freeze when trying to leave his mother to enter the school building. The adults there to greet him accepted that he found it hard but their strategy wasn't working, which was to keep trying to encourage him to leave his mother, even though he was visibly expressing that he couldn't do it. It seemed that, in school, the focus on support was to do what they could to fix his situation rather than listen to what he was trying to say: *that school was too much for him, and he couldn't do it anymore.*

## Conditional Acceptance

On the occasions Charlie was able to attend school, he would really struggle in class, which raised his anxiety even further. He had help available in class, but only if he asked for it. Again, staff accepted his anxiety and wanted to help, but it came with conditions: if he did not "tell" them he was anxious, then they would not be able to help him. It was deemed Charlie's responsibility to tell them he was anxious so he could get help. But again, they missed that he could not do this, and often Charlie would have to *mask* his anxiety and bottle it all up just to get through the lesson.

He was also given a time-out card he could use to go to a safe space, which the school believed would also help him, but again, he had to tell the teacher if he was struggling, something he just could not do when anxious because he would shut down, unable to speak to anyone. The message he was receiving through all these strategies was "*We accept that you find it difficult to ask for help, but you have to take responsibility to ask; if you don't tell us, then we can't help you*".

Charlie was experiencing here what many autistic children and young people experience in schools: *conditional acceptance*. The message is "*I know you are autistic, and we will do what we can to help, but you must still follow the rules and conditions we have created for you, in order to get the help*". Charlie was only really accepted if he learned to manage his feelings. His issues were seen as problems to be fixed, with Charlie as the main person responsible for making the changes.

Like so many autistic children in schools, he was accepted on the surface, but then expected to adapt whenever he felt anxious, which is actually saying that he was *not* accepted, or at least only accepted up to a point. With conditional acceptance, the message given to a child is that to be accepted, you have to "work for it", put the effort in, and then you will be accepted. Charlie was learning that to be accepted, he must meet conditions set by the adults around him and not follow his true feelings.

Inevitably, Charlie did not respond to this type of support and became another autistic child who felt misunderstood and eventually disengaged completely from school and all professionals involved. His anxiety worsened to the point that he began to develop a more complex issue where he started to believe that everything was *his* fault, developing new feelings of self-blame and self-guilt. These new issues made it increasingly more difficult for him to leave his mother now, and he could not go anywhere without her, seeing himself more and more as a failure, not because he was disobedient or manipulative, but because he did not know how *not* to feel anxious. He was labelled a "*troubled child*", even though there was nothing troubling about him.

## The Beginning of Acceptance

When we were asked to support Charlie, I knew he needed a lot of support initially to build his confidence and help ease his anxieties around attending school. After a meeting with his parents, I knew that this would take time. We agreed that I would meet Charlie at his home, where he felt safe and could be with his mother.

The support used to help him was *the Accept Approach*, which is an acceptance-based support model you will be familiar with throughout the book. Within the approach, there are the Four Foundations of Acceptance.[16] These are practical processes used to apply acceptance specifically to support children and young people through a problem or an issue they need help with. They are as follows:

1. **Remove**: What is causing anxiety/stress
2. **Remind**: It is not their fault.
3. **Reassure**: It is going to be OK.
4. **Reaffirm**: You accept them unconditionally.

At the heart of these foundations are two empowering affirmations: "*It is not your fault*" and "*It is going to be OK*". These are then paired with two grounded messages of acceptance: "*I will remove whatever is making you anxious*" and "*I accept you unconditionally*". The foundations are *intentionally* fluid, designed to support any situation where an autistic child requires help. When applying them, however, it is important to note the "Remove" foundation must be applied first. If a child is anxious, distressed, or overwhelmed, nothing you say will help if the reason they are feeling anxious is still there. You cannot reassure a child that it is going to be okay if the thing hurting them has not been taken away. You cannot remind them

that it is not their fault while they are still in the situation causing the stress. Therefore, the first step is to identify what is causing the anxiety and remove it.
In Charlie's initial support, I used all four. I will now show how each one was applied.

### Reflection

The idea with the Four Foundations of Acceptance is to offer solutions to a problem directly by applying acceptance to help an autistic child or young person feel completely supported, listened to, reassured, and emotionally safe, allowing them to learn to deal with an issue on their own terms, in their own way, and at their own pace.

### *1. Remove*

The first time I met Charlie was at his house. I was greeted at the front door by his mother, who informed me that he was extremely anxious about our visit as he did not like speaking to professionals. However, she also told me he was aware of our team and said he wanted to see if we could help. At first, I peered around the doorway into the living room where Charlie was, to say "*hi*". He was seated on the floor cross-legged in the middle of the room, hiding under a large grey blanket.

I could immediately see he was anxious about my presence, so my first focus was to *remove* what was making him anxious, which, in this moment, was *me*. So, I moved away from the living room and positioned myself outside the door. I told him, "*You don't have to speak to me, it's OK*". I then asked, "*Would it be OK to stay outside the room to just tell you and your mum a few things I would like you to know*?" His mother who was in the room with him, said he nodded to say that was OK.

I knew that the expectation for him to go to school was too much for him, and I also wanted to remove this pressure. I told him very clearly, "*You do not have to go to school ever again if you don't want to*". This decision had already been made by the school and his parents, but his mother was not sure he was fully aware that he never had to return. I thought it was important for me as a visiting professional to make this point very clear to him. Interestingly, after I spoke briefly, his mother acknowledged that Charlie had whispered to her that I go back into the room.

### *2. Remind*

Now sitting on a large swivel chair, Charlie was half appearing through his grey blanket. I sat with his mother on the other side of the room. I could see his anxiety was reduced enough to allow me back into his space, and it felt appropriate to continue with the next foundation, to *remind* him that what he is going through was "*not his fault*". To apply this, I said to him,

> *I just want you to know that nothing you have been going through is your fault. There is nothing you have done to cause what has happened. It is not your fault that you cannot go to school.*

I was reminding him here that the reasons why he cannot go to school or leave the house are *not his fault*. None of what he is going through was his fault: none of it, and I made sure he knew this, even if he didn't yet believe it. His mother said to me, "*We have never been told this before. It's refreshing to hear this, because we agree, it's not his fault*". She went on to tell me that up until now, he had always been made to feel that it was his fault, and that he was the one who had to make the changes and to do the work to get the support.

### 3. *Reassure*

After receiving this feedback from his mother, I moved to applying the third foundation of acceptance: reassuring him that, despite what he was going through, no matter how bleak the situation felt, that "*it was going to be OK*". I reassured him that we could help him find a way past this time and that *together* we would help him see that learning is possible and that his life was not over. Telling a child that things are going to be OK is a way of sharing the message of hope and is conveyed through conversations when a child feels anxious or doesn't know what to do. The adult says to them, "*Don't worry, it's going to be OK. We will find a way.*" We will discuss the concept of "*hope*" in more detail in Chapter 9.

### 4. *Reaffirm*

The final foundation was to reaffirm to Charlie that I accept him, through applying unconditional positive regard, which underpins the whole process. The way we apply this foundation is to tell the child or young person that they are in complete control of what they want to learn in our sessions. For Charlie, this message was shared, addressing *the Two Rules of Learning*, which are part of the Acceptance-Based Curriculum, which we discuss in more detail in Part Three. The rules are set during all sessions, with all children. They are as follows:

1. The student is the boss of their learning.
2. We will not do anything they don't want to do.

Charlie was clearly informed about this, where I told him he is the boss of what we will do, and he doesn't have to engage in anything he doesn't want to. The message given was that he is in charge, and it's my role to guide him and offer any suggestions or help if he needs. I also said he could choose the best time for his sessions, and we could have them anywhere he would like. There were no conditions on how he should be during the sessions, and we would follow his lead in everything we did.

> **Reflection**
>
> With the Two Rules of Learning, (1) direction comes from the student, while *guidance comes from the adult*, and (2) their interests set the agenda, *and the support brings them to life.*

## Charlie's Response

Bearing in mind that up until now nothing had worked, when I left the house, I didn't know how he would respond to our first meeting. Later that day, I received a call from his mother, who told me, "*He wants to see you again*". I asked what had led him to this decision, and she said it was when you told him, "*It's not his fault*". His mother said he had held onto this idea because he had *never* been told this before, and it really helped him to hear it from a professional.

When I arrived for our second session, something profound happened that I would never have expected. I knocked on the door, and as his mother opened it, Charlie was there to greet me with a smile. I said "*hello*" and asked him where he would like our session to be. He turned and walked into the living room, so I followed. We spent most of the session discussing what we could do to help him. His words were still very limited, but he did choose to speak to me, which in itself was amazing, because he had not managed to talk to any other professionals who had visited his house up until this point. We discussed his interests and what he would like to do during our sessions. He had lots of ideas, mostly about his Xbox and playing board games, which I told him was completely OK. I reminded him, "*He is the boss*", which he seemed to like. It was good to see how well he had responded to the message of acceptance after the first session.

However, something more profound and transformative happened during that session that I hadn't expected and hadn't even noticed. On my way out, his mother said, "*I need to show you something*". She pointed to the object of safety that had been used countless times to get him through difficult conversations and interactions: his grey blanket. It was folded neatly on a chair on the other side of the room, unused. His mother said he no longer needed it, and to this day, I have never seen it again during our sessions.

## Overview of Support

As our support developed, Charlie's engagement increased. We added more sessions during the week, and he worked with different specialist teachers from our team. At every stage, he controlled what he learned, when he learned it, and how. This began with Xbox sessions and progressed to board games, then to walks, visits to shops, and even a newfound passion for photography. He was so far removed from the boy who hid under that grey blanket. It was inspiring to see him slowly begin to accept himself. He was beginning to experience self-acceptance.

Charlie had *not* responded to traditional strategies to reintegrate him into school. Attempts to face his anxieties, especially those related to leaving his mother, only made things worse. Leaving his mother was something he just couldn't do. He found it even harder to ask for help, and his inability to talk to people also worsened. He did, however, respond to acceptance, as he learned that his struggles were not his fault, and that he never had to return to school, because he knew it was not the right place for him.

We supported his decisions. Embracing autonomy, he took charge of his learning, growing in confidence, knowing all learning was interest-led, and that he had the *final say*. He also responded positively to knowing he no longer had to overcome anything that made him anxious, thanks to his newfound freedom to say "no" to things he didn't want to do.

The Four Foundations of Acceptance are inspired by the psychological principles discussed earlier. Charlie responded positively to me because he was shown *unconditional positive regard:* I accepted him, showing his value regardless of his condition, behaviour, or feelings. This view helped Charlie begin to see a way through, knowing that things would be OK.

## Three Years On

At the time of writing this, we are passing three years of successful support for Charlie and have been able to explore the impact that applying acceptance has had on his learning and his mental health. The shift did not happen by chance; the profound effects of acceptance became more apparent when Charlie began to see that we accepted him even when he couldn't engage. Acceptance-based support has helped Charlie to reframe his views on what it is for him to be autistic. He no longer fears anxiety; instead, he accepts it. Charlie now knows it's OK *not* to do things that make him anxious, because it just made things worse for him. He was experiencing firsthand the *curious paradox* Rogers mentioned, where change comes about almost unnoticed, which, for Charlie, it did and continues to do so.

Of course, there are still times when he struggles; the difference now is that he no longer feels hopeless. His parents also feel empowered to remove anxieties, rather than thinking they are "bad" parents who need to try harder. The difference is now that Charlie and his family know he is autistic, and that's OK. They are no longer waiting for a time when he will be *fixed*. They know now there is nothing broken about Charlie. He is exactly who he is meant to be, with his achievements and his limitations, just like the rest of us.

For a clearer understanding of how acceptance-based support impacted Charlie, the following overview is provided within the SEND Four Areas of Need.

| *Area of Need* | *Before Support* | *After Support* |
|---|---|---|
| **Communication and Interaction** | Stopped engaging with school, and all professionals.<br>Selectively mute.<br>No engagement with extended family.<br>Isolated from peers. | Engaging in weekly sessions with staff.<br>No longer selectively mute during sessions.<br>Spending more time with family and friends. |
| **Cognition and Learning** | Could not engage in any form of learning. | Engaging in learning again.<br>Happy to explore interest-led learning. |
| **Social, Emotional, Mental Health** | Severe anxiety.<br>Low self-esteem.<br>House bound.<br>Disengaged with family. | Calmer, able to express feelings.<br>More confident and happy.<br>Able to leave house.<br>Socialising with family and friends. |
| **Sensory and Physical** | Hiding under a blanket for safety.<br>Not coping with anxiety when in sensory triggering environments. | Has stopped using blanket during sessions.<br>Is more aware of anxious feelings, and how to cope with them when having too much sensory information. |

Charlie's story as you will read throughout the book, is not an isolated case; it reflects what is possible when we choose to listen, and to accept a child for exactly who they are, *warts and all*, instead of focusing all our efforts on outcomes, fixing problems, and changing behaviours to fit flawed narratives much like "*school is the best place for a child*", when for so many children it really isn't.

Here is some feedback from his mother:

> *From the trauma of school to where we are now, with acceptance-based support being introduced to us, the difference is absolutely outstanding. He's accepting himself; he's accepting that he is autistic and that he has anxiety. There are days that are really difficult for him, but he knows that's OK, and on those days when he is unable to go out and do things, that's OK, we stay at home, and he's in his safe space doing what he needs to do. He is learning to accept himself for who he is, and it has made a massive difference to everyone's lives. We are all positively impacted. As a family, we now get to do things together that we never thought we'd ever be able to do again.*

## Summary

I think it is important as professionals to be aware that we can often fall into the trap of thinking our role is only to find solutions to problems that autistic children present as having, when this is often not the case, especially when supporting the complexities of autistic individuals. There is another approach, a humanistic one, where we focus not on fixing problems but instead listening, understanding, and accepting the child or young person exactly as they are, without conditions.

These first two chapters have introduced you to the concept of acceptance and its practical application in supporting autistic children and young people. In the following chapters, we shift our perspective to examine further the need for new models of support, as we explore the reality behind the present systems that shape autistic children's lives in mental health and education. In the coming chapters, we look at what is broken, why, and what needs to change if we are to effectively support autistic children and their families.

We begin our journey by exploring the complex world of the mental health system.

## Notes

1 Warts and All Article (Accessed July 2025). https://www.historyextra.com/period/stuart/where-does-phrase-warts-and-all-come-from-history-etymology/
2 Origin Article for Warts and All. https://wordhistories.net/2017/08/11/warts-and-all-origin/
3 House, R., Kalisch, D. & Maidman, J. (2017). *Humanistic Pyschology: Current Trends and Future Prospects*. Routlege.
4 Mistry, L.N., Neelkanthan, S., Deshpande, S.S., Jawdekar, A.M., Shah, P.P. & Khachane, N.A. (2024). Matters of the Mind: A Look into the Life of Sigmund Freud. *Cureus*, October 15, 16(10), p. e71562. https://doi.org/10.7759/cureus.71562. PMID: 39552960; PMCID: PMC11563769.
5 Simply Psychology Article on Operant Conditioning (Accessed January 2026). https://www.simplypsychology.org/operant-conditioning.html
6 Waters, R.H. (1958). Behavior: Datum or Abstraction. *American Psychologist*, 13(6), pp. 278–282. https://doi.org/10.1037/h0046500
7 Overskeid, G. (2007). Looking for Skinner and Finding Freud. *American Psychologist*, September, 62(6), pp. 590–595. https://doi.org/10.1037/0003-066X.62.6.590. PMID: 17874899.
8 Overskeid, G. (2007). Looking for Skinner and Finding Freud. *American Psychologist*, September, 62(6), pp. 590–595. https://doi.org/10.1037/0003-066X.62.6.590. PMID: 17874899.
9 Solms, M. (2018). The Scientific Standing of Psychoanalysis. *BJPsych International*, February, 15(1), pp. 5–8. https://doi.org/10.1192/bji.2017.4. PMID: 29953128; PMCID: PMC6020924.
10 Freud, S. (1960). Letter to Marie Bonaparte, 13 August 1937. In E.L. Freud (Ed.), *Letters of Sigmund Freud*. Translated by Tania and James Stern (p. 436). New York: Basic Books.
11 Hoffman, L. & Lac, V. (2019). *The Evidence-Based Foundations of Existential Humanistic Therapy*. Abingdon: Routledge.
12 Hoffman, L. & Lac, V. (2019). *The Evidence-Based Foundations of Existential Humanistic Therapy*. Abingdon: Routledge.
13 Rogers, C.R. (1961). *On Becoming a Person: A Therapist's View of Psychotherapy*. Boston: Houghton Mifflin.

14 Rogers, C.R. (1961). *On Becoming a Person: A Therapist's View of Psychotherapy*. Boston: Houghton Mifflin.

15 Rogers, C.R. (1961). *On Becoming a Person: A Therapist's View of Psychotherapy*. Boston: Houghton Mifflin.

16 Yorke, A. (2021). A Case Study of Two Autistic Children Supported by the Accept Approach: A New Acceptance Based Strategy. *Good Autism Practice*, 22(2), pp. 34–45.

Chapter 3

# The Madness of the System

One planet, many different worlds. Some people live life accessing 24-hour supermarkets, electric cars, free education, organic food, and clean clothing, while others are left uneducated, with no clothes, fighting for food, and chained to wooden posts for having a mental health condition. A man in an institution in Kenya recently shared *his* world with the Human Rights Watch in February 2020:

> *I've been chained for five years. The chain is so heavy. It doesn't feel right; it makes me sad. I stay in a small room with seven men. I'm not allowed to wear clothes, only underwear. I have to go to the toilet in a bucket. I eat porridge in the morning, and if I'm lucky, I find bread at night, but not every night . . . It's not how a human being is supposed to be. A human being should be free.*[1]

In a different part of the world, a 10-year-old autistic girl in the United Kingdom, struggling with debilitating anxiety, is hiding under a classroom table, frozen by fear, unable to move. The adults around her are confused, not knowing how to help. Grasping a pad and pen, she attempts to express in words how she is feeling:

> *What stupid person invented school? They have ruined my day. I thought I was going to have an amazing day. But now December is ruined. It's very cosy under the table where no one cares about me. I am crying again. Hell is better than here. I don't know what's happening. I can't breathe. There is a random person I've never seen before in the room, and I don't know where my teacher is. I am sitting here under the table crying. I don't know what to do; there is no internet, so I can't text Mum or Dad to help me. Help me, help me, help me, help me, help me. I can't breathe. I am gonna go to sleep now. I need to go home, but I don't know who to ask.*[2]

The man with mental health issues, chained to a post in Kenya, and the autistic girl trapped under a table in the UK, are both experiencing the *burden* of mental health. Both are misunderstood. Both are scared. Both are calling out to be freed from their *restraints*, one physical, one mental. Their real experiences of mental pain and strife are unlike anything most of us will ever experience in our lifetimes.

DOI: 10.4324/9781003686064-5

## What Is Mental Health?

The World Health Organization defines mental health as "A state of mental well-being that enables people to cope with the stresses of life, realise their abilities, learn well and work well, and contribute to their community".[3] This definition frames mental health through the lens of flourishing and functioning in life, *without* any illness.

However, in reality, *not* experiencing stress, accessing our full potential, and being happy at work in education and our communities is far from the *norm*. To be completely psychologically well nowadays is a rare commodity. We never read in the news "*Man Has an Ordinary Day, and Feels no Stress*" or "*Couple Share Their Secrets to a Loving Life With no Relationship Issues at All*".

What we actually read are stories with headlines sharing a different reality where people are not coping, and nobody seems to be able to help. We read "*Global burden of mental health on governments*",[4] "*Families begging for mental health support*",[5] "*Man who died by suicide faced a total lack of care and compassion*",[6] and "*More than a million people every week show suicidal intent when chatting with ChatGPT*".[7]

The positive experience of mental health is clearly something that many people do *not* have. Even as of September 2025, there is predicated over 1 billion people living with a mental health condition, with anxiety and depression being the most common.[8] The situation is bleak. Things need to change. But what?

### Reflection

I always knew these two chapters on mental health would not be easy to write, especially when sharing real-life experiences of autistic children and young people being let down. But I think it's really important to share the realities that are faced because if we don't realise what is really going on, we are never going to start making any meaningful change.

I am also aware not everyone feels this way or has negative experiences of mental health support, and there are many skilled and passionate mental health professionals and practitioners try to make a difference.

## How Is Mental Health Understood?

When thinking about what mental health actually is, and why there are over a billion people worldwide who experience mental health difficulties,[9] it depends on the lens you view it through. With the medical model lens, mental health is viewed as *pathological*, with issues such as depression and anxiety needing to be diagnosed and treated. Through the medical lens, mental health issues are located in the brain caused by internal dysfunction, such as chemical imbalances or neurological anomalies,[10] with psychiatry traditionally relying on diagnostic systems such as the DSM-5 to classify conditions.[11]

Another lens with a different view is the social model, which sees mental illness not as a defect but as a response to social barriers, exclusion, and unmet needs.[12] The focus here in supporting mental illness is to look at ways of removing barriers that restrict a person's life, so that they lead more independent lives and have more freedom of choice.[13] However, to bring meaningful mental health support through the social model lens would require more organisational support, time, training, and systems that value safety and relationship-building rather than symptom control, which is challenging because mental health support is dominated by the medical model, which focuses primarily on symptom treatment.[14]

## A Humanistic Perspective

Another perspective to consider is mental health through the lens of humanistic psychology. Carl Rogers argued that a person experiences psychological distress because they are in a state of incongruence between their real self and the self they think they need to be to become truly accepted. Rogers believed that this is why people feel anxiety, shame, and self-criticism.

Abraham Maslow also argued that mental health is strongly related to the self. He argued that the reason a person is struggling with mental health issues is that they don't feel safe or accepted, unable to reach their potential.[15] Through the humanistic lens, when someone experiences mental health issues, it is not because there is something *broken* inside of them; it is more an indicator that a person requires acceptance, to feel a sense of belonging, and to find *meaning* in their lives. We discuss humanistic principles in more detail in Part Two.

## Real-Life Experiences

When we look at real-life accounts shared by autistic families, we can see that many are facing exclusion and a lack of understanding when seeking mental health support. In July 2025, ITV News reported on Josh, a 21-year-old with severe learning disabilities and autism.[16] His parents were desperate to help him, so they sought support. What was meant to be a three-month assessment, where his parents thought he would receive the help he so desperately needed, turned into four years of incarceration in a secure unit. His parents said seeking help from professionals was the "*biggest regret of their lives*". They describe his treatment as abusive and degrading, where he was overmedicated, repeatedly restrained, and placed into segregation for long periods of time, even spending his 21st birthday in isolation.

Much like Josh, Kasibba, an autistic adult, was detained in a mental health hospital at the age of 7,[17] without even being diagnosed with a mental health condition. She spent 45 years imprisoned, with 25 of those years locked in long-term segregation. She was even assessed in 2013 and deemed safe to live in the community, but it took another nine years before she was released.[18] Dr Staite, who helped free Kasibba, said,

> *I hadn't ever seen anyone living in the situation that she was living in. And I think what was really shocking was it was all legitimised.*[19]

Kasibba's case is one of the most extreme examples of the inappropriate detention of an autistic person with mental health issues. Sadly, she is not alone; the same report exposed the lack of care for another young girl called Amelia, who was placed in long-term segregation at the age of 14, and another called Maeve, an autistic young person also detained as a child, and sectioned for much of her adult life.[20]

As mentioned at the beginning, in many parts of the world, today, people are exposed to inhumane treatment as a result of their mental health. One example of this comes from the stark realisation that there are still people bound and shackled around the world for having mental health issues. The Human Rights Watch (HRW), in 2020, uncovered harrowing evidence of people with mental health and intellectual disabilities chained and shackled in the following places around the world: Afghanistan, Argentina, Armenia, Bangladesh, Benin, Bolivia, Brazil, Brunei, Burkina Faso, Cambodia, Chile, China, Colombia, Côte d'Ivoire, the Dominican Republic, the Democratic Republic of Congo, East Timor, Ecuador, Egypt, El Salvador, Ethiopia, Ghana, Guatemala, Haiti, Honduras, India, Indonesia, Iraq, Israel, Japan, Jordan, Kenya, Laos, Liberia, Mexico, Morocco, Mozambique, Nicaragua, Nigeria, Oman, Pakistan, Palestine, Paraguay, Peru, the Philippines, Russia, Saudi Arabia, Senegal, Sierra Leone, Somalia, South Africa, South Sudan, Sudan, Tajikistan, Tanzania, Thailand, Togo, Turkey, Uganda, Yemen, and Zimbabwe.[21]

It defies belief that today, hundreds of thousands of men, women, and children are shackled and held in "*overcrowded, filthy rooms, sheds, cages or animal shelters and are forced to eat, sleep, urinate, and defecate in the same tiny area*".[22] What makes it worse is that governments know this is happening because of inadequate support from mental health services and continuing widespread negative beliefs that stigmatise people with mental health issues, and still nothing meaningful is being done to help; these people remain shackled and forgotten.

## The Story of James Norris

In the UK, physically shackling people with mental health issues was outlawed during the 1820s.[23] Inspired by the Enlightenment movement, public opinion was changing during this time, with many people standing up against the poor treatment of people with mental health issues. A new approach, called *moral treatment*,[24] was emerging in France, England, and the United States, rejecting the brutality of confinement and punishment of people with mental health issues, and replacing support with more understanding and compassion, with spacious, well-kept hospitals with gardens and fresh air.

At the time, a well-documented case of an American sailor held at Bethlem Hospital became a turning point for mental health reform in the UK. Recognised as one of the most horrific icons in Bethlem's History,[25] James Norris was viewed as one of the most violent patients, and after killing a keeper and attacking two other men, he spent all his time in solitary confinement. He was restrained many times, but due to his feeble arms and hands, he would often break free and use his shackles as weapons. Until John Haslam, the resident apothecary, created a device that locked Norris in place for over ten years, leaving him helpless and unable to move.[26]

When prison reformer Edward Wakefield visited Bethlem, he witnessed semi-naked men and women chained to the walls as if they were vermin and was horrified by the appalling treatment of these patients. When he came upon James Norris, he found him with "*a stout ring was riveted around his neck, from which a short chain passed to a ring made to slide upwards or downwards on an upright massive iron bar, more than six feet high, inserted into the wall. Round his body, a strong iron bar about two inches wide was riveted; on each side of the bar was a vertical projection, which, being fashioned to and enclosing each of his arms, pinioned them close to his sides*".[27]

James Norris was held in this device for over ten years. Unable to move. Wakefield wanted this to stop, so as part of a calculated propaganda move, he commissioned an artist to paint a picture of Norris, which was then printed in several newspapers. It was this story of James Norris that sparked public outcry, and as Francis Schiller wrote, "*set all London agog*",[28] prompting a Parliamentary Select Committee inquiry and ultimately leading to the end of the use of chains in the UK.[29] James Norris' case is credited with leading to the Madhouses Act 1828, which further attempted to regulate the treatment of mental health patients in private institutions.

### Reflection

Although a difficult read, James Norris' story demonstrates that when we stand up against poor treatment of mental health things *can* change, replacing support with more understanding and compassion, which is where I believe we need to be helping autistic people with mental health issues. More support. More compassion.

## Mistakes and Misunderstandings

Although the 1800s are a long time ago now, we can look back and see where the obstacles existed for people with mental health issues. We know there was a clear lack of scientific understanding,[30] poor conditions as a result of overcrowded asylums,[31] the fear and social stigma of mental illness,[32] underfunding,[33] and emerging conflicts in treatment.[34]

I believe that, sadly, some of these same obstacles exist today, just in different ways. A 2024 systematic review of improving mental care for autistic children and young people, funded by the National Institute for Health Research (NIHR), identified, "*Children with autism are left in mental distress and miss out on crucial years of education, and parents and carers find themselves blamed by the educational establishment (and often the medical professionals) for what is seen as bad behaviour rather than a distressed child in need of help*" (p. 27).[35]

The NIHR is not alone in identifying these issues. In 2019 the All-Party Parliamentary Group for Autism (APPGA) released a report, "The Autism Act 10 years on", and found that "*many thousands of autistic people who need support in the classroom, at home, at work and in every aspect of everyday life, simply are not getting it*", and when considering why this is, they found the problem is a "direct" cause of a "*Poor autism understanding by professionals and a low awareness of the duties*".[36]

This report showing the lack of professional understanding, is not in isolation. In 2025, we can see other reports arguing there is a "poor professional understanding", with mental health services rejecting referrals for autistic people, leading to them being "*bounced around between* services",[37] and the whole SEND system in the UK recognised as "*one of the worst it has ever been*",[38] having reached a crisis point,[39] and now even deemed not to be financially sustainable.[40]

## The Role of the Mental Health Professional

Given that professional roles are identified in these reports as one of the causes of the mental health issues and lack of support for autistic people, it seems important to consider briefly what exactly the role of a professional supporting autistic children and young people is meant to be.

UK legislation states that a professional's role in this context is to "*improve the quality of life of those being supported*",[41] and to work within frameworks in which all are expected to listen,[42] adapt,[43] collaborate with families,[44] protect children's rights,[45] and provide child-centred support rather than a system-led model.[46]

There is also support for professionals in their roles, with several key framework guides to follow. The Equality Act 2010[47] underpins *all* support guidance, placing a legal duty to safeguard the rights of autistic children and ensure that reasonable adjustments are made to remove barriers. The SEND Code of Practice 2015[48] outlines all statutory duties for mental health practitioners, educators, and local authorities, with a focus on child-centredness and collaboration with families. In addition, the NICE Guidelines on Autism[49] aim to ensure that professional practice aligns with evidence-based recommendations.[50]

Following these guidelines, we would presume professionals have the right understanding and know how to perform the role effectively, especially when these frameworks also hold them accountable, ensuring consistent, appropriate, and effective support for all autistic children and their families. This, for me, raises another question: if the role of a mental health professional is grounded in well-informed frameworks, why do we hear of so many autistic children and their families being let down?

## The Problem That Won't Go Away

Today, across the world, professionals are tasked with supporting autistic people with mental health issues and are failing at an alarming rate. Although we do not physically shackle people in the UK, as we still see happening across the world, there are lived experiences of thousands of autistic children who *feel* shackled, not by chains but by systems that misunderstand and dismiss their experiences. On our own doorstep, many children are trapped in their own homes, in their bedrooms, paralysed by anxiety, drowning in depression. Families are falling apart under the pressure, watching helplessly as their children are bound in their own chains, and we are doing nothing about it. I believe these issues still remain because *autistic children and young people are still viewed as problems needing to be fixed.*

**Real-Life Experience 3**

As a specialist teacher and an autism advisor working in schools, and supporting families, although not a therapist, there have been many times over the years I have had to support autistic children and young people with mental health issues, on the ground in their classrooms and in their homes. It's never easy, and although trained in applying autism strategies, it was always a challenge to help them effectively, especially when there was no mental health support available for them to access. Either they were refused support because of being autistic, or they were on a long waiting list. We had to do the best we could.

I now want to share a story about a young person whom I helped using acceptance-based support. He was 16 years old when I first started supporting him. He was in a constant state of anxiety, and his family felt lost, not knowing what to do to help him. He was supported at the time by social services, and at one point, things were so bad that there was talk of removing him from the home because he was a possible risk. He would constantly climb out of his bedroom window and sit on the roof. He would often run away, only to be found walking the streets or by his local train tracks.

When I started supporting him, his mental health support had been withdrawn because they did not know how else to help. He was put on medication, but it didn't seem to do much for him. Most days, he spent in his room, and at night, he could not be alone, so he slept on the floor in his parents' room. At first, he was very reluctant to engage with me. For the first few months, my only focus was to get him to a place of psychological safety.

I applied the Four Foundations of Acceptance during every session, and over time, he began to respond to the two rules of learning. He really embraced "being the boss", and I could see for this young person – that was my way in. Giving him complete autonomy was what changed a lot for us. He engaged in most sessions and loved doing what he wanted. We would spend time in his garden playing basketball, or he would show me tricks on his bike, and back flips on his trampoline. We would play puzzle games, go for walks, and drive to the shops to get his favourite drink.

We then got to the point where he would leave his house with us, and that was all he needed – to be given some purpose, and to be able to control what we do. He is such a joy to be around, and although very complex, and his mental health issues were always lingering, I noticed after around six months of support, his past behaviours had become less. He no longer escaped from the house or climbed onto his roof and was a lot more interested in life.

At age 17, he asked his parents to learn how to drive. Although it was very challenging for him, his strong determination drove him to do everything possible to achieve his goal. He excelled in his driving lessons and only needed some of the instructor's support, but he found it difficult to pass his theory test. This was his biggest challenge. However, he never gave up, and after many attempts, he passed and got his full driving license. That day was more than an achievement. His family had been through so much. He had been let down, left without an education for years. That day, he fought through it all and achieved the impossible. Now, he helps his family. He drives them places, goes to the shops for them, and takes them out. He is calmer. Happier and has found some purpose in his life for the first time.

## Summary

My goal for this chapter was to start showing that, based on the findings and stories shared, mental health support today continues to fall short for many autistic children and young people. The primary focus remains on fixing, correcting, adjusting, and improving them. Addressing this issue in mental health is crucial to prevent failing another generation of children and young adults. I believe autistic children and young people with mental health issues need to feel psychologically safe, to be unconditionally accepted, and to learn that they can find purpose that is meaningful to *them*, and to be given opportunities for growth to move towards self-acceptance. All this is achievable if we only learn to think differently and to address the issues we face.

In the next chapter, we will discuss the mental health crisis in more detail, delving into our past and examining how it still impacts what we do today. Although it may be a challenging read, the lessons learned from past mistakes are crucial for progress and for securing a better future for our autistic children and young people. As George Santayana said in his book, *The Life of Reason*:

> *Those who cannot remember the past are condemned to repeat it.*[51]

## Notes

1 Human Rights Watch Report (2020). https://www.hrw.org/report/2020/10/06/living-chains/shackling-people-psychosocial-disabilities-worldwide
2 **This is a journal entry taken from the diary of a 10-year-old autistic child. She was writing this in real-time hiding under a table, during a lesson in class. This was then shared with her parents, who gave me permission to share her *word-for-word* record log.
3 World Health Organization Definition of Mental Health. https://www.who.int/health-topics/mental-health#tab=tab_1
4 Fan, Y., Fan, A., Yang, Z. & Fan, D. (2025). Global Burden of Mental Disorders in 204 Countries and Territories, 1990–2021: Results from the Global Burden of Disease Study 2021. *BMC Psychiatry*, May 15, 25(1), p. 486. https://doi.org/10.1186/s12888-025-06932-y. PMID: 40375174; PMCID: PMC12080068.
5 BBC News Article. Children's Mental Health: 'I Was Begging for Help for My Daughter' (Accessed November 2025). https://www.bbc.co.uk/news/uk-england-59896025
6 BBC News Article. We Begged for Help for Years, But It Wasn't There (Accessed November 2025). https://www.bbc.co.uk/news/articles/cjekvjyxk0po
7 Guardian Article. More Than a Million People Every Week Show Suicidal Intent When Chatting with ChatGPT. *OpenAI Estimates* (Accessed October 2025). https://www.theguardian.com/technology/2025/oct/27/chatgpt-suicide-self-harm-openai
8 https://www.who.int/news/item/02-09-2025-over-a-billion-people-living-with-mental-health-conditions-services-require-urgent-scale-up
9 Mental Health Issues. Statistics from the World Health Organization. https://www.who.int/news/item/02-09-2025-over-a-billion-people-living-with-mental-health-conditions-services-require-urgent-scale-up
10 Gordon, J.A. (2024). The Neuroscience of Mental Illness: Building Towards the Future. *Frontiers in Psychiatry*, [online]. https://pmc.ncbi.nlm.nih.gov/articles/PMC11490687
11 Diagnostic and Statistical Manual of Mental Disorders (DSM-5-TR). https://www.psychiatry.org/psychiatrists/practice/dsm
12 Oliver, M. (1990). *The Politics of Disablement*. London: Macmillan.
13 https://www.disabilitynottinghamshire.org.uk/index.php/about/social-model-vs-medical-model-of-disability/
14 Hogan, A.J. (2019). Social and Medical Models of Disability and Mental Health: Evolution and Renewal. *CMAJ*, January 7, 191(1), pp. E16–E18. https://doi.org/10.1503/cmaj.181008. PMID: 31009368; PMCID: PMC6312522.
15 Rogers, C.R. (1961). *On Becoming a Person: A Therapist's View of Psychotherapy*. Boston: Houghton Mifflin.
16 ITV News Article. We Wish We'd Never Asked for Help: Family's Hurt as Thousands with Learning Disabilities Locked Up (December 2025). https://www.itv.com/news/2025-07-14/familys-hurt-as-thousands-with-learning-disabilities-locked-up
17 ITV News Article. We Wish We'd Never Asked for Help: Family's Hurt as Thousands with Learning Disabilities Locked Up (December 2025). https://www.itv.com/news/2025-07-14/familys-hurt-as-thousands-with-learning-disabilities-locked-up
18 Learning Disability Article. Autistic Woman Stuck in a Mental Health Hospital for 45 years (Accessed December 2025). https://www.learningdisabilitytoday.co.uk/news/autistic-woman-stuck-in-a-mental-health-hospital-for-45-years
19 Kasssiba's Story. https://www.bbc.co.uk/news/articles/cly43png991o
20 Kasssiba's Story. https://www.bbc.co.uk/news/articles/cly43png991o
21 https://www.hrw.org/report/2020/10/06/living-chains/shackling-people-psychosocial-disabilities-worldwide
22 https://www.hrw.org/report/2020/10/06/living-chains/shackling-people-psychosocial-disabilities-worldwide
23 Compton, N. (2017). *Off the Deep End: A history of Madness at Sea*. Bloomsbury.

24 https://socialwelfare.library.vcu.edu/issues/moral-treatment-insane/
25 Allderidge, P.H. (1991). Sketches from the History of Psychiatry: A Cat Surpassing in Beauty and Other Therapeutic Animals. *Psychiatric Bulletin* (now *BJPsych Bulletin*), 15, pp. 759–762.
26 Allderidge, P.H. (1991). Sketches from the History of Psychiatry: A Cat Surpassing in Beauty and Other Therapeutic Animals. *Psychiatric Bulletin* (now *BJPsych Bulletin*), 15, pp. 759–762.
27 Allderidge, P.H. (1991). Sketches from the History of Psychiatry: A Cat Surpassing in Beauty and Other Therapeutic Animals. *Psychiatric Bulletin* (now *BJPsych Bulletin*), 15, pp. 759–762.
28 Schiller, F. (1984). Haslam of "Bedlam", Kitchiner of the "Oracles": Two Doctors under Mad King George III, and Their Friendship. *Medical History*, 28, pp. 189–201.
29 Compton (2024). Rum, Lunacy and the Lash: History and Philosophy, Mental Health. *The British Psychological Soceity* (Accessed 12 August 2025). https://www.bps.org.uk/psychologist/rum-lunacy-and-lash
30 Porter, R. (2002). *Madness: A Brief History*. Oxford: Oxford University Press.
31 Scull, A. (1981). *Madhouses, Mad-Doctors, and Madmen: The Social History of Psychiatry in the Victorian Era*. Philadelphia: University of Pennsylvania Press.
32 Bartlett, P. & Wright, D. (1999). *Outside the Walls of the Asylum: The History of Care in the Community 1750–2000*. London: Athlone Press.
33 Parry-Jones, W.L. (1972). *The Trade in Lunacy: A Study of Private Madhouses in England in the Eighteenth and Nineteenth Centuries*. London: Routledge & Kegan Paul.
34 Hale, N.G. (1995). *The Rise and Crisis of Psychoanalysis in the United States: Freud and the Americans, 1917–1985*. Oxford: Oxford University Press.
35 Hale, N.G. (1995). *The Rise and Crisis of Psychoanalysis in the United States: Freud and the Americans, 1917–1985*. Oxford: Oxford University Press.
36 Hale, N.G. (1995). *The Rise and Crisis of Psychoanalysis in the United States: Freud and the Americans, 1917–1985*. Oxford: Oxford University Press.
37 National Autistic Society: Constant Fight Article (Accessed November 2025). https://www.autism.org.uk/what-we-do/campaign/empowering-autistic-voices/a-constant-fight
38 The Guardian Article (2024). The Worst It's Ever Been: Teachers Decry SEND Crisis in England's Schools. *The Guardian*, 23 December (Accessed 7 August 2025). https://www.theguardian.com/uk-news/2024/dec/23/the-worst-its-ever-been-teachers-decry-send-crisis-in-englands-schools
39 House of Commons Public Accounts Committee (2024). House of Commons. (2024). *Support for Pupils with Special Educational Needs and Disabilities in England*. HC 353. London: House of Commons (Accessed 7 August 2025). https://publications.parliament.uk/pa/cm5804/cmselect/cmpubacc/353/report.html
40 National Audit Office (2023). *Support for Pupils with Special Educational Needs and Disabilities in England*. London: NAO (Accessed 7 August 2025). https://www.nao.org.uk/reports/send-support-2023
41 Children and Families Act 2014, Sections 19*, 22, 25–27, 36(8), and 66. Equality Act 2010, Sections 19–20 (reasonable adjustments), Section 149 (PSED.
42 National Institute for Health and Care Excellence (2011). *Autism Spectrum Disorder in under 19s: Recognition, Referral and Diagnosis (CG128)*. London: NICE. https://www.nice.org.uk/guidance/cg128. And National Institute for Health and Care Excellence (2013). *Autism Spectrum Disorder in under 19s: Support and Management (CG170)*. London: NICE. https://www.nice.org.uk/guidance/cg170
43 HM Government (2010). *Equality Act 2010*. London: The Stationery Office. https://www.legislation.gov.uk/ukpga/2010/15/contents
44 Department for Education and Department of Health (2015). *Special Educational Needs and Disability Code of Practice: 0 to 25 Years*. London: DfE/DH. https://www.gov.uk/government/publications/send-code-of-practice-0-to-25

45 Department for Education and Department of Health (2014). *Children and Families Act 2014*. London: The Stationery Office. https://www.legislation.gov.uk/ukpga/2014/6/contents/enacted and HM Government (2018). *Working Together to Safeguard Children: A Guide to Inter-Agency Working to Safeguard and Promote the Welfare of Children*. London: HMSO. https://www.gov.uk/government/publications/working-together-to-safeguard-children-2
46 Department of Health (2015). *Future in Mind: Promoting, Protecting and Improving Our Children and Young People's Mental Health and Wellbeing*. London: DH. https://assets.publishing.service.gov.uk/government/uploads/system/uploads/attachment_data/file/414024/Childrens_Mental_Health.pdf
47 HM Government (2010). *Equality Act 2010*. Chapter 15. London: The Stationery Office (Accessed 27 August 2025). https://www.legislation.gov.uk/ukpga/2010/15/contents
48 Department for Education and Department of Health (2015). *Special Educational Needs and Disability Code of Practice: 0 to 25 Years*. London: Department for Education/Department of Health (Accessed 27 August 2025). https://www.gov.uk/government/publications/send-code-of-practice-0-to-25
49 National Institute for Health and Care Excellence (2013). *Autism Spectrum Disorder in under 19s: Support and Management (CG170)*. London: NICE (Accessed 27 August 2025). https://www.nice.org.uk/guidance/cg170
50 National Institute for Health and Care Excellence (2021). *Autism Spectrum Disorder in Adults: Diagnosis and Management (CG142, updated)*. London: NICE (Accessed 27 August 2025). https://www.nice.org.uk/guidance/cg142
51 Santayana, G. (1905). *The Life of Reason: Or the Phases of Human Progress*. New York: Charles Scribner's Sons.

Chapter 4

# The Echoes From the Past

Emily Dickinson, one of America's greatest and most original poets of all time,[1] wrote the poem "Much Madness is divinest Sense" around 1862, in the midst of the American Civil War, where strict societal rules dictated people's behaviour. She wrote, "*Much Madness is divinest Sense to a discerning Eye . . . Assent, and you are sane, demur, you're straightway dangerous and handled with a Chain*".[2] Attempting to show that what most call madness could actually be an intelligent way to think, Dickinson highlights a truth that I see remains today, just as it did in the 18th century: that what society deems "normal" is what is considered "normal". If you agree with society, you are deemed sane. If you disagree, you are considered a threat and dealt with. In this chapter, we delve further into mental health and explore why we continue to repeat the same mistakes, echoing patterns from the past.

When psychologist Hermann Ebbinghaus wrote that psychology has a long past but a short history,[3] He was pointing out that psychology became a science only in 1879 when Wilhelm Wundt set up the first psychological laboratory, and that humans have been thinking and feeling long before the study of behaviour began properly. This highlights that our present ideas have been shaped by thousands of years of history. Although modern psychological theories have come a long way, it is important to recognise that they are based on only a relatively limited scope of human experience.

Historical psychology attempts to address this, as an emerging field[4] exploring how historical thinking has shaped today's beliefs and values. For the context of Part One, this matters because we need to understand that our ideas on mental health and disability today are built on historical *guesswork,* limited understanding, and strong societal bias. In this chapter, I aim to further explore the past and ask: is the lack of understanding and support for autism and mental health we see today due to our historical mistakes?

In the 1800s, Samuel Howe was among the first to publish his work on children's mental health. Howe classified children deemed *mentally defective* into three main groups: "idiots", "fools", and "simpletons", as described in his 1858 paper "On the Causes of Idiocy" in *The Journal of Psychological Medicine and Mental Pathology*. He stated:

> *Idiots of the lowest class are mere organisms, masses of flesh and bone in human shape, in which the brain and nervous system have no command over the system*

DOI: 10.4324/9781003686064-6

> *of voluntary muscles; and which consequently are without power of locomotion, without speech, without any manifestation of intellectual or affective faculties. Fools are a higher class of idiots, in whom the brain and nervous system are so far developed as to give partial command of the voluntary muscles; who have consequently considerable power of locomotion and animal action; partial development of the affective and intellectual faculties, but only the faintest glimmer of reason, and very imperfect speech. Simpletons are the highest class of idiots, in whom the harmony between the nervous and muscular system is nearly perfect; who consequently have normal powers of locomotion and animal action; considerable activity of the perceptive and affective faculties; and reason enough for their simple individual guidance, but not enough for their social relations.*
>
> *(p370)*[5]

It seems unbelievable that only 200 years ago, mental health professionals saw it appropriate and normal to categorise children severely disabled as *idiots*, those with basic emotions as *fools*, and those deemed socially inadequate as *simpletons.* This type of language, known as "deficit discourse",[6] reveals the dehumanising way society back then did not accept children who were mentally ill *or* disabled, which although not recognised autistic children and young people would have been amongst these people, having no chance of a life, with society seeing them as a problem to be locked away, taken from their families and left to rot in asylums, not fit for purpose.

Michel Foucault described these asylums as a mechanism for segregation of "the mad", in what he called "the Great Confinement",[7] where Victorian asylums would actively seek to take children from their family homes, due to the belief that institutional care was morally necessary.[8] Within these asylums, children and young people would experience unimaginable environments, with widespread overcrowding, neglect, and abuse. Far removed from the initial aim of building asylums for moral treatment, these asylums were often described as vast human warehouses, not places of healing but of social disposal.[9] The state of the systems back in the 1800s is summed up perfectly by Lord Shaftesbury, who wrote in his diary on 5 September 1851:

> *Madness constitutes a right, as it were, to treat people as vermin.*[10]

Although we are no longer in the era of asylums and calling children idiots, viewed as untreatable, have we really moved away from dehumanising autistic children with mental health issues? Or have we merely changed the *appearance* of the oppression faced by autistic children and young people today? Of course, today, when describing autistic children and those with mental illness, we no longer use terms like "idiot", "simpleton", and "fool" because they are rightly considered offensive, discriminatory, and dehumanising. However, we still rely on deficit discourse when describing autistic children and their issues.

Today, it is now just more acceptable to use terms such as “defiant”, “disorder”, “challenging behaviour”, “pathological”, “non-compliant”, “oppositional defiance”, and “disruptive”, to name just a few. However, don’t these terms come from the same mindset, still framing children who are “different” as problems to be fixed? I don’t think we are as far removed from the 1800s as we might think. If we examine the core issues of the past, I don’t see that we have changed much at all. There were two main issues in the 1800s: (1) lack of understanding of differences and (2) mental health was seen as a burden on society. I still see these same issues today.

## A Lack of Understanding

Not too long ago, I was speaking with a young autistic adult. A few days previous to this, she had attempted to end her life and was found unconscious in the middle of a road. She was admitted to the hospital, in urgent need of mental health care, only to be sent home because they couldn’t find a bed for her. Instead, the decision was to treat her at home. As we spoke, I noticed there were bruises all over her arms and legs. She told me that when in the hospital, she had been physically restrained by who she said were “like big scary security guards”. I asked if she had been a danger to herself or tried to escape. She replied, “*No, I was just pacing up and down trying to get my thoughts together*”. No violence or risk to life. No danger to herself or anyone else. She was pacing, trying to self-regulate during a time of unimaginable stress, only to be physically restrained because they wanted her to stop pacing.

It is not uncommon to hear about experiences similar to those this young lady had. As we read in the previous chapter, harrowing stories of Josh and Kasibba, autistic young people with real-life accounts, show there is a clear lack of understanding of autism and mental health and how to support them in the right ways.

Another alarming discovery that shows this comes from the International Coalition Against Restraint and Seclusion (ICARS), which found in its report that the autistic community is a group most subjected to the use of restraint and seclusion. They identified many cases of young people being restrained in school settings in England, with parents directly sharing their children’s harrowing experiences.

> *Bruises to arms, chest, and ribs, black eyes, and nail marks in his shoulders that were bleeding. Locked in time-out room for the whole school day, just to be let out for lunch and put back in again until home time*
>
> *Red markings in the wrists/arms, bruising, a hole on the inside of his cheek, and he collapsed, complaining he couldn’t breathe and feel dizzy and sick. No medical attention was given.*[11]

## Mistreatment of Autistic Children

Today, there are still many autistic children being detained in mental health units. The National Autistic Society revealed that as of April 2025, there were 1,428 autistic people locked away in mental health hospitals.[12] They make a bold statement challenging the NHS and UK Government, because they have failed to meet their target to reduce the number of autistic people in mental hospitals.[13] What is going on? Why is nothing being done to prevent this, despite the widely accepted view that mental health hospitals are inappropriate settings for most autistic people, with rising cases of overmedication, seclusion, and unnecessary restraint.[14]

When considering data based on autism and mental health, according to the NHS in June 2025, the UK had 2,040 people with a learning disability or autistic people in mental health hospitals, with 250 autistic children under 18 held in inpatient units.[15] Although the National Autistic Society found that there has been some progress in moving people with learning disabilities out of hospitals, the number of autistic people detained has increased. In 2016, it was recorded that there were 38% of autistic people in hospitals; that percentage has now risen to 73%.[16]

In the 1800s, it was deemed necessary to restrain people with disabilities and mental health conditions physically. It was normal to see people strapped to chairs, locked in isolation rooms, and placed in straightjackets. These methods were accepted as effective forms of treatment for people experiencing seizures, or when in distress, or having communication difficulties. Although we now live in a world that does understand disabilities and mental health more, why is restraint still seen as an effective way to manage distressing behaviours in education and mental health settings?

Today, we still see autistic children being physically restrained for disobedience or placed in isolation for non-compliance. Are we truly that disconnected from the 1800s? Do we continue to misunderstand children and young people because our default response is simply to manage behaviours we consider "unacceptable"? Currently, in many settings, restraint is justified within safeguarding policies; while it may seem more humane, I have always believed the underlying aim of restraint, even though I was trained in the methods myself, remains unchanged: *eliminate undesirable behaviours and enforce compliance.*

## The Old Man

I recall a conversation I had with my critical care nurse whilst sitting outside my local pub. It was during my 30s that I experienced a nervous breakdown. I was acutely anxious and had developed a fear of leaving my home, a psychological problem known as *agoraphobia*.[17] At the time, I was receiving support from an NHS home crisis team, as it was agreed that I was too anxious to be placed into a mental health hospital. Just before my breakdown, I had been under the care of an NHS psychiatric team. After months of going back and forth, I was finally diagnosed as autistic with ADHD (attention deficit hyperactivity disorder) by a child paediatrician specialised in assessing adults for autism.

Back then, the home crisis team had not worked with many autistic adults due to the lack of adults being diagnosed. To be honest, much of the support was hit and miss for me; they tried all the traditional approaches to support anxiety, such as CBT, challenging my thoughts, etc., but it just made me worse. What did work, however, was the support I received from my critical care nurse. He was kind and thoughtful. He would take my calls whenever I was in a bad way and would listen to me reel off all my anxieties and obsessions, until I ran out of words. He didn't give me advice; he just listened. Without knowing it back then, that was exactly what I needed: just to be *listened* to. Not judged or given advice. I didn't need to be told to challenge my thoughts or face my fears. I just needed to be heard.

On this particular day, he came by to see how I was doing. I felt well enough to leave the house, so I agreed to take a walk to the local pub. Sitting outside, in the empty beer garden, we discussed various mental health issues and shared stories. One such story he told has stayed with me ever since, capturing much of what I am trying to highlight in this chapter.

The story was about an old man he was supporting who was experiencing severe mental health issues. He lived alone and was receiving mental health support for his schizophrenia. During a crisis, there were concerns raised that he had spoken about hearing a voice and his medical team decided that he needed to be put on medication to "fix" this issue. He was not depressed or anxious; he just had this voice. Interestingly, he told me the voice was not harmful to him in any way; he just heard it constantly. Eventually, he was treated with medication, and the voice went away. For the mental health team, this was deemed a success, or so they thought. He went on to explain,

> *After the voice stopped, an interesting thing happened. He began to develop severe depression, and his mental health deteriorated even more than it had before. He would not answer his door to his support worker, stopped going out of his flat, and became even more reclusive. You see, the thing that everyone forgot to consider was how he would cope without the voice in his head. He told me the voice was his best friend, and now his friend had gone. In the end, he stopped taking the medication, and his friend's familiar voice returned. The depression lifted, and he was back to his old self again.*

## Spinning Too Many Plates

My personal experience of being diagnosed and having a nervous breakdown back then was an awakening moment for me. Although I did not like the experience, I can see now that many of my issues came from thinking I had to "get rid" of my anxious feelings and "push myself" to leave the house because I wrongly believed that if I didn't, I would get worse. The message was always about seeing my problems as things needing to be fixed. When actually, all I needed was some regular conversation and to be listened to.

Looking back, I would say that it made complete sense to want to lock myself up in my house and not go to work. My panic attacks only got worse when I tried to stop them, because I thought it wasn't *normal* to have anxiety and not to be able to face going out of the house; there must be something wrong with me, and I needed help to get better. But what if that message is wrong? What if, when someone reaches a mental health crisis, we don't jump to labelling their issues and looking for ways to get rid of the feelings, but instead take the time to look at *why* a person feels that way, and begin support from there? Why don't we first listen to their life experiences, consider how their story has impacted their mental health, and then help to create space and time for them, through patience and real human support, instead of asking if they want to go on a two-year waiting list for talking therapy?

I took medication because my anxiety would not go away, which is all I wanted it to do. I hated having panic attacks and feeling like I was going to die. I could not shut my noisy brain off, and all I wanted was some peace and quiet from my mind. I was told that it is to do with the lack of serotonin in my brain, and taking medication would help to make this better. So I took the pills because I was desperate to get better. I know they do work for some people, which is a good thing. I see medication now more like an art than a science. I guess that unless you try them, you will not know whether they will help. For me, they helped a little, but I did not see any real change until I started to look at my anxiety in a completely different way: to *accept* it and be OK with the feelings and the thoughts, no matter how dark or unsettling they were.

I started to see my anxiety as something trying to "protect" me in some way from the overwhelming challenges I was facing at the time. I was *spinning too many plates*, and instead of just letting some of them drop and smash on the floor, I was desperately trying to keep them spinning, which I just couldn't. It was only when I started to accept that my anxious feelings were OK, and to tell myself it was good to sometimes stay in my house in my pyjamas with the curtains closed, eating too much pizza if that's what I needed at that time.

I now see it was OK for me to lock myself in my house and avoid the world. Why? Because my mum was dying of cancer, my autistic child was being failed in education, and I had just been diagnosed autistic, with no signpost for support. I was just left to deal with all this on my own. To somehow come to terms with all the bad things that were happening to me, and to now realise that it was down to my autistic brain and my inability to cope. All this was just too much to deal with. That is why I had severe anxiety and agoraphobia. Because my brain was telling me it's time to stop. It's time to rest. It's time to heal.

## Reframing Mental Illness

From a psychological perspective, I can see now that the way I chose to deal with my anxiety, through acceptance, is much like the thinking of humanistic psychologist Rollo May. May did not view anxiety as a "pathological" condition; instead, he argued it is an essential part of the human experience, signalling the potential for growth and self-awareness. He separated anxiety into normal and neurotic. Normal anxiety, he believed, was triggered when someone is faced with existential challenges, with neurotic anxiety developing as a result of avoiding or repressing these challenges.[18]

What helped me during this time was learning to accept my anxiety and not fight it. I began finding ways through, and to this day, over 15 years later, I have not had another panic attack. When I do feel anxious, which is a lot of the time, I now accept it as a natural response to stress, not as evidence that something is wrong with me, and instead listen to it and look at what it may be trying to tell me.

Rollo May would suggest that both the normal anxiety (my natural fear of my mum dying) and the neurotic anxiety (that I couldn't stop it from happening or feared being able to cope in life without her) were mixed together, and I just needed time to separate them. For example, the fear of losing my mother is a normal feeling, whereas being overly concerned about losing my mother and wanting it *not* to happen is neurotic anxiety. It was the result of this inner conflict within me, as I attempted to avoid the fact that my mother was dying, and I was denying that this was going to happen. The turning point for me came when I realised that all the things I was going through, my mother dying, my child's battles, my own diagnosis, were knowing that my defence strategies, not going out, shutting myself away, were from what was *really* happening. I can relate to what Rollo May said when referring to Søren Kierkegaard's views on anxiety:

> *Anxiety is our best teacher. If you don't have any anxiety at all, you're in very bad shape.*[19]

I believe we need to reframe anxiety and view it more as a natural and *inevitable* response to life's uncertainties, losses, and changes. It's OK to feel anxiety. As Rollo May suggested, it only becomes a problem when it forms into neurotic anxiety, as we try to push away or avoid it, which I think was what I was doing. The moment I began to accept it was the moment it went away.

## Pathologising Mental Illness

My own experience, of course, is just that, my own. However, when we look more widely into the reported mental health crisis across the world, we can see two main issues: (1) Anxiety and depression are the most recorded mental health issues. (2) We treat them through the medical model approach of pathologising them as something wrong with a person who experiences them. While we've made progress in treatment, I see that we still tend to view mental health issues as something abnormal inside, instead of recognising them as a different way of being. I believe this perspective is why we face a global mental health crisis and why autistic children are not adequately supported by existing mental health systems. Past mistakes in mental health support haven't helped us improve at all; instead, I believe they have contributed to our current state of chaos.

## Summary

Across the previous chapter and this one, I have attempted to show that the main reason autistic children are not supported in mental health is that, although we have undoubtedly moved forward since the 1800s, there are still two key underlying problems that are not being addressed, which are that autistic children are being failed because people are still trying to *fix* them, and that society still struggles to accept that autistic individuals perceive and interpret the world differently.

We no longer label children as idiots or simpletons, but deficit discourse still persists just under different terminologies, such as "disorder", "pathological", and "non-compliance". We have replaced asylums with hospitals, but still use physical restraint and overmedication, prioritising control over acceptance and understanding. We still mistake the behaviour of distress as a defect, and difference as something to be feared. Emily Dickinson's poetic words, in my opinion, remain just as relevant today as they were back in 1862: if you agree with what society deems "sane", you will be OK; if not, then you will be considered a threat and punished.

## Notes

1 Santayana, G. (1905). *The Life of Reason: Or the Phases of Human Progress*. New York: Charles Scribner's Sons.
2 Emily Dickinson Poetry Foundation 'Much Madness is Divinest Sense' (Accessed July 2025). https://www.poetryfoundation.org/poems/51612/much-madness-is-divinest-sense-620
3 Ebbinghaus, H. (1908). *Psychology: An Elementary Textbook*. Boston, USA: D.C. Heath & Co. https://www.gutenberg.org/files/52823/52823-h/52823-h.htm
4 Jackson, J.C. & Atari, M. (2025). Historical Psychology: How the Events of Yesterday Shaped the Minds of Today. *Current Research in Ecological and Social Psychology*, 9, p. 100247. https://doi.org/10.1016/j.cresp.2025.100247
5 Jackson, J.C. & Atari, M. (2025). Historical Psychology: How the Events of Yesterday Shaped the Minds of Today. *Current Research in Ecological and Social Psychology*, 9, p. 100247. https://doi.org/10.1016/j.cresp.2025.100247
6 Graham, L.J. & Slee, R. (2008). An Illusory Interiority: Interrogating the Discourse/s of Inclusion. *Educational Philosophy and Theory*, 40(2), pp. 277–293. https://doi.org/10.1111/j.1469-5812.2007.00331.x
7 Foucault, M. (1961/2006). *Madness and Civilisation: A History of Insanity in the Age of Reason*. London: Routledge.
8 Wright, D. (2011). *Mental Disability in Victorian England: The Earlswood Asylum, 1847–1901*. Oxford: Oxford University Press.
9 Scull, A. (1993). *The Most Solitary of Afflictions: Madness and Society in Britain 1700–1900*. New Haven: Yale University Press.
10 Scull, A. (1993). Museums of Madness Revisited. *Social History of Medicine*, 6(1), pp. 3–23. Epigraph credits: "Lord Shaftesbury, Diaries, 5 September 1851."
11 The ICARS Report England. Restraint and Seclusion in Englands Schools. https://againstrestraint.com/icars-report/
12 National Autistic Society Article 1,435 Autistic People Remain Locked Away in Mental Health Hospitals (Accessed December 2025). https://www.autism.org.uk/what-we-do/news/1-435-autistic-people-remain-locked-away-in-mental
13 National Autistic Society Article (Accessed December 2025). https://www.autism.org.uk/what-we-do/news/missed-target-to-reduce-number-of-autistic-people
14 National Autistic Society Article (Accessed September 2025). https://www.autism.org.uk/what-we-do/news/1-435-autistic-people-remain-locked-away-in-mental
15 Learning Disability Services Monthly Statistics, AT: July 2025, MHSDS: June 2025 (Accessed January 2026). https://digital.nhs.uk/data-and-information/publications/statistical/learning-disability-services-statistics/at-july-2025-mhsds-june-2025

16 https://www.autism.org.uk/what-we-do/news/1-435-autistic-people-remain-locked-away-in-mental
17 DSM 5 Definition of Agoraphobia. https://www.ncbi.nlm.nih.gov/books/NBK519704/table/ch3.t10/
18 May, R. (1950). *The Meaning of Anxiety*. New York: Ronald Press.
19 Schneider, K.J, Galvin, J, & Serlin, I. (2009). Rollo May on Existential Psychotherapy. *Journal of Humanistic Psychology*, 49(4), pp. 419–434.

Chapter 5

# A Disconnected Education System

Since the 1960s, when pioneering psychiatrist Lorna Wing and others fought to improve the lack of support for autistic children in education,[1] not much has changed. Today, support is still lacking, focused mostly on fitting autistic children and young people into an education system that often fails so many of them. With standardised curricula, overstimulating environments, overcrowded classrooms, and policies attempting to shape all children to fit societal norms, many autistic children and young people are falling out of education because they cannot cope with the demands placed on them by these systems. Something has to change, and quickly. It is time to move these children away from a disconnected education system and create *new* ones.

I don't believe that the solution for autistic children is to fix them. I also don't believe that we need to adapt or adjust the current system to fit their needs. I think this is where we are going wrong. We need a complete education *overhaul*: an entirely new education system, grounded in psychological safety, acceptance, and interest-led learning. Although this may appear somewhat radical, I do believe it is more than possible, and in this chapter, I aim to show how by returning to the wisdom of past educational thinkers and rediscovering the *original* purpose of education. However, before we do that, we need to look at what is in front of us and examine the realities of the current state of the education and SEND system in the UK.

## Our Present Reality

Our present reality is not good. Consider this statement from the House of Lords Select Committee on the Autism Act 2009-Report of Session 2024–26:

> *Autistic children and young people do not have equal access to education. Most autistic children and young people attend mainstream schools; many are unhappy there. Increasing numbers of families of autistic children are turning to home education, not because they want to, but because school is no longer an option for them. Rates of suspension and exclusion are also too high. A new generation of young autistic people is being set up to struggle.*[2]

DOI: 10.4324/9781003686064-7

Although the Autism Act 2009 was a step in the right direction, it has made little impact.[3] Sixteen years on, we can see there is still systemic failure in delivering the changes it proposed. We don't need to look far to see evidence of this.

Caroline Stevens, the chief executive of the National Autistic Society (NAS), in their 2021 school report, summed up the issue of autism support stating:

> *The education system in England is simply not working for autistic children.*[4]

This NAS report found that parents of autistic children continue to experience distressing and drawn-out battles to find the right educational support for their children, and concludes that the current education system remains unfit to support autistic children and young people.

Another report I want to use to highlight the state of our education system for autistic children and SEND in general comes from the Education Committee, which monitors the Department for Education. In a 2025 report, named "Solving the SEND Crisis",[5] it states:

> *The current system is not designed with inclusion in mind.*

Revealing a further problem, which lies with inclusion not being what it is meant to be. The report highlights that, while it is regarded as normal for large numbers of pupils with SEND to be educated in mainstream school settings, the current education system remains unsuited to effective inclusion. The report also found that since the Children and Families Act 2014, the number of children with special educational needs has risen dramatically, from 1.3 million to 1.7 million. Additionally, over 1.2 million children receive SEND support in schools, with almost half a million having an education, health, and care plan. The report also identified that families are battling for their children's right to an education, with little to no success. Their findings reveal that parents and families are exhausted from fighting for support, teachers are overwhelmed by the increasing demand to support more children with SEND, and professionals feel their services are nearing breaking point.

We are facing a crisis in the UK, with families struggling to fight for their children's right to a basic education, only to be let down at every turn. Another report by Ambitious About Autism[6] found that the education system is hiding a present-day *hidden* crisis[7] for many autistic pupils in mainstream settings, and also calling for a complete "overhaul" of the whole education system.

The message is clear: *the present education system is not working for many autistic children and their families.* The pressure to meet the high demands for support is too much for the current systems to cope with, and the worst part of this crisis is that, unless something changes now, things will only get worse, leaving more families without the help their children so desperately need.

What we need now is a new education system specifically designed for autistic children and young people who cannot engage with the traditional education model. They don't need reasonable adjustments, adapted timetables, wobble cushions to sit on, or quiet spaces to hide in. These children need something completely new, driven by their interests, where learning happens in their time and in their way. This is absolutely possible, and the guidance on how to do it is already in our grasp. We simply need to revisit history, explore the original purpose of education, and begin from there.

## The Purpose of Education

Education is one of humanity's oldest and most important pursuits,[8] and throughout the centuries, each generation and culture has sought to preserve its *true* meaning. Before children were expected to attend a school building and be taught specific subjects *not* of their choosing, education was viewed as a natural human process through which knowledge and meaning were passed down across generations. In ancient China (551–479 BCE), Confucius,[9] China's most revered sage,[10] believed learning should not be passive; instead, he taught that education must build virtue and social harmony. When describing education, Confucius said, "*Education breeds confidence. Confidence breeds hope. Hope breeds peace*"."[11] He saw education as empowering people and, in turn, creating hope for a better future, ultimately leading to peace.

During the same period, in India, there were Vedic scholars, often referred to as gurus or rishis.[12] Their approach to education was also that it should not be passive but should be collaboratively shared between the teacher and the student through reflection and recitation. Learning was delivered in small residential schools, where the focus of education was on holistic development of the whole person rather than just preparing them for exams or employment, as we see today. One of the most influential teachers of this time was the Buddha[13] (Siddhartha Gautama, 563–483 BCE), who viewed education as *a path to enlightenment and understanding*, focusing on experiential learning through dialogue and personal insight.

In Greece (470–399 BCE), Socrates showed that, through education, we can develop critical thinking and knowledge through dialogue rather than the passive transfer of information. He believed that a human could achieve intellectual independence by questioning their own assumptions and beliefs. Socrates believed that true learning comes from within the individual. He encouraged people to ask questions and to seek understanding, wisdom, and truth. He saw that people should be free, thoughtful, and independent thinkers, driven by a love of learning and personal growth,[14] and said:

> *Education is the kindling of a flame, not the filling of a vessel.*[15]

Then we have John Amos Comenius,[16] in the 1600s, who was a Czech philosopher believing that learning should be guided by the principles of nature, being natural, gentle, and universal. Developing a philosophy of education known as "Pansophism", he believed in universal, lifelong learning, accessible to everyone, arguing against the idea that education should be limited by class, age, or gender.

He believed the advancement of any civilisation is dependent on equal access to knowledge and understanding, he said:

> *Knowledge should be a living tree which grows out of the root, branches, blooms and bears fruit, rather than a pile of chopped wood.*[17]

A century later, we are introduced to the ideas of Jean-Jacques Rousseau (1712–1778), who believed that children are inherently good and that education should protect their natural development. In his work *Emile,* he confronts the process of formal education, arguing that it educates *the nature out of children.*[18] Rousseau proposed that for education to be effective, it needed to follow the natural stages of a child's growth, allowing play, curiosity, and exploration to guide learning. He also believed the child should be at the centre of their learning and not the teacher. His ideas challenged the notion of teacher-led learning and opened the door for child-centred learning.

Influenced by Rousseau, we then have Johann Heinrich Pestalozzi (1746–1827), who opened schools for poor children and believed also that education should nurture the *whole child.* Pestalozzi argued against the traditional educational approaches of his day, which did not respect the whole child, advocating instead an educational approach built on "love", "care", and "respect". He believed that education must go beyond academic learning, nurturing the mind, heart, and hands together to help children grow both socially and emotionally.[19]

## The Birth of the School

It was during the Industrial Revolution (1760–1840)[20] that mass schooling in the UK began to emerge, and many of the problems we face today began to develop. Mass schooling was what shaped the development of school reformers and idealists, and during this time, Adam Smith[21] argued that a stable and productive society required the growth of *an educated population.* He stated, "*The more they are instructed, the less liable they are to the delusions of enthusiasm and superstition*".[22]

Education was fast becoming a system that supported national stability as industrial growth increased and the demand for skilled workers grew, making it the primary purpose of education. Consequently, more funds were directed to schools, turning education from a private privilege into a public responsibility. This transition was the beginning of modern education[23]

Despite all these changes, many educational scholars continued to fight for the true meaning of education. Friedrich Fröbel, a student of Pestalozzi, was one such scholar. He believed that play was the most effective form of learning and disagreed with the mass schooling approach. In his book *The Education of Man,*[24] he emphasised the importance of a holistic approach to learning that included a child's spiritual, physical, emotional, and social development. Advocating for children to learn through nature and the outdoors, he developed the first "children's garden", which later developed into what we now know as "kindergarten", which fosters education through curiosity, creativity, and a sense of unity.

## Evolving Education

Then, in the early 20th century, American philosopher John Dewey began developing the concept of progressive education.[25] In his book *Democracy and Education,*[26] he argued that the foundations of learning must be experience and social participation. He stated, "*Education is not preparation for life; education is life itself*", creating classroom environments based on inquiry, reflection, and collaboration.[27]

In Italy, around the same time as Dewey, Maria Montessori created an educational approach that also emphasised respecting children as independent learners. She believed that when children were placed in thoughtfully designed environments, their development would naturally progress. In her book *The Montessori Method,*[28] she wrote, "*Never help a child with a task at which he feels he can succeed*".

In support of similar ideas to Montessori's, Rudolf Steiner developed "Waldorf education",[29] which blended art, rhythm, and imagination. He believed children learn best through imitation and creativity. Resisting the industrial education mindset, he fought for his method of learning, arguing that it was more effective than passive instruction. In his book *The Education of the Child,*[30] he said, "*Two magic words indicate how children enter into a relationship with their environment. These words are imitation and example*", arguing that children learn best through observing and copying the people around them.

Around the same time, Lev Vygotsky and Jean Piaget also began developing the psychological foundations that play a large role in what is now considered modern pedagogy.[31] Piaget demonstrated that children's learning progresses in stages as they develop and mature. He argued that children, during each of these stages, will see and understand the world in new ways. He showed, again, just as Confucius, Rousseau, Fröbel, Pestalozzi, and Dewey did before him, that children do *not* benefit from passive learning; they learn through building their own understanding through experiences as active explorers.

Vygotsky demonstrated that learning can be facilitated through social experiences. He believed that learning can be developed through communication and collaboration with others. He created the zone of proximal development, which explains that children respond when teachers act as guides and not controllers. He showed that as educators, our role is to find the "sweet spot"[32] between what a child can do independently and what they can do with some gentle support. He believed that "scaffolding" to support children in learning is how they can develop new skills, and with this support, gradually, the child begins to work independently.

## Post-War Reconstruction

Following the Second World War, education in the UK expanded rapidly. In 1944, the first Education Act[33] came into force, introducing major reforms that transformed schools in Britain. The act first made education free and compulsory for all children and created three stages of education: primary, secondary, and further education. The act also established a Ministry of Education,[34] giving local authorities the duty to provide free education to every child.

In 1967, England was also introduced to the Plowden Report,[35] which called for child-centred primary education. Influenced by the work of Piaget and Vygotsky, the report emphasised the importance of play in education and learning.[36] Sadly, around the same time, the battle between child-centred learning and standardised learning began to shift more towards the latter, due to concerns that there needed to be greater focus on testing and accountability. We see this in the Black Papers,[37] which argued a "*progressive collapse*" in education, suggesting that child-centred learning was leading to academic decline.

## A Battle for the Right Education

A battle over what education should be for was fast becoming a global issue, which led Paulo Freire to write his book *Pedagogy of the Oppressed*. Freire argued strongly that we cannot let traditional education (which focuses on standardised learning) ruin children's learning experiences. He argued the traditional model treated students as empty vessels to be filled, calling this problem the "*banking model*". This is where the teacher is viewed as the expert who deposits information into the student's mind (the empty vessel), and students are expected to listen, memorise, and repeat what they are taught, rather than being encouraged to question and think for themselves.

Freire was concerned that education had become a passive activity, serving as a tool for control and conformity and argued that instead, education should be based on dialogue and mutual respect, where the teacher and student can learn together, moving away from control or domination. He also argued that traditional education only served the interests of those in power. What he said needed to happen was what he termed the "problem-posing method". In this educational method, he suggested that teachers and students learned *together*, discussing real issues that affected their lives. Fighting to preserve the *true meaning of education,* Freire believed that education must be grounded in love and empathy, fostering understanding and freedom.[38]

## Losing the Battle

Unfortunately, the fight to preserve educational freedom was a losing battle after the Education Reform Act 1988[39] introduced the National Curriculum. Schools soon began to be judged based on data, making learning outcomes quantifiable. A decade earlier, the Warnock Report[40] had advocated for including children with special educational needs, but critics felt it didn't go far enough. Instead of fostering inclusive education, the report allowed segregation through special units and schools rather than ensuring that all children could be educated together in mainstream settings, which is the core goal of inclusion.[41]

Today, our education system is in a difficult place. Systems are overstretched, classrooms are overcrowded, and the focus is more on compliance than on well-being and the real meaning of education. Autistic children are expected to fit into these environments that are not set up to meet their needs, and this is why many children are falling away from education at a rapid pace, because they can't keep up. Learning is now more about control than the freedom of exploration. It appears we have completely overlooked the visionary thinkers who regarded education as life itself, rather than merely a way to measure progress and count the number of students achieving certain grades.

## Thirty Years of Failure

I have been supporting autistic children in education for over two decades. During that time, as a specialist teacher and an autism local authority advisor, I began to notice, about 10 years into my career, that the same problems kept resurfacing, with nothing being done about them. Millions of pounds were spent annually on reports, inquiries, training initiatives, and government schemes, yet those efforts appeared to make little to no impact in tackling the real problems. For nearly 30 years, the UK Government has stated that it will "prioritise" and "improve" support for autistic children in mainstream schools, with funding for inclusion and better access to specialist and mainstream education, but they have not managed to do so. I want to show you the evidence of this now.

In 1997, we were introduced to the Department for Education and Employment's Green Paper "Excellence for All Children".[42] This paper aimed to increase inclusion for all children with special educational needs, but it *failed*. How do we know it failed? Because just three years later, in 1999, we still see the problems existing.[43] There was still a lack of mainstream support, and children with SEND were still not getting the support or education they needed.

Responding to this, the Disability Rights Task Force argued that children with SEND must now have a "legal" right to mainstream education, stating clearly that it is now a civil rights issue.[44] Prior to this, children with SEND did not have a legal right; there was only a presumption that they should be given access to mainstream education. As a result, the Education Act 1996 was amended, making mainstream schools the default option for all children, which we could say was a positive step to offer further support. Still, even with the legal right now to a mainstream education, we were still failing autistic children.

We then see in 2001 that inclusion becomes a key part of law and policy.[45] However, the Audit Commission found that, despite all the changes, schools and local authorities *still* lacked the necessary training and funding to implement inclusion effectively.[46] As a result of the same failures, the Government, in another attempt to deal with the issues, released its "Every Child Matters Green Paper"[47] in 2003, which became just another government paper that revealed more of the same: a lack of support for SEND children that was still *not* being addressed. This paper found that many services for children and young people continued to struggle with effective collaboration, with local authorities, partner agencies, and service providers failing to communicate properly.

Consequently, children continued to fall through the gaps between services, and there was still a lack of support for children with SEND, which was reported to be inconsistent across regions, depending on priorities and funding. This paper also found that schools were being judged too narrowly on test results rather than on supporting the whole child's well-being, and that support systems were failing children with SEND, responding too late to their needs.

Then, in 2004, we received *another* overview of education support, "Removing Barriers to Achievement".[48] This report, once again, revealed many of the same issues we saw way back in the 1997 reports: *a system still struggling to meet the needs of children with SEND.* This 2004 paper found the same issues: education was *still* struggling, but now with children waiting too long for support and with teachers feeling they still lacked the proper training and confidence to teach autistic children in the classroom. The paper also found support varied across areas, with Ofsted identifying serious inequalities in access.[49] Furthermore, parents were fighting further battles for even the most basic support for their children, while special schools were beginning to express uncertainty about their roles and expectations in the education system.

Now, more than two decades later, we have the Department for Education's 2024–2025 report "Solving the SEND Crisis",[50] identifying the *same issues* that existed back in 1997. The SEND system is still in crisis and financially unsustainable, with local authorities still facing rising deficits, and a postcode lottery persists due to inconsistent assessments and a lack of national standards.

We now have the "Time to Deliver" report from the House of Lords Select Committee on the Autism Act 2009,[51] released in 2026, which reveals the stark truths that autistic people and their families are still facing in education, with the report stating, "*Outcomes have not improved, and a new approach is now urgently needed*",[52] calling for the Government to improve capacity and expertise across all forms of education provision, due to the autistic children and young people not experiencing the same level of access to education as their peers.

Nothing has changed in the past 30 years, and things are getting worse. Something has to be done. These reports are merely a dip in the ocean of failure and promises *unfulfilled.* Autistic children are *still* being failed and let down at an alarming rate, as much today as they have been historically. The same problems persist, with insufficient specialist support and an education system primarily focused on a *mainstream-first* model. What all of these reports, white papers, and reform strategies overlook is the one real issue that remains unaddressed: the education system does *not* need fixing for autistic children; it needs to create completely *new* models of education for these children and young people.

## Summary

For many autistic children and other neurodivergent learners, the education system is now unbearable. For the children who are intrinsically motivated to learn, through interest-led approaches, the system has had a catastrophic impact on their lives, not because they need extra support to fit in, but because it is "wrong" for them. I believe the answer lies in creating *new* education systems, not reforming the outdated and harmful ones we have today. In the next chapter, we explore how this can be achieved by addressing a common problem that has become so normalised in education that no one does anything about it. I refer to the old adage "You cannot put a square peg into a round hole" or, a better way to put it, "Square pegs need square holes".

## Notes

1 Gillberg, C. (2015). Lorna Wing OBE, MD, FRCPsych Formerly Psychiatrist and Physician, Social Psychiatry Unit, Institute of Psychiatry, King's College London, Co-Founder of the UK National Autistic Society. *BJPsych Bulletin*, February, 39(1), pp. 52–53. https://doi.org/10.1192/pb.bp.114.048900. PMCID: PMC4495836.
2 House of Lords Select Committee on the Autism Act 2009 (2025). *Time to Deliver: The Autism Act 2009 and the New Autism Strategy*. Report of Session 2024–26. London: House of Lords. Ordered to be printed 10 November 2025 and published 23 November 2025.
3 Report on the Autism Act Review. https://www.autistica.org.uk/news/new-autism-act-report
4 National Autistic Society School Report 202. https://www.autism.org.uk/what-we-do/news/school-report-2021
5 Education Committee Report 'Solving the Send Crisis'. https://publications.parliament.uk/pa/cm5901/cmselect/cmeduc/492/report.html
6 Education Committee Report 'Solving the Send Crisis'. https://publications.parliament.uk/pa/cm5901/cmselect/cmeduc/492/report.html
7 Ambitious Abut Autism School Report 2025. https://www.ambitiousaboutautism.org.uk/sites/default/files/reports/files/ambitious-about-autism-autism-in-education-report-may-2025.pdf
8 Bowen, J. (1981). *A History of Western Education: Volume I – The Ancient World: Orient and Mediterranean, 2000 B.C.–A.D. 1054*. London: Methuen.
9 Confucius (1997). *The Analects*. Translated by A. Waley. New York: Vintage Books.
10 Definition of Sage. https://www.merriam-webster.com/dictionary/sage
11 Confucius Quotes. https://www.open.edu/openlearn/education/12-famous-confucius-quotes-on-education-and-learning
12 Radhakrishnan, S. (1951). *Indian Philosophy*. Vol. 1. 2nd edn. London: George Allen and Unwin.
13 Sharma, R.N. (2002). *Philosophical Foundations of Education*. Delhi: Atlantic Publishers.
14 Kelam, I. & Vučić, J. (2019). The Applicability of the Socrates Method of Education in Education Today. *Pannoniana*, 3, pp. 115–145. https://doi.org/10.2478/pannonia-2019-0008
15 Illuminar Education article Education is the Kindling of a Flame, Not the Filling of a Vessel Socrates Enduring Educational Philosophy. https://illuminareeducation.com/education-is-the-kindling-of-a-flame-not-the-filling-of-a-vessel-socrates-enduring-educational-philosophy/
16 Comenius, J.A. (1632). *Didactica Magna*. Prague: Karolinum Press.
17 Comenius, J.A. (1632). *Didactica Magna*. Prague: Karolinum Press.
18 Rousseau, J.-J. (2007). *Emile; or, on Education*. Translated by B. Foxley. 1911; repr. Sioux Falls, SD: Nu Visions Publications, p. 11.
19 Pestalozzi, J.H. (1801). *How Gertrude Teaches Her Children: An Attempt to Help Mothers to Teach Their Own Children and an Account of the Method*. [Edition information if available].

20 https://www.worldhistory.org/British_Industrial_Revolution/
21 Carl, J. (2009). Industrialization and Public Education: Social Cohesion and Social Stratification. In R. Cowen & A.M. Kazamias (Eds.), *International Handbook of Comparative Education*. Springer International Handbooks of Education, Vol 22. Dordrecht: Springer. https://doi.org/10.1007/978-1-4020-6403-6_32
22 Kandel, I.L. (1933). *Studies in Comparative Education*. London: George G. Harrap.
23 Carl, J. (2009). Industrialization and Public Education: Social Cohesion and Social Stratification. In R. Cowen & A.M. Kazamias (Eds.), *International Handbook of Comparative Education*. Springer International Handbooks of Education, Vol 22. Dordrecht: Springer. https://doi.org/10.1007/978-1-4020-6403-6_32
24 Froebel, F. (1887). *The Education of Man*. New York: Appleton.
25 Dewey, J. (1916). *Democracy and Education*. New York: Macmillan.
26 Dewey, J. (1916). *Democracy and Education*. New York: Macmillan.
27 John Dewey Information. https://www.pedagogy4change.org/john-dewey/
28 Montessori, M. (1912). *The Montessori Method*. New York: Schocken.
29 The Steiner Approach. https://theeducationhub.org.nz/the-steiner-approach/
30 Steiner, R. (1907). *The Education of the Child*. London: Anthroposophical Press.
31 Modern Pedagogy Article. https://teachhq.com/article/show/the-educational-theorists-behind-modern-pedagogy
32 Simply Psychology Vygotsky Information. https://www.simplypsychology.org/vygotsky.html
33 Gov Report. https://www.legislation.gov.uk/ukpga/Geo6/7-8/31/enacted
34 Education Act 1944. https://www.britannica.com/topic/education/Education-Act-of-1944
35 Plowden Report (1967). *Children and Their Primary Schools*. London: HMSO.
36 Plowden Report (1967). *Children and Their Primary Schools*. London: HMSO.
37 Cox, C.B. & Dyson, A.E. (Eds.) (1969). *Fight for Education: Black Paper 1*. London: Critical Quarterly.
38 Harris, D.B. & Roter, D.L. (2024). Profound Love and Dialogue: Paulo Freire and Liberation Education. *Health Literacy Research and Practice*, July, 8(3), pp. e118–e120. https://doi.org/10.3928/24748307-20240613-02. Epub 2024 July 5. PMID: 38979815; PMCID: PMC11230641.
39 UK Government (1988). *Education Reform Act 1988: Chapter 40*. London: HMSO.
40 Department of Education and Science (1978). *Special Educational Needs: Report of the Committee of Enquiry into the Education of Handicapped Children and Young People (The Warnock Report)*. London: HMSO.
41 Warnock Report. https://disability-studies.leeds.ac.uk/wp-content/uploads/sites/40/library/Barton-Warnock.pdf
42 Department for Education and Employment (DfEE) (1997). *Excellence for All Children: Meeting Special Educational Needs*. London: HMSO. https://www.education-uk.org/documents/pdfs/1997-green-paper.pdf
43 Disability Rights Task Force (1999). *From Exclusion to Inclusion*. London: DRTF. https://dera.ioe.ac.uk/id/eprint/4553/1/drtf.pdf
44 Disability Rights Task Force (1999). *From Exclusion to Inclusion*. London: DRTF. https://dera.ioe.ac.uk/id/eprint/4553/1/drtf.pdf
45 Department for Education and Skills (DfES) (2001). *Inclusive Schooling: Children with Special Educational Needs*. London: DfES.
46 Audit Commission (2002). https://publications.parliament.uk/pa/cm200607/cmselect/cmeduski/memo/specialedneeds/ucm2802.pdf
47 Every Child Matters (2003). https://assets.publishing.service.gov.uk/media/5a7c95a4e5274a0bb7cb806d/5860.pdf
48 Removing Barriers to Achievement (2004). https://dera.ioe.ac.uk/id/eprint/4955/13/8b56f1b2944d88f593e89ae3009fa5c3_Redacted.pdf

49 Ofsted Findings (2009). https://assets.publishing.service.gov.uk/media/5a7c1aa840f0b61a825d67a0/0195.pdf
50 Solving the Send Crisis (2025). https://committees.parliament.uk/publications/49536/documents/265373/default/
51 House of Lords Select Committee on the Autism Act 2009 (2025). *Time to Deliver: The Autism Act 2009 and the New Autism Strategy*. Report of Session 2024–26. London: House of Lords. Ordered to be printed 10 November 2025 and published 23 November 2025.
52 House of Lords Select Committee on the Autism Act 2009 (2025). *Time to Deliver: The Autism Act 2009 and the New Autism Strategy*. Report of Session 2024–26. London: House of Lords. Ordered to be printed 10 November 2025 and published 23 November 2025.

Chapter 6

# Square Pegs Need Square Holes

The familiar saying, "*you can't put a square peg into a round hole*", is often used to refer to autistic children and young people who do not fit into the traditional education system,[1] this analogy is attributed to the writings of Sydney Smith, who, in his book, *Elementary Sketches of Moral Philosop*hy,[2] wrote, "*If you choose to represent the various parts in life by holes upon a table, of different shapes, some circular, some triangular, some square, some oblong, and the persons acting these parts by bits of wood of similar shapes, we shall generally find that the triangular person has got into the square hole, the oblong into the triangular, and a square person has squeezed himself into the round hole*".

What I find frustrating about the square peg, round hole analogy is that it doesn't inspire *meaningful* change. It is as though there is a unified agreement on what it stands for, but no actionable response. I believe this statement is essentially highlighting a specific point and would be clearer if rephrased as:

*Square pegs need square holes.*

When someone says, "*You can't put a square peg into a round hole*", people generally agree. But that's all they do. Much like a new Head Teacher brought in to improve a failing school, when he first addresses his staff, he says, "*Who wants change?*" and everyone raises their hands in agreement. He then asks, "*Who wants to change?*" and all the hands go down.

Whereas saying "*square pegs need square holes*", I believe, is more specific. This is saying clearly, from the start we need to find a square hole for this peg, there is no point trying to fit it into any other hole, because it won't work. For context I am not saying square pegs can't exist in the same environment as round pegs. I am suggesting we cannot treat them the same, because they are not, much like a CD and a vinyl record.

## Same Music, Different Players

Music has always been a big part of my life. As a child, I would spend hours in my bedroom listening to Phil Collins on my cassette player. Whenever I had the

DOI: 10.4324/9781003686064-8

opportunity, I would also sit in our living room, absorbed in the music of my dad's records, listening to Queen, Led Zeppelin, and Supertramp, mesmerised by the *sound* of these songs blasting out of the hi-fi speakers. As a child, we only had cassette tapes and records. As a teenager, I was introduced to the world of CDs. They were different but served the same purpose as a record: they released the sound of music. However, I would never put a CD on my dad's turntable and expect it to play the same way as his records because it wouldn't. This doesn't mean the CD is broken or defective; the music is still there; it just needs a *different player* to hear it.

This is how I see autistic children and young people in education, and why I prefer the term square pegs need square holes. When an autistic child is placed into an environment designed for children who are not autistic, are we not doing the same thing as putting a CD onto a turntable and expecting to hear the music? No matter how good the turntable is, how well the needle is designed, or even how carefully we try to turn the CD, it still won't play the music contained within. All it will do is scratch and *damage* the CD. This is what I see in education today: too many autistic children being placed in environments that are wrong for *them,* and all that happens is people focus too much on *repairing* the scratches, trying to support children through adjustment, and then placing them back onto the same player to cause more damage. This raises another question I've always found hard to understand: *what is so reasonable about reasonable adjustments?*

## The Problem With Reasonable Adjustments

The idea of *squeezing* a square peg into a round hole is extremely problematic. Especially when we look at the purpose of *reasonable adjustments*, and what they actually stand for. Consider an autistic child who has stopped attending school due to high levels of anxiety. The system will typically direct educators and professionals to apply what are termed *reasonable adjustments* to support the child and help them overcome their anxiety, with the main goal of getting them back to school. Since 2002, schools and education authorities have had a duty to provide such reasonable adjustments for pupils with disabilities. Defined here in the SEND Code of Practice 2015,

> *reasonable adjustments, including the provision of auxiliary aids and services for disabled children, to prevent them being put at a substantial disadvantage. These duties are anticipatory; they require thought to be given in advance to what disabled children and young people might require and what adjustments might need to be made to prevent that disadvantage.*[3]

When an autistic child stops attending, the school will usually try to make reasonable adjustments to help reduce the child's anxiety, such as introducing a more relaxed approach to attendance, offering a flexible timetable, or even allowing them to attend only the lessons they like. Another reasonable adjustment would be to have an adult support the child throughout the day, assisting them with emotional regulation strategies to manage anxiety and helping them identify and deal with their feelings. Additionally, the child may be offered regular check-ins and quiet spaces to retreat to when things become overwhelming in school.

However, when none of these approaches work, nobody knows what to do, which, I see, lies at the heart of the problem with reasonable adjustments. A real-life example of this is a 14-year-old whom I supported with this very problem. He couldn't get into school. His anxieties were just too much for him to cope with. The school had tried reasonable adjustments, but nothing had worked. They were now pinning all their hope on one strategy, which was for him to keep coming to the school gate every morning in the hope that he would one day miraculously walk in free from his anxieties.

When I began supporting this young person, he had been walking to school every day for the past year, totalling 190 school days of waking up, putting on his uniform, walking to the school gate, meeting a staff member, realising he can't go in because of his anxieties, then going back home, and repeating the routine the next day. At what point does this *not* become a reasonable adjustment? For this young person and his family, there is nothing reasonable or effective about this approach.

For many autistic children like this young person, it is here that support becomes ineffective because the focus is on supporting the child to *overcome* their anxiety so they can *return* to school. All they are really doing is shaving off some corners here and there (reasonable adjustments) from the square peg (the child) to squeeze the child into the round hole (the school). For these children, reasonable adjustments often prove ineffective, serving more as a short-term solution for a long-term problem. The long-term problem being that the education system continues to frame children's success *solely* in terms of school attendance, perpetuating the myth that school is *the best place for all children*, when, for a lot of "square peg" children, it is not.

**Reflection**

For context, I am not critiquing reasonable adjustments in general. They have their part to play and are invaluable for many students who *want* to engage in school, which I believe is a crucial factor to consider. If a child wants to learn in a school environment but faces barriers, reasonable adjustments are essential. For example, a child may require auditory aids, a specialised chair, or need to be in front of the class to be closer to the teacher. Others may need adult support during transition times or help at lunchtimes to manage routine and social situations. These are reasonable adjustments that work well, and I fully support them.

## Anxiety as a Guide

Square peg children are those who don't fit into existing systems like mental health and education, not because they are flawed, but because the systems are. These children require something new, rather than just modifications to fit into current systems; they need square holes. One way to demonstrate how this thinking can be applied is to examine further the support that would help an anxious, school-avoiding child.

Instead of pathologising the issue, thinking the child needs to *overcome* their anxiety, we could instead see it not as a threat but as an *ally*. For example, what if we viewed anxiety in situations where a child cannot go to school often acts as a *warning sign* to protect the child from a perceived real problem: the school. Instead of viewing anxiety as a *negative* emotion, we see anxiety as a red flag, a sign that a child needs us to help them find their way to safety, which is often *not* to go back to school.

**Real-Life Experience 4**

Max had a breakdown at the age of 12 and could no longer attend school. When we began supporting him, he was self-harming, deeply depressed, and, in his words, wanted to "*unalive*" himself. He hated that he was autistic and blamed himself for everything that went wrong in his life. Despite every attempt by his parents, the school, and external professionals, he failed to return to school.

During our initial sessions, we applied *the Four Foundations of Acceptance*, which will be discussed in depth in Part Three of the book. The first step was to *remove* whatever was causing his anxiety, which in this instance was the fear that he would have to attend school again. To remove this pressure, the message was clear: "*You do not have to go to school again if you don't want to*". He took hold of this message straight away, and over the coming weeks we could see him begin to internalise it independently, accepting that it was OK because he believed he didn't have to go back to school. Instead of developing strategies for him to *overcome* his anxiety and return to school, we listened to him. We validated how he was feeling by removing the primary source of his anxiety. We never encouraged Max to change anything about who he was. We accepted 100% of who he was from our very first session.

The next step was to create something *new* for him. The focus here was to create a "square hole" that he could fit into comfortably, without any stress of expectations. This evolved into tutoring sessions at his home, at his pace, focusing only on activities that genuinely interested him. We did not need to make reasonable adjustments to fit back into the school model that had failed him, because we were creating a *new way* for him to learn that would fit him perfectly. Here is what his square hole looked like.

## Interest-Led Learning

All of his learning was interest-led. During sessions, traditional subjects like maths and English were never discussed. He was not interested in those, so we never approached them. If he had wanted to do those subjects, we would have. We consistently followed his lead in all activities, ensuring that everything we did was specifically educationally aligned with his interests. Some days, this involved playing online games, visiting his bike shop, or stopping at a café for a drink. On other days, we stayed in his house, looking at books, making some of his favourite foods, or simply sitting in his living room, talking.

## Complete Autonomy

On days when he couldn't engage, he knew we were available for him if he needed us. When he couldn't go to school in the past, he was filled with anxiety and dread, because he believed he had to go to school, and he had no choice. He was back then, between a rock and a hard place. This time, he didn't feel that level of anxiety because in our sessions, he was in control of his learning. He was given complete autonomy. We never pushed him out of his comfort zone or encouraged him to do things he didn't want to do. Max could decide when the sessions started, how long they would last, and what we would do in them.

We also offered him a choice of a morning or afternoon slot and arrived at the agreed time, but he didn't have to be ready; he could take his time and join the session when he felt he was ready. In some sessions, I wouldn't see him for the first half, but then he would come down happy and ready to engage. When I asked what he was doing before, he would often say, "*Just lying on my bed*". For the first time, he was given the permission to do what he feels is right for him. If he needed time to gather his thoughts and feelings, he was given that time – completely and unconditionally.

## Applying an Acceptance-Based Curriculum

Max's education was based on the Acceptance-Based Curriculum[4] (the ABC), which we will discuss in more detail in Part Three. For context, this curriculum is designed to begin with the child or young person's interests and build on them. The most effective aspect of this curriculum is its focus on learning driven by curiosity and intrinsic motivators, which helps create real-life meaning in education and moves these children away from the traditional compliance-based model. When applying the ABC, learning follows the child, rather than the other way around. This approach fosters engagement, confidence, and a genuine interest in learning, which are often lacking when students are forced to fit into a system not created for them. Max settled in well with the ABC; we had found him the perfect learning model for his *square hole*.

## Max's Response

Over time, we noticed that his anxiety began to ease. He would emerge from his room more often and interact consistently with tutors. He accessed learning in his own way and chose what he wanted to do in each session. The response to acceptance-based support has been really positive for him. He no longer experiences daily anxiety, has stopped self-harming, and is now happier and more content with his life. Max has been supported by us for over two years and is doing really well, engaging in more learning than he did at school. He also spends more time with his family and is generally much happier. However, the most notable impact of acceptance-based support is that he no longer wishes to unalive himself.

Here is some feedback we received from Max's parents.

> *He had been traumatised by the school environment, and this was made worse as he was being told to attend special schools, which caused him further distress and disengagement from learning. He was very low and suffering from mental health issues, and generally did not want to be alive.*
>
> *My son is now transformed. He is engaging regularly with learning and is excited about having his sessions. He has been able to go out, which is a remarkable achievement for him. Thank you so much, you are just amazing, it is priceless the amount of positivity and acceptance you have given to our family, we feel very well supported by you, thanks without end.*

His parents tell us they have their son back and can see such a difference. Max does still have his tough days; the only difference is that he knows he can take his time and engage with what *he* can cope with. There is no need to mask anymore; there is no need to get stressed and put pressure on himself thinking he has to do things he cannot.

## Education Today

Society still thinks the "round hole" is where all children will receive the best education, meaning you will have an equal chance at life, regardless of who you are or where you come from. If an autistic child is struggling, the idea is that reasonable adjustments will help address any inequalities they may be experiencing and remove barriers, so that they too can reach the ultimate goal of full human potential, which is only found in the round hole.

However, this is not true for many groups of children and young people. It is estimated that approximately 20% of the population is defined as neurodivergent, with figures suggesting 10% are dyslexic, 4–5% have attention-deficit hyperactivity disorder (ADHD), and 1–2% of the general population are autistic.[5] In reality, the traditional education model for these people does not remove inequality, as it only "suits" certain types of learners.

Autistic children and young people who cannot engage in traditional education do not need support to return to school, or reasonable adjustments to do GCSE's, unless *they* want to. These children need other options that work for them. Policymakers, service providers, and local authorities are often too focused on fitting them into the existing education models, when, in fact, these children need square-hole environments, new models, and new approaches. It is as though the square peg cliché merely covers up what is really going on: that too many autistic children are being failed at an alarming rate, and nothing new is being done about it.

In the current UK education model, autistic children who cannot engage are not given a new education model; they are treated as children with problems, needing to be fixed, with their true feelings suppressed rather than being understood. Paulo Freire,[6] mentioned in the previous chapter, discussed a crucial issue that all humans encounter: the question of how they can truly be human, live with dignity, awareness, and freedom.

Freire suggests that our first step in education should be to concentrate more on our shared humanity and recognise the existence of *dehumanisation*. He believed that throughout history and in every society, we can either strive to help others become more human by emphasising freedom and respect or, alternatively, dehumanise them through oppression and control.

I believe it is the latter approach that is particularly relevant today when considering autistic children who struggle. The autistic child who avoids school because they see the place as overwhelming, where managing demands is difficult for them, is expected to return without addressing the real reasons why they can't attend anymore. Freire would say this type of child isn't being listened to, which results in unfair treatment, oppression, and the loss of their human dignity. The child is neither lazy nor manipulative. The parents are not "bad parents" for not sending their child to school. What's really happening for many children is that they yearn for freedom and want to be *released* from school because it is wrong for *them*. Freire would argue that supporting these children is essential to preserving their "humanity".

**Real-Life Experience 5**

Many children we support come to us feeling dehumanised, as if their lives are over, with parents often distressed and feeling hopeless that their child's life is on hold due to trauma from not being understood. One such 16-year-old, whom I call *the Countdown Kid*, struggled to engage with traditional education, often withdrawing from subjects like Maths and English because the pressure to study them would trigger lengthy meltdowns. He had attended both mainstream and special needs schools, but neither could accommodate his demand-avoidant profile, and none of the teachers who worked with him could get him to do any of the core subjects. When we began supporting him, he mostly stayed in his room, unable to leave the house, and was in a constant state of distress.

When we first started supporting him, we applied the same approach: interest-led learning, with the child as the boss and making the final decision on what we did during the sessions. Although engagement was initially limited, he showed signs of interest in certain activities, such as going for walks, climbing trees, and playing his Xbox. However, this was not considered learning in the traditional sense; he did not engage well with anyone who tried to put a worksheet in front of him.

After some months had passed, I noticed he enjoyed playing one game with the staff: *Countdown*. In a section of the game, contestants must choose two large numbers and five small ones, then, within 30 seconds, reach a randomly generated target number. He would play this game for hours. Our sessions would begin with a piece of paper, and he would instruct me to write down numbers in the same way and then choose a random number. He would become fixated, completely in the moment, timing himself to get the answer within 30 seconds. Without fail, he would get to the answer within or very near the 30-second limit. He would solve each problem effortlessly. It was a marvel to witness.

For me, this experience raises an important question: is this young person a *failure* because he may never sit or pass a maths GCSE exam, or is he more than capable of maths because he can solve *Countdown* problems faster than most adults can? The answer depends on how you want to define his intelligence.

## A Different View of Intelligence

The traditional education system would say he is behind in his learning and not reaching his full potential. The traditional educational model does not value young people like him; they see him not as clever, but as a failure because of what he *cannot* do, specifically his maths GCSE paper. They would say he has barriers to his learning, and if he continues to only do maths countdown activities, he will fail and underachieve.

Then there is another way of viewing his ability: to see him as *exceptional* in the sense that he is talented and can complete maths challenges that very few people can. Howard Gardner, an American developmental psychologist, suggested that human potential cannot be measured through standardised tests, because intelligence is not a single fixed ability.[7] He identified that intelligence is found in forms of linguistic, logical–mathematical, spatial, musical, bodily–kinaesthetic, interpersonal, intrapersonal, and naturalistic. Gardner argued that we all possess a unique blend of these intelligences, demonstrating that people learn and express understanding in diverse ways. Using this way of thinking, a new educational approach that would value young people's skills rather than undermine them.

This example emphasises the "square peg in a round hole" problem. The student's robust mathematical intuition and commitment to long hours of effort showcase a different form of intelligence, one that standard tests don't measure but rather through independent learning. His real potential is overlooked by the traditional education system, which isn't set up to recognise or nurture his exceptional talent.

I believe that, as professionals and educators, we should reconsider whether school is the most suitable environment for these children. An autistic child's initial eagerness to learn is driven by curiosity; most children are eager to learn initially, but some face obstacles that make them feel overwhelmed. They may become confused by many other children, overwhelmed by classroom noise, or disengaged from lessons. These stresses can lead to frustration and feelings of restriction, especially when they are made to learn topics that do not interest them and are criticised for slow progress.

## Summary

The idea of creating something new where square pegs can find their perfect fit is not easy, given the dominance of the current educational system. To be clear, I am not saying the whole system doesn't work. It does, for most children and young people. Many fit fine in the round hole and often come out the other side intact, ready for the next stage of their life. However, what we often fail to recognise is when education isn't accommodating for those who are different.

In this chapter, I have attempted to show that the phrase "*you can't put a square peg into a round hole*" would better support autistic children and young people if changed to "*square pegs need square holes*". This provides a fresh perspective on the real issue and what we need to do, as families, educators, mental health practitioners, policymakers, and service providers. Shifting our focus to creating and developing "square holes" will enable us to direct our efforts toward building *new* systems across mental health, education, and society as a whole. Only then can we finally leave behind these outdated views of trying to get autistic children to fit. Instead, we can build exactly what they need. Not within any current systems, instead, make completely new ones. Then they will fit just perfectly.

## Notes

1 McHugh, M., Machuca Palmeros, M., Pandey, S. & Chaudhary, G. (2024). A Square Peg in a Round Hole? Autistic Students in Third-Level Education in Ireland. *International Journal of Technology and Inclusive Education*, 13(1), pp. 679–693.
2 Smith, S. (1850). *Elementary Sketches of Moral Philosophy: Delivered at the Royal Institution in the years 1804, 1805 and 1806*. London: Longman (Harper & Brothers, New York edition). Lecture IX, "On the Conduct of the Understanding", p. 45.
3 SEND Code of Practice: 0 to 25 Years. https://www.gov.uk/government/publications/send-code-of-practice-0-to-25
4 Yorke, A. (2023). Using an Acceptance Based Curriculum to Support Autistic Students Who Have Not Engaged in the National Curriculum. *Good Autism Practice*, 24(2).
5 McHugh, M., Machuca Palmeros, M., Pandey, S. & Chaudhary, G. (2024). A Square Peg in a Round Hole? Autistic Students in Third-Level Education in Ireland. *International Journal of Technology and Inclusive Education*, 13(1), pp. 679–693.
6 Freire, P. (1970). *Pedagogy of the Oppressed*. Translated by M.B. Ramos. New York: Continuum.
7 Simply Psychology Information on Multiple Intelligences. https://www.simplypsychology.org/multiple-intelligences.html

Chapter 7

# The Burden of Behaviourism

During my first year as a local authority autism advisor, I visited an autism base, attached to a mainstream school. Upon arrival, the teacher introduced herself and showed me around. In her classroom, I saw photos of five children on the wall. In each image, the child was seated on the same chair, with their legs together and arms by their sides. Above the photos was a sign that said, *Good Sitting*. The teacher told me she used the photos to help teach good sitting whenever she needed to engage her students in a group activity. When looking around the room, I could see one child lying under a table playing with some paper, another walking back and forth across the classroom, another sitting cross-legged on a chair with her shoes off singing into a portable microphone, one rolling back and forth on the carpet with his socks and shoes off, and a child looking out the window watching the outside world. I looked back at the photos and asked the teacher, "*Is that really good sitting, or is this good sitting?*" Looking back at the children, none of them were sitting as they looked in the photos.

I walked out of the classroom that day, wondering where the idea that there is only one *right* way for a child to be came from. Who decided what *normal* looks like? Why must children sit in the same way in class? Be told to put their hands up to speak? To be taught to obey a set of rules? Why can't children sit how they want to? And learn how they want to? These questions have followed me ever since that day, and in this chapter, I attempt to find the answers by examining the history of psychology as I believe this is where a lot of these ideas originated, evolving from the scientific study of the human mind and behaviour[1] and then developing into systems of behavioural modification that we see today, much like the idea that all children must learn there is only one way to sit good.

## The Birth of Psychology

Before psychology emerged, there were philosophers. For centuries, they asked the same question: *why do humans think, feel, and act the way they do?* From philosophy to physiology, science, and psychology, these great thinkers over the centuries have sought to understand this question by offering new ideas and perspectives on why they believe humans behave the way they do. Today, psychology is so deeply

DOI: 10.4324/9781003686064-9

ingrained in our thinking that we often fail to appreciate how long the search for answers has been going on, and although we have made many strides forward, I believe we still don't *really* know why humans *do what they do.*

The mind and the brain have been studied as distinct fields for over 140 years,[2] yet psychology still struggles to define the basic concepts of what they actually are.[3] In an attempt to consider other ideas, some researchers argue that psychology is too focused on being "scientific"[4] and that we need to bring back a more human and reflective side.[5] Could this be why we fail to support many autistic children and young people? Has psychology become too rigid and too scientific, forgetting the importance of understanding real-life human experience, like what it *really* means for a person to be autistic?

Our exploration of psychology begins in the 1600s with philosopher René Descartes. In his work, he was interested in the study of consciousness, thought, attention, and emotion, all key areas of psychology today. His ideas influenced how early scientists approached understanding the differences between humans and other living beings; however, Descartes was heavily criticised for his idea of dualism, the belief that the mind and body are separate entities, and for suggesting that animals do not have consciousness.[6]

Despite his critiques, Descartes made significant contributions during the Enlightenment that helped psychology emerge as a science, enabling research to focus on mental processes rather than physical ones and leading us to the idea that the mind could be studied and understood separately.[7] Furthermore, his ideas helped establish the study of the mind as a distinct discipline from anatomy and biology, laying the groundwork for modern psychology. And we must not forget one of the most famous philosophical quotes taken from *Discourse on the Method:*[8]

> *Je pense, donc je suis.*"
>
> (I think, therefore I am.)

John Locke (1632–1704), influenced by Descartes' work, wanted to study how the mind works. He developed what is known today as empiricism, the idea that we learn through our experiences of seeing, hearing, and touching, and through observing the world.[9] This is where he expanded on Descartes' work, arguing that these processes involve more than just thinking and reasoning. For example, a child learns that a fire is hot after touching it and feeling the pain of being burned; therefore, the experience teaches the child not to touch the fire again. Locke is known for his description of the newborn mind as much like a blank slate, a *tabula rasa.*[10] He explained in *An Essay Concerning Human Understanding,*

> *Let us then suppose the mind to be, as we say, white paper, void of all characters, without any ideas: How comes it to be furnished? Whence comes it by that vast store which the busy and boundless fancy of man has painted on it with an almost endless variety? Whence has it all the MATERIALS of reason and knowledge?*[11]

Then came the German philosopher Immanuel Kant (1724–1804), who disagreed with Locke, arguing that the mind is more active than passive, responding to experience through internal frameworks such as space, time, and causal relations. Kant wrote, "*Though all our knowledge begins with experience, it does not follow that it arises from experience*".[12] He emphasised that the mind constructs meaning, highlighting that perception involves more than just visual input; it also includes how we *interpret* that input. Take, for example, the child who touched the fire might interpret the experience differently from another child with high impulsivity, such as one with ADHD. That child may *know* the fire can cause burns but still feel compelled to touch it repeatedly.

From Kant's work, we move to the 19th century, where philosophical ideas begin to evolve into scientific ones. Theories of human behaviour that Descartes, Locke, and Kant had debated in abstract ways were now being tested through *observation.*[13] One such observer was Charles Darwin[14] (1809–1882), who stood at the centre of this transformation, revolutionising our understanding of human evolution with his groundbreaking proposal that humans and animals share a common biological heritage.[15]

Darwin's work is very important to psychology because it made it acceptable to study human and animal behaviour *together*. He also laid the foundation for the scientific study of emotion with his ideas about universal expressions, the biology of emotions, and the evolution of emotional signals, which still guide modern psychology today.[16]

## Experimental Psychology

We now come to the emergence of experimental psychology. Inspired by the work of Darwin, Wilhelm Wundt, in 1879, founded the first recognised psychology laboratory in Leipzig.[17] There had been others conducting individual experiments before him, but these were only single studies and not considered sufficient to form a new science. At the same time, Wundt achieved this by providing both a shared direction and a shift in how people worked. Leipzig became the first research community to believe that psychological questions could be answered through systematic experimentation, and Wundt made this possible.[18]

As Wundt was establishing the first psychology laboratory, another philosopher and psychologist, William James, was developing a different approach at Harvard, viewing psychology as "*the Science of Mental Life, both of its phenomena and of their conditions*".[19] What made James different from Wundt was that he believed psychology should include the study of feelings, thoughts, decisions, and desires, arguing that when people examine their *inner* experiences, they often find them "chaotic" and difficult to interpret.[20]

Where Wundt aimed to study consciousness through controlled scientific experiments, James argued that this is impossible because human consciousness is never *still*. James argued that consciousness is always moving and reacting to what is happening inside your body and around you. For example, when walking alone late at night, you may feel nervous, your thoughts may race, and you may find yourself constantly scanning your surroundings for safety. James would say in this situation, your thoughts are not separate from your body or the environment you are in; they depend on what you are doing and where you are. James helped psychology move towards the examination of real-life experiences. His work opened doors to studying the mind as an active, constantly changing phenomenon.

However, as many psychologists sought to better understand consciousness, another movement emerged with a very *different* view of the mind. Where James emphasised the role of subjectivity and consciousness as central to the human experience, a new movement argued that another primary driver of thoughts and behaviours was *unconscious*, guided by repressed memories, thoughts, and primal urges, which were really what determined human behaviour. This new movement of thought was known as *psychoanalysis.*

## Psychoanalysis

Sigmund Freud, in his *study of the unconscious mind*,[21] proposed that repressed memories and unconscious drives are what shape behaviour. He believed that our early childhood experiences make up our personality and that unresolved childhood conflicts can affect how we act and behave in adulthood.[22] Freud is best known for his ideas of the id, ego, and superego. He argued that the mind works in three parts. The *id* is the part that wants things immediately for comfort and pleasure. The *ego* is the part that helps you make sensible decisions and make sense of real life, and the *superego* is the part that pushes you to do what you believe is right. The ego is the part of the mind that acts as the "inner guide", sitting between the id and the superego.

A simple example of the id, ego, and superego at work would be when you see a big piece of cake. The id says, "*I want it now!*" The superego says, "*You should not eat it because you are trying to be healthy*". The ego tries to balance both sides and might say, "*Have a smaller piece or wait until after dinner*"."

Much like thinkers before him, Freud faced his share of critiques. Despite this, his work moved psychology in another direction, focusing on deeper forces that may influence human behaviour. Freud's work helped shape psychological thinking by looking beyond surface behaviour to consider the complex inner worlds that influence people's behaviour, and influenced modern psychology's view of human behaviour, mental processes, and emotional growth.[23]

## Moving Away From Freud

The next psychologist of importance during this time is Alfred Adler (1870–1937), one of Freud's students. He began his career working with Freud, and then later developed his own approach. He disagreed with Freud's idea that people are driven by hidden desires. Instead, Adler proposed that human behaviour was shaped by social life and how people managed their feelings.[24]

Adler's approach was known as *individual psychology*,[25] as it viewed people as whole social beings who can make their own choices as they attempt to find their individual place in the world. He argued that how people act and feel is influenced by their relationships, family experiences, and social belonging. In his book *Understanding Human Nature*,[26] Adler saw behaviour as the quest for belonging and significance.

## The Rise of Behaviourism

As Freud and Adler debated the complexities of the internal world of human behaviour, yet another movement was emerging. This movement abandoned the concepts of unconscious drives and social meaning, believing that psychologists ought to focus only on what is *observable*. This new movement believed that psychology should study what people *do,* not what they think or feel. This new movement was behaviourism.

Ivan Pavlov[27] (1849–1936) was the first to provide the foundational empirical data and the stimulus-response model that made behaviourism possible. Pavlov is known for his work revealing how dogs could learn to salivate when they heard a tone paired with food. His work introduced the concept of *classical conditioning*, showing that the brain can associate one event with another to elicit new responses. His findings inspired later research on the idea that animals could learn behaviours,[28] demonstrating that reflexes could be trained.[29]

John B. Watson (1878–1958), inspired by Pavlov's ideas, argued that we can only learn about humans by observing their behaviour and how they interact with their environment. He was openly frustrated at psychology wasting its time on what he termed "*intangibles and unapproachables*",[30] saying that we either give up on psychology or make it a science. He openly refuted the idea of consciousness:

> *All schools of psychology except that of behaviorism claim that "consciousness" is the subject matter of psychology. Behaviorism, on the contrary, holds that the subject matter of human psychology is the behavior or activities of the human being. Behaviorism claims that "consciousness" is neither a definable nor a usable concept.*[31]

Watson's key argument was that psychology needed to stop studying consciousness and study only observable behaviour. He fought for psychology to become a purely objective science, like physics or chemistry, in which data are based solely on measurable actions and the conditions that produce them. As stated, he called thoughts, emotions, and feelings "intangibles" and "unapproachables"[32] because he argued they cannot be scientifically tested or observed and therefore are not reliable sources of information. For Watson and other behaviourists of his time, the true goal of psychology should be to predict and control behaviour by understanding the links between stimuli and response.[33]

## Skinner's Radical Behaviourism

Approximately 25 years after Watson, we are introduced to the work of B.F. Skinner (1904–1990). In his book *The Behaviour of Organisms*,[34] he also opposed psychologists who attempted to explain behaviour via invisible forces. He argued they did not succeed because these *inner forces* required as much explanation as the behaviours themselves. A key argument Skinner made was that these approaches do not clarify human behaviour because they fail to treat it as a scientific subject. Instead, he believed that behaviour could only be understood as a valid and reliable field when studied directly, without resorting to concealed explanations in science.[35]

Skinner expanded the scope of Watson's behaviourism by creating *radical behaviourism*, focusing on the role of genes and the biological components of behaviour. He developed *operant conditioning,* described as "the regulation of behaviour by its consequences".[36] In his work, he showed that rats respond at their own pace and that actions followed by a reward are repeated, whereas those punished are avoided. The idea of operant conditioning, when applied to human behaviour, is that it also changes as a result of what happens after it. For example, if a person is rewarded for doing something, they are more likely to repeat that behaviour; if they are punished, they are more likely to avoid it. This is why we see operant conditioning widely used in education.

The concept of *reward and punishment* spread rapidly through educational establishments, mental health systems, and workplaces and remains the dominant approach to managing behaviour. However, one of the main issues with this is often the misuse of the idea, especially when the focus is more on the punishment aspect than the reward. The term "punishment" is no longer used today; instead, it has been replaced with "consequence". We will discuss this further later.

For example, when a child in school is placed in isolation because of their behaviour, or when we see a reward chart, a behaviour report, a smiley sticker, a sanction, or read the words "*good sitting*", we are seeing the direct influence of Skinner's radical behaviourism. The core beliefs of Skinner's radical behaviourism are often seen as relics of the past, but upon closer inspection, we can see that his ideas are very much alive today.

Interestingly, Skinner saw that when a person is under the threat of punishment, they are not truly free or dignified. When a person feels this way, they may act or respond out of fear rather than choice. In other words, their behaviour is being shaped by threat, not by understanding or growth. In *Beyond Freedom and Dignity*, he explained,

> *A person who has been punished is not thereby simply less inclined to behave in a given way; at best, he learns how to avoid punishment.*[37]

## Behaviourism Today

For context, it is important here to recognise that behaviouristic approaches can be effective when applied *correctly*. For example, consider the idea of positive reinforcement. A young child is learning to put on a jumper for the first time but finds it difficult. A parent can initially divide the task into manageable steps. The child begins by picking up a jumper. Next, they insert one arm, then the other. The parent gives them time to complete each step and then offers praise to reinforce their progress.

Another example could be a student studying for an exam. They set a two-hour study timer, then reward their efforts with a 1-hour break. During the break, they do something they enjoy, such as eating some chocolate or watching an episode of their favourite TV programme. Then they repeat the process, helping the student develop discipline to study more effectively, knowing they can reward themselves for studying every two hours.

However, the issue I am trying to raise in this chapter is when behaviourism is used to *modify* the behaviour of autistic children and young people in order to encourage conformity and compliance. This is what I refer to as the burden of behaviourism. For example, the autistic child who storms out of class, swearing at the teacher, I believe, does not need to be given a detention for their behaviour, or to be put on report. The behaviour in this context is driven by anxiety and not feeling safe, and this cannot be understood unless we step back and ask what caused the behaviour in the first place. Behaviourism does not do that when used only to reward desired behaviour and *punish* unwanted behaviour.

## Do Rewards Really Work?

Skinner's operant conditioning is widely used in schools today. It can be seen in many different forms, such as detentions, exclusions, isolation rooms, and report cards. We see the names of children who misbehave in red zones on the classroom wall, and the names of good children in green zones, visible to all. Then there are strategies that focus on *positive reinforcement*,[38] which is the process of rewarding desired behaviour to encourage repetition, such as stickers, smiley faces, and positive behaviour charts. Many educators see these as "positive" reward strategies. However, research indicates they might not be as effective as we tend to think.

Alfie Kohn, in his research on rewards,[39] found that rewards often *reduce* motivation and *increase* the pressure to comply, leading children to feel they must get a reward rather than enjoy an activity for its own sake. Research also shows that autistic people actually experience better motivation when they have complete *autonomy*, not when they are controlled by external rewards.[40]

In *Punished by Rewards*,[41] Kohn, cites a study by Lepper, Greene, and Nisbett.[42] In the study, preschool children who already enjoyed drawing were divided into three groups. The first were rewarded for drawing. The second were promised a surprise reward after drawing, and the third group received no reward at all. Afterwards, when children returned to drawing activities, those who had been given the reward were less likely to want to draw. The results indicate that when people do something solely for a reward, it reduces the natural desire to do the activity.

In support, when reviewing 128 studies[43] examining how positive reinforcement influences children's motivation, researchers found that when rewards are given for participation, completing tasks, or doing well, children *lose interest* in the activity once the reward is removed. Many of the studies reviewed found that children would stop choosing an activity and enjoy it less, and that rewards such as stickers and tokens were less effective than simple positive feedback, encouragement, and recognition.

## Punishment or Consequence: Is There a Difference?

In operant conditioning, if a positive reinforcement is ineffective, punishment is applied. Skinner's idea of punishment was that it helps to reduce or remove an unwanted behaviour, making it less likely to occur again.[44] Today, we no longer use the term "reward and punishment"; instead, we use "reward and *consequence*". This shift did not happen overnight; the change began when corporal punishment was banned in state schools under the Education (No.2) Act 1986,[45] which came into force in 1987. The act forced schools to adopt alternative ways of managing behaviour, and over time, the term "punishment" evolved into "consequence". These terms are often viewed as different ideas; consequence is defined as "*a result of a particular action or situation, often one that is bad or not convenient*",[46] and punishment is "*suffering, pain, or loss that serves as retribution*".[47]

Today, applying a consequence to an unwanted behaviour is considered more *suitable,* as it teaches a child to make positive decisions about their behaviour. Whereas punishment would focus more on reducing behaviour through direct blame or threat. However, I find that consequences are often not really that different from the idea of punishment, especially through the eyes of the autistic child. For example, an autistic child who cannot sit still in class is rocking back and forth on their chair. The teacher quickly tells them to stop rocking in front of everyone. This leaves the child overwhelmed and embarrassed, so, as a protective response, they run out of the lesson to calm down. Then they are confronted by another teacher, who gives them an instant detention as a *consequence* for not being in class. To that child in that moment, the consequence does not teach them a gentle lesson about how to make better decisions next time; it places them between a rock and a hard place. They can't be in the lesson because of their heightened anxiety levels, and now they have to go to detention as a *consequence* of being anxious. Instead of helping the child learn through experience, this child is now feeling *punished*, in detention for trying to cope in a situation that was too much for them.

## Summary

In this chapter, I have attempted to show that many problems autistic children and young people face in education today are embedded in behaviourist ideologies. We began by exploring the rise of behaviourism from early philosophical thinkers to the behaviourist movement of Pavlov, Watson, and Skinner, who have shaped modern discipline approaches, especially in schools. The chapter is named "The Burden of Behaviourism", not because it is a bad approach in general, but because it isn't. We only need to look at the benefits of behaviourism on dog training; it works wonders!

Part One of this book has now come to an end. I have highlighted the persistent issues in the mental health and education systems that continue to fail autistic children and young people. It hasn't been easy to sift through real-life stories and critical reports, all of which reveal the harsh realities many children and their families face. Yet it is vital to acknowledge the current and past mistakes ingrained in these systems to demonstrate why *urgent* action is now necessary.

In Part Two, we move on to providing a solution to the problems discussed. We consider the ideas of humanistic psychology, far removed from behaviouristic models, in which the practical application of acceptance is valued over compliance with control. Where demands are removed, and unconditional acceptance, autonomy, and interest-led learning take their place. You will read in the coming chapters that behaviourism is not the only way to support autistic children and young people, and it is now time to step in a different direction.

## Notes

1 The British Psychological Society Description of What Psychology Is. https://www.bps.org.uk/what-psychology
2 https://www.learner.org/series/discovering-psychology/explorations/history-of-psychology-contemporary-foundations/
3 Uher, J. (2020). Psychology's Status as a Science: Peculiarities and Intrinsic Challenges in the Study of Human Behaviour. *Frontiers in Psychology*, 11, p. 874.
4 Pereira, R. & Vaz, M. (2018). Psychology as a Science of Subject and Comportment, Beyond the Behaviour-and-Mind Dualism. *Frontiers in Psychology*, 9, p. 1521.
5 Held, B.S. (2022). Making Sense of Charges of Scientism in Psychology and Beyond: Logical and Epistemological Implications. *Theory & Psychology*, 32(4), pp. 535–555. https://doi.org/10.1177/09593543221088555 (Original work published 2022).
6 Brown, D. & Key, B. (2020). Descartes' Dualism of Mind and Body in the Development of Psychological Thought. *Oxford Research Encyclopedia of Psychology*, July 30 (Accessed 8 November 2025). https://oxfordre.com/psychology/view/10.1093/acrefore/9780190236557.001.0001/acrefore-9780190236557-e-486
7 Brown, D. & Key, B. (2020). Descartes' Dualism of Mind and Body in the Development of Psychological Thought. *Oxford Research Encyclopedia of Psychology*, July 30 (Accessed 8 November 2025). https://oxfordre.com/psychology/view/10.1093/acrefore/9780190236557.001.0001/acrefore-9780190236557-e-486
8 Descartes, R. (1637/1912). *Discourse on the Method.* Translated by J. Veitch. London: J.M. Dent & Sons.
9 APA Definition of 'Empiricism'. https://dictionary.apa.org/empiricism
10 Definition of 'Tabula Rasa'. https://www.britannica.com/topic/tabula-rasa
11 Locke, J. An Essay Concerning Humane Understanding, Printed by Eliz. Holt, for Thomas Basset, at the George in Fleet Street, Near St. Dunstan's Church. https://www.gutenberg.org/files/10615/10615-h/10615-h.htm

12 Kant, I. (1781/1787). *Critique of Pure Reason*. Translated by N.K. Smith. London: Macmillan, 1929, p. 41 (B1).
13 Barton, A. (2018). Evolving Perspectives on the History of Psychology: The Transformation of Psychology: Influences of 19th-Century Philosophy Technology and Natural Science. *American Journal of Psychotherapy*, 72(2).
14 Bolhuis, J.J., Brown, G.R., Richardson, R.C. & Laland, K.N. (2011). Darwin in Mind: New Opportunities for Evolutionary Psychology. *PLoS Biology*, July, 9(7), p. e1001109. https://doi.org/10.1371/journal.pbio.1001109. Epub 2011 July 19. PMID: 21811401; PMCID: PMC3139638.
15 Darwin, C. (1859). *On the Origin of Species by Means of Natural Selection, or the Preservation of Favoured Races in the Struggle for Life*. London: John Murray.
16 Ekman, P. (2009). Darwin's Contributions to Our Understanding of Emotional Expressions. *Philosopical Transaction of the Royal Society of London Series B, Biological Sciences*, December 12, 364(1535), pp. 3449–3451. https://doi.org/10.1098/rstb.2009.0189. PMID: 19884139; PMCID: PMC2781895.
17 Rosa, P.J. (2023). Editorial for Special Issue "Psychophysiology and Experimental Psychology". *International Journal of Psychology Research (Medellin)*, October 10, 16(2), pp. 1–3. https://doi.org/10.21500/20112084.6584. PMID: 38106961; PMCID: PMC10723746.
18 Danziger, K. (1980). Wundt's Psychological Experiment in the Light of His Philosophy of Science. *Psychological Research*, 42, pp. 109–122.
19 James, W. (1890). *The Principles of Psychology*. New York: Henry Holt (Accessed 15 November 2025). https://www.gutenberg.org/files/57628/57628-h/57628-h.htm
20 James, W. (1890). *The Principles of Psychology*. New York: Henry Holt (Accessed 15 November 2025). https://www.gutenberg.org/files/57628/57628-h/57628-h.htm.
21 Freud, S. (1915). The Unconscious. In *The Standard Edition of the Complete Psychological Works of Sigmund Freud*. Vol. 14. London: Hogarth Press.
22 Freud, S. (1905). *Three Essays on the Theory of Sexuality*. Vienna: Deuticke.
23 Mistry, L.N., Neelkanthan, S., Deshpande, S.S., Jawdekar, A.M., Shah, P.P. & Khachane, N.A. (2024). Matters of the Mind: A Look Into the Life of Sigmund Freud. *Cureus*, October 15, 16(10), p. e71562. https://doi.org/10.7759/cureus.71562. PMID: 39552960; PMCID: PMC11563769.
24 Description of Adler's Individual Psychology: Striving for Superiority and Social Interest. https://psychology.town/fundamentals-of-mental-health/adlers-individual-psychology-superiority-social-interest/
25 Description of Adler's Individual Psychology: Striving for Superiority and Social Interest. https://psychology.town/fundamentals-of-mental-health/adlers-individual-psychology-superiority-social-interest/
26 Adler, A. (1927). *Understanding Human Nature*. New York, NY: Greenberg.
27 Pavlov, I.P. (1927). *Conditioned Reflexes: An Investigation of the Physiological Activity of the Cerebral Cortex*. Translated by G.V. Anrep. London, England: Oxford University Press. http://psychclassics.yorku.ca/Pavlov/
28 Hauser, L. (1997). Behaviorism. In J. Fieser & D. Bradley (Eds.), *Internet Encyclopedia of Philosophy*. http://www.iep.utm.edu/behavior/
29 Smith, G.P. (2000). Pavlov and Integrative Physiology. *American Journal of Physiology-Regulatory, Integrative and Comparative Physiology*, 279(3), pp. R743–R748.
30 Watson, J.B. (1924). *Behaviorism*. New York: Norton.
31 Watson, J.B. (1924). *Behaviorism*. New York: Norton, p. 3.
32 Watson, J.B. (1913). Psychology as the Behaviourist Views It. *Psychological Review*, 20(2), pp. 158–177. https://doi.org/10.1037/h0074428
33 Watson, J.B. (1913). Psychology as the Behaviourist Views It. *Psychological Review*, 20(2), pp. 158–177. https://doi.org/10.1037/h0074428.

34 Skinner, B.F. (1938). *The Behavior of Organisms: An Experimental Analysis*. New York: Appleton-Century.
35 Skinner, B.F. (1938). *The Behavior of Organisms: An Experimental Analysis*. New York: Appleton-Century.
36 Pear, J.J. (2001). The Science of Learning and Behavior. *The Behavior Analyst*, 24(2), pp. 143–152.
37 Skinner, B.F. (1971). *Beyond Freedom and Dignity*. New York: Harper & Row.
38 Doggett, R. & Koegel, L. (2013). Positive Reinforcement. In F.R. Volkmar (Ed.), *Encyclopedia of Autism Spectrum Disorders*. New York, NY: Springer. https://doi.org/10.1007/978-1-4419-1698-3_130
39 Kohn, A. (1993). *Punished by Rewards: The Trouble with Gold Stars, Incentive Plans, A's, Praise, and Other Bribes*. Boston: Houghton Mifflin.
40 Goldfarb, Y., Gal, E. & Golan, O. (2021). A Self Determination Theory Approach to Work Motivation of Autistic Adults. *Autism*, 25(8), pp. 2220–2231.
41 Kohn, A. (1993). *Punished by Rewards: The Trouble with Gold Stars, Incentive Plans, A's, Praise, and Other Bribes*. Boston: Houghton Mifflin.
42 Lepper, M.R., Greene, D. & Nisbett, R.E. (1973). Undermining Children's Intrinsic Interest with Extrinsic Reward: A Test of the "Overjustification" Hypothesis. *Journal of Personality and Social Psychology*, 28(1), pp. 129–137.
43 Deci, E.L., Koestner, R. & Ryan, R.M. (1999). A Meta-Analytic Review of Experiments Examining the Effects of Extrinsic Rewards on Intrinsic Motivation. *Psychological Bulletin*, November, 125(6), pp. 627–668; discussion 692–700. https://doi.org/10.1037/0033-2909.125.6.627. PMID: 10589297.
44 A clear explanation of reward and punishment. Taken from the Simple Psychology Website (Accessed January 2026). https://www.simplypsychology.org/operant-conditioning.html
45 United Kingdom Parliament (1986). *Education (No. 2) Act 1986, c. 61*. London: HMSO.
46 Definition of Consequence. https://dictionary.cambridge.org/dictionary/english/consequence
47 Definition of Punishment. https://www.merriam-webster.com/dictionary/punishment

# Part Two

# The Rebirth of an Idea

Life is difficult.
We all face many struggles,
and answers can be hard to find.

*However,*

through acceptance,
we can see things differently.
We can find comfort in knowing
it is OK when things are not OK
and it is OK when things are.

DOI: 10.4324/9781003686064-10

Chapter 8

# Bringing Back the Third Force

Throughout the 1940s and 1950s, the study of human behaviour was dominated by psychoanalysis and behaviourism.[1] One studied the complex inner world that influences human behaviour, and the other observed only what people did, paying little attention to how a person thought or felt. Around the same time, a new movement emerged with a different psychological perspective, openly rejecting the assumptions of psychoanalysis and behaviourism, which began to shape academic thinking[2] and influence wider cultural attitudes[3] through its ideas on personal development. This new movement became known as humanistic psychology and earned its title as the *third force of psychology*.[4]

Gordon Allport first introduced the phrase *humanistic psychology* to the study of personality in the 1930s.[5] Believing in the importance of each person's uniqueness and individuality, Allport argued that we can better understand human personalities by considering them as dynamic and constantly evolving throughout one's lifespan.[6] Then, in the late 1940s, humanistic psychology began to develop rapidly as a distinct movement, reacting to the reductionist views of behaviourism and psychoanalysis.[7] The movement opposed any psychological model that reduced humans to a single explanation. Arguing that behaviourism reduced people to conditioning and psychoanalysis reduced them to unconscious conflict.[8] Humanistic psychologists instead sought to restore the idea that people are whole beings with thoughts, feelings, values, and potential, and to challenge traditional approaches that overlooked the *wholeness* of the human experience.

During the 1960s, many humanistic psychologists contributed to the development of these principles, including James Bugental,[9] Alfred Adler,[10] Rollo May,[11] Abraham Maslow,[12] Carl Rogers,[13] Arthur Combs,[14] and Charlotte Bühler.[15] In the next few chapters, we will consider key ideas and, importantly, how these can be applied to support autistic children and young people. We begin with James Bugental and his five basic postulates of humanistic psychology.[16]

## The Five Postulates of Humanistic Psychology

James Bugental sought to establish clear principles that distinguished humanistic psychology from behaviourism and psychoanalysis.[17] Each of these principles

DOI: 10.4324/9781003686064-11

serves as the blueprint for humanistic psychology, with much of its development stemming from them. The five postulates are as follows.

### 1. *Humans Are More Than the Sum of Their Parts*

A person is viewed as more than just their behaviour, traits or diagnosis, and we cannot begin to understand someone by simply breaking them into different parts. We must see the whole person, including their feelings, needs, and subjective experiences.

> **Reflection**
>
> How could this be applied to an autistic child or young person? By learning to look past an autistic child's behaviour. As adults supporting, we can be more effective when see the child as a whole human, asking *why* they may have behaved in a certain way.

### 2. *Humans Exist in a Human and Cosmic Context*

The second postulate holds that human beings need to be understood within the contexts in which they live, e.g. their social relationships, cultures, and environments.

> **Reflection**
>
> We can apply this by seeing an autistic child within the full context of their lives, instead of focusing on narrow issues, such as their behaviours or academic skill levels. We can instead pay attention to their complete world made up of their relationships, their sensory world, and their routines. Getting to know them and finding out what it is like to live in *their world.*

### 3. *Humans Are Conscious and Self-Aware*

In this postulate, Bugental suggests that it is essential to recognise that humans can become aware of their own feelings, thoughts, and experiences, and that this awareness shapes how they make sense of their world.

**Reflection**

We can apply this postulate by recognising how a child makes sense of their world guided by their thoughts, feelings, and experiences, and recognising that their views and experiences will not be the same as yours, and that is OK.

### 4. *Humans Have Choice and Responsibility*

People have the ability to make their own choices, and it is crucial to acknowledge that individuals are free to decide what to do and what not to do. This recognition is important because it enables people to take responsibility for their lives and their reactions to various situations.

**Reflection**

Here, we can help autistic children gain autonomy and control over the choices they make in their daily lives at school and at home. We can also respect their right to say no. Children need to know they have a genuine choice in their lives and can take responsibility for their choices. We may also apply this postulate by helping autistic children to reflect when things go wrong in a *nonjudgemental way*.

### 5. *Humans Are Intentional and See Meaning*

The idea here is that people already want purpose, value, and understanding in their lives. They are driven by *meaning,* not just external rewards or consequences.

**Reflection**

Here we can help autistic children by focusing on intrinsic motivators and moving away from controlling what they learn. Whenever an autistic child is struggling in lessons, think about what they are interested in and move away from what they are *not* interested in.

These five principles invite us to see autistic children through their own ideas, awareness, and meaning, rather than through their behaviours or diagnoses. The importance lies in how *they* understand the world, and it is there that we can begin to effectively support them by validating their views and creating environments that allow them to make their own choices. Applying these postulates could be revolutionary within education and mental health models if they were only given the chance. We will now consider other humanistic principles that I believe can be applied to help support autistic children and young people who have not responded to anything else.

## Unconditional Positive Regard

Carl Rogers was best known for his therapeutic approach, which emphasised *unconditional positive regard.*[18] Shifting psychology away from control and diagnosis, Rogers emphasised the importance of relationship-building through an understanding of people's subjective, lived experiences. Within therapy, unconditional positive regard enables individuals to realise that they are valuable and accepted, even after making mistakes and feeling worthless. He best describes the process in his book *On Becoming a Person,*[19] where he writes,

> *When the therapist is experiencing a warm, caring, non-possessive acceptance of the client, no matter what the client is experiencing or expressing, this is unconditional positive regard.*

He explained that each individual has an innate motivation to become their true self, and this journey is fostered when we create an environment free of pressure and full of acceptance. When people feel understood, they start to comprehend themselves better. When they feel valued, they begin to recognise their own worth. His contributions laid the groundwork for humanistic psychology, person-centred therapy, and the wider belief that humans are inherently inclined toward growth, authenticity, and connection.

Rogers believed that psychological growth requires complete acceptance without conditions.

A good example of how to apply this concept is to accept a child's behaviour as communication rather than as defiance. Another way would be to stop using reward systems to control children; instead, tell them the message that "*I accept you completely exactly as you are*".

**Real-Life Experience 6**

I supported an autistic boy in primary school, reported to me as being unmanageable in class, not attending 80% of his lessons, and at risk of permanent exclusion. He would disrupt the class and was sent out daily; he could not stop moving around in class and was constantly rocking in his chair, getting told off for not sitting properly. The school did not know what else to do, and asked for my input.

To begin, I met him in the playground and introduced myself. His initial response was "*Who the f**k are you?*" I did not try to correct him at all. I stood with him and waited a moment to offer him unconditional positive regard.

He then asked me, "What car have you got, sir?"

I said, "Oh, I have a Porsche!"

"Really?"

"No, actually, I have a boring Ford Focus."

He seemed to like my joke and told me Fords are OK cars. It was as though when he swore at me, he was waiting for a negative response. To be told off, like he usually is. It felt like this quiet acceptance from me broke the ice and put him at ease. From then on, we had a great chat. I walked around the playground with him and played some football. He even told me about school, and that he doesn't like being there. I said I was there to try to help if I could. He seemed OK with this.

At the time, the school had him on a behaviour report, which he had to give to the teacher after every lesson so they could *rate* his behaviour. I was handed some of his weekly behaviour reports, where they scored his behaviour on a scale from 1 to 5. One being the worst and five the best. I could see from his reports that he rarely reached a 5, and in almost every lesson, he was only scoring 1s and 2s. This resulted in more sanctions, more timeouts.

The school really wanted to help him, but nothing they had tried was working. They could see the negative impact the report was having on him because when he was given a low rating, he would become so distressed that he would storm out of class, and it would take a long time to calm him down enough to go to his next lesson. After meeting with the child and the staff on a couple of occasions, I suggested the following approaches.

### Change the Behaviour Plan

The first thing I suggested was changing the wording in his report. The requirements were written in a very negative way, focusing only on the boy *changing* his behaviour, and he was the one who had to put in all the effort. Here are the initial targets on his plan.

1. *Completely unacceptable*
2. *Very limited cooperation*
3. *Some co-operation*
4. *Better than expected*
5. *Almost perfect.*

I can only imagine how he must have felt when reading these. This behavioural modification approach is very subtle but can be damaging to autistic children because a lot of the time, they *can't* do what is expected of them. Please also note the top rating: "almost perfect". Even when the boy was rewarded for doing his best, he would still have read this as *almost* perfect, so meaning *still* not good enough.

Do you notice the influence of behaviourism here? The issue lies with the *child,* and fixing the *behaviour* is the primary focus, by rewarding good behaviour and punishing bad behaviour.

I advised ceasing the behaviour report completely and trying something else. However, the school wanted to keep the report, so I did the next best thing and rewrote the targets. The targets were rewritten so that he could use them more effectively, to help the teacher know he was struggling, and then, instead of expecting to improve, he could be offered help and support. By rewriting the targets, the expectation that he would improve his behaviour was *removed.* Here are the new targets we used.

1. *I am not coping, and I want to leave.*
2. *I don't want to be in this lesson, but I am OK to stay.*
3. *Things are too much, and they are affecting me.*
4. *I am a little bit on edge, but I am OK.*
5. *I am really coping well in this lesson.*

### Allow Him to Move on His Chair

The second issue I needed to look at was *why* he was constantly moving around in class, and *why* he could not stay still on his chair. This was the main problem in class, as he would rock in his chair, sometimes falling over or accidentally hitting other children. They wanted him to sit still and remain in his chair. Again, following the idea of unconditional positive regard, I wanted him to know he is valuable and accepted, even after making mistakes and feeling worthless. So, to do this, I suggested taking away his chair and replacing it with a gym ball.

At first, the staff said they might not be able to do this due to health and safety concerns. They were also concerned that this might not be fair to the other children in the class, and the teacher was worried they would ask for their own gym ball, since he had one and they didn't. In the end, they followed the advice and monitored it carefully.

### Feedback

I was not due to return to the school for a few weeks. When I did return, I went into the classroom to see how he was doing. The teacher requested to speak with me outside. At first, I was a little worried that things had gotten worse. Instead, she told me, "*It is amazing! He is like a different child!*"

After only a few weeks of using the new behaviour targets, the teacher told me he had been scoring 5s in *every* lesson. She told me he now saw the report as something that helped him express how he was truly feeling. As a result, he had now been attending 80% of his lessons, which was astounding, a complete turnaround from his previous lack of attendance.

The teacher also told me he responded really well to the gym ball and loved to sit on it. He didn't walk around as much in class and was less fidgety on the ball. The teacher also noticed that when he was on the gym ball, he focused more on his work and spent more time at his desk. I asked about their initial concerns, including health and safety issues, and was told there were none. He did not throw the ball around the classroom or use it in a negative way. Regarding the other children and their concerns over fairness, the feedback was that none of them asked for their own gym ball; in fact, she told me, "*They were just happy he was not upset anymore*".

Two simple strategies for applying unconditional positive regard are: first, accepting him completely by turning a behaviour report into something that supported his behaviour rather than trying to improve it, and secondly, allowing him to move in class using a gym ball instead of a chair. Both were cost-effective and helped this boy engage in his learning *without* feeling like a problem to be fixed or an issue to be dealt with. I was also informed by the SENCO that the student was no longer at risk of exclusion and was much happier at school. Whenever I saw him around school, we would still talk about cars, and he never masked with me; he was completely himself.

## Summary

There is so much more to say about humanistic psychology, which is why the next few chapters are dedicated to its principles. To end this chapter, I want to sum up humanistic psychology through the words of Charlotte Bühler, who, when speaking at the First International Conference on Humanistic Psychology in 1970, said,

> *One of the most generally agreed upon aspects of humanistic psychology is that we strive to find access to the study and understanding of the person as a whole.*[20]

Humanistic thinking has been supported by decades of research, but up until this point has been mostly overlooked in mental health and education support for autistic children and young people. It is time to revisit the key principles and apply them in our professions. Over the coming chapters, we will look more closely at the work of Abraham Maslow and Carl Rogers to show why their insights still matter and how they can be used today in current practice.

It is more important now than ever that these values are brought back to the forefront of autism support. We have forgotten the importance of understanding people as whole human beings, with inner experiences. These concepts are important to human development, but they have been mostly forgotten. There is no better time than now to revive them. John Rowan and Dina Glouberman, in their essay taken from the book *Humanistic Psychology: Current Trends and Future Prospects*,[21] explain this urgency perfectly:

> *It might, therefore, be more necessary than ever that Humanistic Psychology become the standard bearer for a radical vision of what it means to be human.*

## Notes

1 Royce, J.R. & Mos, L.P. (Eds.) (1981). *Humanistic Psychology: Concepts and Criticisms*. New York: Plenum Press.
2 Koch, S. (1974). Psychology and Emerging Conceptions of Knowledge as Unitary. In T Mischel (Ed.), *Understanding Psychology*. New York: McGraw Hill.
3 Roszak, T. (1969). *The Making of a Counterculture*. New York: Doubleday.
4 House, R., Kalisch, D. & Maidman, J. (Eds.) (2017). *Humanistic Psychology: Current Trends and Future Prospects*. London. Routledge.
5 DeRobertis, E.M. & Bland, A.M. (2019). The Humanistic Perspective on Personality. *The Humanistic Psychologist*, 47, pp. 295–314.
6 Gordon Allport Humanistic Trait Models. https://www.ebsco.com/research-starters/history/gordon-allports-humanistic-trait-models
7 House, R., Kalisch, D. & Maidman, J. (Eds.) (2017). *Humanistic Psychology: Current Trends and Future Prospects*. London: Routledge.
8 Royce, J.R. & Mos, L.P. (Eds.) (1981). *Humanistic Psychology: Concepts and Criticisms*. New York: Plenum Press.
9 Bugental, J.F.T. (1964). The Third Force in Psychology. *Journal of Humanistic Psychology*, 4, pp. 19–26.
10 Adler, A. (1927). *Understanding Human Nature*. New York: Greenberg.
11 May, R. (1958). *Existence: A New Dimension in Psychiatry and Psychology*. New York: Basic Books.
12 Maslow, A.H. (1968). *Toward a Psychology of Being*. New York: Van Nostrand Reinhold.
13 Rogers, C.R. (1961). *On Becoming a Person*. Boston: Houghton Mifflin.
14 Combs, A.W. (1962). *Perceiving, Behaving, Becoming: A New Focus for Education*. Washington, DC: ASCD.
15 Bühler, C. (1962). *Humanistic Psychology*. New York: Basic Books.
16 Bugental, J.F.T. (1965). *The Search for Authenticity*. New York: Holt, Rinehart and Winston.
17 Bugental, J.F.T. (1965). *The Search for Authenticity*. New York: Holt, Rinehart and Winston.
18 Rogers, C.R. (1959). A Theory of Therapy, Personality and Interpersonal Relationships. In S. Koch (Ed.), *Psychology: A Study of a Science. Volume 3: Formulations of the Person and the Social Context*. New York: McGraw Hill.
19 Rogers, C.R. (1961). *On Becoming a Person*. Boston: Houghton Mifflin.
20 Bühler, C. (1971). Basic Theoretical Concepts of Humanistic Psychology. *American Psychologist*, 26(4), pp. 378–386. https://doi.org/10.1037/h0032049
21 House, R., Kalisch, D. & Maidman, J. (Eds.) (2017). *Humanistic Psychology: Current Trends and Future Prospects*. London: Routledge.

Chapter 9

# Hope

## The Human Experience of Hope

Hope is central in humanistic psychology. Rollo May described hope as *a state of becoming: an openness to new possibilities within oneself and the world.*[1] May saw hope not as a fingers-crossed mindset, but as something we become when we are open to the idea that things will be OK, whatever is happening. May suggests that hope is an active process that helps people engage with life despite their circumstances. Most traditional scientific methods attempt to measure hope primarily through cognitive processes, rather than its effect on people's *emotions*.[2] A prominent theory is Charles R. Snyder's hope theory"[3] Snyder defines hope as "*the perceived capability to derive pathways to desired goals and motivate oneself via agency thinking to use those pathways*".[4]

He argued that hope has two key cognitive components: *pathways thinking*, the ability to generate routes to reach desired goals, and *agency thinking,* a belief in one's capacity to follow those routes. In doing so, he framed hope primarily as a cognitive process, involving the belief that one can achieve desired goals and the motivation to do so.

However, other researchers argue that hope involves *more* than cognitive processes. In a particular study, the Trait Emotion Hope Scale (TEHS) was introduced as an innovative approach to measuring hope.[5] Their results showed that people often perceive hope as an emotion rather than merely a thought, indicating that hope may not solely be a cognitive act but also carries a significant emotional component, involving feelings alongside thinking.

### *Understanding Hope*

The idea of hope as an emotional component resonates with one of Anne Frank's diary entries, where she writes, "*Will this year, 1944, bring us victory? We don't know yet. But where there's hope, there's life. It fills us with fresh courage and makes us strong again*".[6] Her hopeful outlook seems ultimately futile, given that she sadly died without ever experiencing the freedom she longed for. However, although hope did not alter her fate or save her life, it influenced how she *responded*

DOI: 10.4324/9781003686064-12

to her circumstances. She employed hope as a form of defiance, using it to resist the suffering of her reality.

Another example of hope as a driven emotion comes from Václav Havel, a playwright during the communist regime in Czechoslovakia. He became one of the leading figures in the human rights movement Charter 77.[7] His political plays attracted global attention, but Havel was repeatedly imprisoned for his activism. In 1989, he led the Velvet Revolution, which brought an end to communist rule. He became president, committed his life to democracy, human rights, and creative expression. In his book, he explored moral responsibility and the power of hope, arguing that living in truth was the key to resisting oppression and bringing about change. When describing hope, he said,

> *Hope is not the conviction that something will turn out well, but the certainty that something makes sense, regardless of how it turns out.*

**Reflection**

With hope it is OK to take a step back and be OK with not having an answer to a problem or situation. Hope allows us to become consistent adults, offering support no matter what is going on for a child in need of our support.

### *The Impact of Hope*

In 2025, a study followed 25,000 adults for 14 years to examine the impact of hope on their lives.[8] They found that people who were more hopeful were happier, healthier, less lonely, more educated, and able to maintain employment. People with higher levels of hope were able to bounce back when bad things happened and showed a stronger sense of how they could influence their lives. This research suggests that hope, as a concept, is not just a feeling; it can shape how people act and think about their futures. As a result, could it be possible then that as professionals, we could apply hope as a way to improve autistic children's well-being?

Another study[9] showed what can happen when autistic people recognise their own *value*. Showing that hope is not just an abstract feeling but can be a lived experience that, as Rollo May suggests, grows, and develops as people begin to recognise not their flaws and problems, but their own value within them.

They compared 276 autistic and non-autistic adults to assess their knowledge of their strengths and whether they applied them in their lives. Both groups had similar strengths, but autistic individuals were less likely to recognise the value of their strengths and utilise them in their lives. They found that by helping autistic individuals identify and utilise their strengths, there were measurable improvements in the quality of their lives, higher well-being, and better mental health, with a significant drop in anxiety, depression, and stress.

In my experience working with many autistic children and young people, the idea of hope offers empowerment. The hope that things will be OK, whatever happens. When a child learns that they are enough and that they will work things out in their own time, this leads to a strong sense of purpose and fulfilment. Hope enables a child in distress to experience personal growth that is meaningful to *them*. In this way, hope gives an autistic child a chance to build inner strength, showing that they already have the capability to handle whatever challenges arise. With adult support, we can create a space for them to develop hope, something they may not have had the opportunity to experience before.

**Real-Life Experience 7**

Leo had not left his house for over two years. He was diagnosed autistic with selective mutism and was unable to attend any type of school setting. He was one of those children whom everyone turned away. Efforts were made to find him a suitable environment, but over 25 placements rejected him. I remember my first visit to his home: he was upstairs, and I attempted to greet him, but he slammed the door in my face. No response. This same reaction lasted for over five months, during which I continued to visit three times a week. Each time, I would do the same thing: call up the stairs to say hello, not expecting a response. All I wanted him to know at this stage was that I am not going anywhere, and its OK if he doesn't want to speak to me or engage. Sometimes his bedroom door was open; other times, it was closed.

He rarely spoke to anyone, only to his mother or his nan. He did not even talk to his siblings or his father. Hope was the attitude I took when sitting in his living room for months on end. Not expecting a reply but hoping I might get one. It was always OK if he didn't; that was not the focus.

If I had followed the traditional support path, I probably would have concluded within the first month or so that he would not engage with me, so I would have stopped the support. Hope kept me going, encouraging me to keep showing up, no matter what happened.

Leo was 14 years old when we first began supporting him. Everyone was at a loss. The Local Authority did not initially see the benefit of our support, and his parents, although they wanted the best for him, continued to fight to secure a college placement. Still, I continued to convey the same message of acceptance. I told them he is the boss of his sessions, and that I will only do what he wants when he is ready. At that point, he only knew me as the man who would visit three times a week, sit in the living room and then leave, saying bye on my way out.

After about four months, I started to have doubts and was unsure whether my consistent approach was helping. Until one day, he miraculously asked his mother, "*Is Aaron coming today*?" She texted me, saying she couldn't believe it! When I arrived, he was sitting in his garden, wearing a baseball cap. I went into the garden and sat opposite him. He did not speak, and I did not ask him to. I generally spoke about anything I could think of and just wanted him to feel safe around me. I was still amazed he was out of his room.

In the next session, the same thing happened; this time, he started to look up at me while I was talking, with an occasional smile. I noticed he had a ball with him, so I said, "*Do you want to go to the park and kick the ball around?*" There was a pause, and then he suddenly got up and walked straight to his front door, opened it, and walked out! His mum was with us at the time, and said he liked to go to the park to kick his ball around. She suggested we follow, so we did and spent the next two hours playing football and having a great time. No words, just kicking the ball around, taking turns to go in the goal.

Over time, Leo responded very well once the pressure on him to engage was removed. He understood that he was the one leading what we did and could choose whether to engage. This experience gave him a sense of autonomy he had never experienced in his earlier educational environments. He started to trust us, as evidenced by his daily interactions with staff and his increased communication with his dad and other family members. It was truly rewarding to witness. He started to show a genuine curiosity in the things he enjoyed and let us into his world. He would be ready for sessions, had more energy, and was keen to try different things, visiting the community and exploring learning in ways he had never done before. Leo had responded to acceptance in ways no other type of support could. When all other education models failed him, autonomy and interest-led learning were exactly what he needed.

What changed in those five months? Why did Leo suddenly go from not speaking to any of us to then suddenly opening up and engaging? I can't say for certain. All I can say is what approach we took as a team to support him. We applied the principle of acceptance, allowing him to be completely who he wanted to be, to engage when he felt ready. Unknowingly, he was beginning to see us as a safe place, and this came only from those weekly sessions, where we would turn up, say nothing, and leave. We didn't expect him to engage. We were not there to fix him. He was fine exactly as he was, and he did not need to do anything he did not want to. To some, it seemed we were just sitting down and doing nothing. Perhaps even thinking that our support was ineffective because he wasn't engaging. In fact, what was happening was we were being consistent adults who turned up no matter what. We were applying some of the core principles of humanistic psychology.

What happened to Leo was that we showed him he could be exactly who he wanted to be, which is the humanistic idea that "*people can continue to grow beyond their usual limits, if they are allowed to*".[10]

## Summary

In this chapter, we have begun our journey into new territory, starting with the idea of hope in supporting autistic children and young people. With hope, we don't need to remain in the unknown. We can begin to imagine that worth may not be based on grades or on how well a child manages anxiety or rehearses the perfect smile. The traditional ways no longer work for these children. We have wasted too much time hoping that there will be a way to fix them, to come up with some amazing strategy to teach them how *not* to be autistic anymore. Hope does not exist in those moments, but when a teenager speaks for the first time in five months, realising, maybe, that things will be OK, because they have learned, through acceptance, that it's ok to be *exactly* who they are.

## Notes

1 May, R. (1953). *Man's Search for Himself.* New York: W. W. Norton.
2 Feldman, D.B. & Jazaieri, H. (2022). Feeling Hopeful: Development and Validation of the Trait Emotion Hope Scale. *Journal of Positive Psychology*, 17(6), pp. 798–812. https://doi.org/10.1080/17439760.2021.1871932
3 Snyder, C.R. (2002). Hope Theory: Rainbows in the Mind. *Psychological Inquiry*, 13(4), pp. 249–275. https://doi.org/10.1207/S15327965PLI1304_01
4 Snyder, C.R. (2002). Hope Theory: Rainbows in the Mind. *Psychological Inquiry*, 13(4), pp. 249–275.
5 Feldman, D.B. & Jazaieri, H. (2022). Feeling Hopeful: Development and Validation of the Trait Emotion Hope Scale. *Journal of Positive Psychology*, 17(6), pp. 798–812. https://doi.org/10.1080/17439760.2021.1871932
6 Frank, A. (1947). *The Diary of a Young Girl*. London: Penguin Books.
7 Charter 77. https://www.csce.gov/publications/human-rights-czechoslovakia-documents-charter-77-1977-1982/
8 Graham, C. & Mujcic, R. (2025). Hope and the Life Course: Results from a Longitudinal Study of 25,000 Adults. *Health Economics*. https://doi.org/10.1002/hec.70041
9 Taylor, E.C., Livingston, L.A., Clutterbuck, R.A., Callan, M.J. & Shah, P. (2022). Strengths Use Predicts Quality of Life, Well-Being and Mental Health in Autism. *Autism*, [online] (Accessed 3 November 2025). https://doi.org/10.1177/13623613221146440
10 House, R., Kalisch, D. & Maidman, J. (Eds.) (2018). *Humanistic Psychology: Current Trends and Future Prospects*. Abingdon: Routledge.

Chapter 10

# How to Become a Person

As an undergraduate studying psychology, I was profoundly influenced by the humanistic psychologist Carl Rogers. He gave me hope that some ideas in psychology could support me as a professional working with autistic children and young people in education. I learned that acceptance can genuinely make a difference in the lives of children who have not engaged in support and have withdrawn from their lives. In this chapter, I delve into Rogers' ideas and explain why I believe they stand out from other psychological perspectives. While cognitive and behaviourist models continue to influence many of our views today, I have a stronger connection to humanistic principles and believe they provide a more effective way to support this particular group of autistic children and young people: the demand avoidant, highly anxious ones who need something different to help them.

Carl Rogers was an American humanistic psychologist whose work in the mid-20th century significantly transformed our understanding of learning and personal development. He believed that people possess an inherent drive for self-guided growth and that this growth occurs best when individuals feel understood, accepted, and free to shape their own experiences as a whole person. Originally developed within psychotherapy, his person-centred approach has been adopted in education to create learning environments in which students are seen as active participants in constructing knowledge, rather than passive recipients. In such settings, teachers serve as facilitators, offering empathy, unconditional positive regard, and support, which allows students to explore and learn in ways that respect their individuality and sense of agency.

Rogers believed that learning and growth develop through lived experiences, not solely through instruction, and that people respond better to empathy, genuineness, and unconditional positive regard. Within therapy, Rogers believed a person responds to empathy, as their experiences are understood by another person, and when they receive unconditional positive regard being accepted by another person without condition or judgement. He also saw that a therapist's role is to be present and authentic, and not to hide behind their professional role. Rogers explained this process:

> *We can say with some assurance that a relationship characterised by a high degree of congruence or genuineness in the therapist, by sensitive and accurate*

DOI: 10.4324/9781003686064-13

> *empathy on the part of the therapist, by a high degree of regard, respect, liking for the client by the therapist, and by an absence of conditionality in this regard, we have a high probability of being an effective therapeutic relationship.*[1]

Rogers later applied these ideas to education, further suggesting that learning is effective when the teacher relates to a student as a therapist would to a client.[2] Research has consistently shown that empathy, acceptance, and authenticity are central to effective learning and therapeutic relationships.[3] What also stands out to me about Carl Rogers was his unique approach to his work. He always strived to be open, constantly questioning himself and never hiding behind a professional façade. He constantly challenged himself as a psychologist and, more importantly, prioritised his role in supporting another person. He said,

> *In my relationships with persons, I have found that it does not help, in the long run, to act as though I were something that I am not.*[4]

## Being in a State of Incongruence

In his book *On Becoming a Person*,[5] Rogers shared insights from his extensive therapeutic experience on how individuals can lead fulfilling lives. He believed that people could thrive when they receive acceptance, understanding, and honesty, rather than being judged or conditioned. He argued that when someone faces difficulties in life, they are in a state of incongruence, a term which describes the barrier between a person's self-image and their actual feelings or experiences. He best described this in his book *A Way of Being*,[6] stating,

> *When the other person is hurting, confused, troubled, anxious, alienated, terrified, or when he or she is doubtful of self-worth, uncertain as to identity, then understanding is called for.*[7]

Take, for example, an autistic child sitting in class, who appears to be calm and coping, is, in fact, inside, feeling completely overwhelmed by the demands and expectations placed on them. They stay silent in class to hide their *true* feelings, possibly to avoid trouble or because they can't articulate how they feel inside: they don't want to be there but feel that they have to.

Their true feelings surface only when away from school, usually at home, as a shutdown or meltdown. Inside, they are anxious and stressed; on the surface, they comply because that is what they think they should do. The gap between *how* the child feels and how they *believe* they must behave is what creates the incongruent state.

In my experience, when a school asks for advice because they feel a child is "fine in class", but the parents say they are anxious, depressed, and withdrawn at home. I follow how the child is at home because it is a more accurate representation of their true feelings and who they want to be but can't. By existing in an incongruent state, in school, they are trying to cope with an environment that does not reflect how they feel inside or what they really need. I have also seen that children in a state of incongruence can only keep it up for so long and, often, without warning, stop attending school, develop mental health issues, and appear not to be able to cope with anything.

> **Reflection**
>
> When an autistic child is withdrawing from lessons, or not attending school, or struggling with something at home, even if they appear fine, they are most likely in an incongruent state, and your role as a professional, parent, or adult supporting is to step back look for ways to help the child first feel safe around you. If you accept them completely, without condition, they are then most likely to open up to you and describe how they really feel.

## Finding Congruence

Rogers believed you help someone in an incongruent state by helping them find *congruence*. For an autistic child masking in school, this would mean aligning the child's inner experience with their outer experience. In therapeutic terms, Rogers saw congruence not just as something the therapist gives to the client; it is something the client grows into as they begin to experience the adult supporting them through unconditional positive regard, something we will discuss later in the chapter. Through this process, a client in therapy becomes more aligned with who they are as they find the freedom to be themselves, knowing they are unconditionally accepted, no matter their state at any given time.

How do we help autistic children to find their own states of congruence in education and mental health? This is a complex question to ask, for obvious reasons, such as the expectation to follow school rules and the limitations in mental health support. There are times when it would seem impossible to accept an autistic child entirely within the confines of these systems. I hear this a lot in my advisory role in educational settings or when I am training. Questions often arise: "*We can't just let them do what they want?*" and "*They can't be themselves; society will not accept them!*" and "*We need to teach children emotional resilience; we all have to do things we don't want to in life*". My answers are always the same. "*Yes, we can*", "*Society needs to change*", and "*No, we don't have to do what we don't want to in life, that is a myth*".

To help an autistic child find a state of congruence, I suggest starting by asking *why* they are struggling in the first place. For example, the child who appears to be fine in class and then all of a sudden, without warning, storms out, is this a sign that they are not able to let their true feelings out? I find that it is very common for autistic children, who mask in school, to reveal how they actually feel when they are at home, staying in their rooms, unable to communicate.

Finding a congruent state for those children begins by removing the pressures and expectations that cause them to mask their true selves. For example, if the child knows the adult supporting them accepts them completely and unconditionally, knowing they *do not* have to hide their true feelings and are not made to stay in class when it's too much for them, then their internal distress begins to settle, and their anxiety is relieved. A congruent state, for this child, can be achieved by the simple act of letting them leave the room whenever they need to, or not to do the work if they can't, or to find ways of reducing their sensory input by offering other spaces to learn in, are just a few simple ideas to help a child reach a congruent state.

In more complex cases, where a child is in an incongruent state and has become completely withdrawn from school, the most effective and immediate way to help is to *remove* the demand to attend. Remove *all* school pressure from them. At this moment, school is not right for them, instead what they need is to feel listened to and understood. Only then, when the very thing making them anxious is removed, can we begin to help these children find what works best for *them,* not the systems they find themselves in. Simply, thinking "school is the best place for a child" does not work for these children. Demand-avoidant children who cannot attend school need to know that school is *not* the best place for them and that this is totally accepted and OK.

When a child hears the adult say, "*I can see this is too much for you. It's OK, we are going to take away the pressure for you to attend school. Enough is enough. I hear you. Let's find other ways for you to learn*", the child will no longer have to mask or hide how they feel. Their inner world and outward experience begin to align, and a congruent state is formed. It is then, in a congruent state, that an autistic child can begin to be who they really are, which, in my experience, is the beginning of a journey of self-discovery that is much more effective than trying to get children to face their anxieties and to make them do what they can't do.

### Real-Life Experience 8

Just after I graduated, I worked as a community songwriter supporting young people who had fallen out of education, either through exclusion or disengagement from their education settings. All the young people were autistic, had ADHD, or had oppositional defiance disorder, and all were excluded from their education settings. The idea behind the project we set up was that, through the art of songwriting and music production, they might find an outlet for their frustrations.

On the surface, these young people were openly argumentative, with their hoodies up, phones out, swearing every other word, and looking to *push* boundaries. But through songwriting, they soon learned they had an outlet to express how they truly felt. When they realised, we were there to let them be completely themselves; with no conditions or boundaries to push, they soon came out of their protective shells.

During one session, tensions between two rival gangs had been building. One afternoon, while we were practising for a performance, a teenager came storming in. He was verbally threatening another young person on stage. As he moved closer, my instinct was to intervene and to protect the other teenager. As he came closer, a more experienced project worker advised that, instead of intervening, we should sit down and let the young person explain why he was so upset. So, as he came closer to the stage, we were sitting there waiting for him. We didn't intervene; instead, I asked, "*Are you OK? Is there anything we can do to help?*"

What happened next was not more anger. He completely changed his demeanour. Moments before, he was angry, big, and threatening to attack the other person. Instead, as soon as I asked if we could help him, he burst into tears and fell onto a chair opposite us. He was no longer acting violently; he was *vulnerable*. Within 20 minutes, the situation was resolved.

In his moment of anger, he saw in front of him adults who wanted to listen to him, not to tell him off, as he was used to. We didn't judge his language or his threats; we didn't tell him to calm down or to get out. He was met with acceptance and understanding, which was what instantly removed his anger. He received unconditional positive regard from us.

This young autistic person was *not* at fault. He was in an emotional state because he couldn't process his feelings. He was unable to calm himself or rationalise what he was thinking. What he needed in that moment was to see that even then, in his anger, he was accepted by the adults in front of him.

## The Six Conditions of Change

As a therapist, Rogers observed that genuine and lasting change occurs when *six specific conditions* are present within the relationship between the client and therapist. I propose that these same conditions can help us to effectively support autistic children and young people, particularly those who struggle with traditional educational and mental health systems.

In an article titled "*The necessary and sufficient conditions of therapeutic personality change*",[8] Rogers outlined the six conditions necessary to support a person in therapy, providing a compelling framework for understanding the human condition and fostering emotional safety essential for growth. We will now discuss these in detail, then look at how we could apply them to support autistic children and young people.

### 1. Psychological Contact

This first condition is when two people are in a *genuine* psychological connection, not just going through the motions. He identified that change occurs within a relationship, where a person can learn to depend and rely on human connection through trust and acceptance. Rogers also said that this first condition can occur at the most basic level, even when a person is withdrawn and does not appear to respond. Rogers also noted, importantly, that this first condition must be established; otherwise, the other conditions have no real meaning.

### 2. *The Client Is in a State of Incongruence*

In this second condition, the client will be feeling unsure, anxious, or uncomfortable with themselves. The therapist identifies that the client is in conflict between how they feel inside and how they *believe* they should feel or behave. The therapist openly accepts the client in their state of incongruence, without judgement or pressure to change. The therapist *accepts* the client exactly as they are.

### 3. *The Therapist Is Congruent, Genuine, and Honest*

In the third condition, the therapist is in a *congruent* state, genuine, and completely their true selves. The critical step here is for the therapist not to hide behind a professional mask or to think they need to perform a role that could be perceived as distant or false. Instead, the aim is to show the client that they are human, with their own struggles and issues. This condition allows the client to begin to feel accepted by another *human* and not an authority figure. Rogers found that when the therapist models congruence, the client begins to learn to accept themselves.

### 4. *The Therapist Has Unconditional Positive Regard for the Client*

In the fourth condition, the therapist needs to demonstrate unconditional positive regard, without judgement or conditions, helping the client realise they don't need to earn their approval. With unconditional positive regard, a client begins to feel safe to explore their feelings without fear of judgement or anxiety. As a result, they start to let go of the pressure to perform or conceal their true emotions.

### 5. *The Therapist Is Empathetic of the Client's Situation*

As the relationship evolves, the therapist shows empathy through understanding the client's experiences, seeing the world from the client's perspective and understanding how it must feel for them. The most effective way to do this is for the therapist to listen closely to the client's experiences and feelings. The therapist does not correct the client in any way or try to interpret their experience for them.

### 6. *The Client Feels the Therapist's Acceptance and Understanding*

In the final condition, the client begins to feel accepted and understood by the therapist. The client learns to accept that the therapist's trust and empathy are genuine and authentic, enabling them to feel they can be completely themselves and allowing meaningful change to occur.

### Supporting the Autistic Child

Rogers demonstrated that when all six conditions are met, individuals start to feel secure enough to explore their feelings, challenge their beliefs, and pursue meaningful growth. I aim to illustrate now that these conditions can also be applied to autistic children and young people in mental health and educational contexts. To do this, we'll consider an example involving an educator and an autistic student.

For context, I am not suggesting that educators become therapists; I am suggesting that the ideas within the conditions can inspire us to build more effective ways to help a child regulate their emotions by knowing they are accepted unconditionally by the adult in front of them, without judgement or conditions. We will consider the following scenario and how to apply these conditions.

**Scenario:** *An autistic child has stormed out of his classroom and is swearing at the top of their voice. Visibly distressed, angry, and crying, you find them standing in the corridor outside their classroom.*

#### 1. Human Connection

The adult and the child first begin to understand each other as people, not based on their roles. The teacher shows a genuine interest in the child and is present and accepting of what the child is going through in the moment. As an adult in this situation, you are looking to *connect* with the child, to try to understand how they are feeling. What could have upset them so much? A demand? An expectation that seems too difficult for them? You are trying here to connect with how the child is feeling, not to solve the existing issue.

#### 2. The Child Is Struggling Inside

The adult identifies and recognises that the child is feeling overwhelmed and sees this as the child communicating that they need *help*. The child swearing in the corridor after they have stormed out of class does not need to be sanctioned for using bad language; they need you to listen to what they are expressing. Your role here is to accept that the distressing behaviour is a cry for help, not defiant behaviour that needs to be dealt with.

#### 3. The Adult Is Genuine and Honest

The adult does not mask who they are and is open and transparent with the child. They are genuine, not hiding behind their role or the rigidity of professionalism, or how they think they should act. The teacher understands the importance of showing their human side. For example, you could say to the child swearing, "*I can see you are upset. I feel like you sometimes and also feel the need to swear! It's OK. Can I help? Do you want to go somewhere quiet to chat?*"

### 4. *The Adult Accepts the Child 100%*

The teacher then accepts the child for *exactly* who they are, unconditionally, in that moment. They do not judge the child's behaviour or limit their acceptance of the child because the child is swearing. As the teacher, you remain consistent in your acceptance, regardless of how the child may be acting towards you.

### 5. *The Adult Understands the Child's Inner World*

The adult tries to understand the child's point of view and takes the child's subjective experiences into account. They value and validate how the child feels, what they fear, and their hopes and dreams, as well as what they enjoy in life. This could be achieved by maybe sitting beside them in a calming manner, offering acceptance of the situation, and not judging them for their negative behaviour.

### 6. *The Child Begins to Feel Accepted and Understood*

The teacher openly accepts the child through their actions, and the child begins to see this. The child begins to see that you are accepting them in their distress and upset. The child then begins to accept that they can be themselves with the teacher, completely, knowing with confidence that they do not need to change. This then allows the child to express how they are feeling and to begin to feel safe in the teacher's presence.

## Openness to Experience

There is so much to Carl Rogers' work, and his ideas go beyond the scope of this chapter. Instead, I have attempted to highlight his key ideas that inspire me in my work supporting autistic children and young people. In Part Three, we will explore in more detail how these ideas influenced my development of the Accept Approach. To conclude this chapter, I want to share another idea of Rogers and what he meant when he described a person's *openness to experience.*

The idea is that a person will be more open to their experiences when they feel safe and, in turn, this state of being helps them accept what they are thinking and feeling without having to block or deny their true feelings. When someone feels no threat, they will not feel the need to be in a defensive mode. As Rogers explained,

> *When the individual is in no way threatened, then he is open to his experience. To be open to experience is the polar opposite of defensiveness.*[9]

The idea could be applied effectively when supporting an autistic child who is in a distressed state. If they do not feel threatened by the adults supporting them, they can begin to accept how they feel inside and their responses to what is happening around them. They will notice their fear, anxiety, sadness, stress, and frustrations without thinking that they are wrong in some way to feel these emotions.

Whereas when an autistic child is in defensive mode, this idea suggests that their mind is trying to protect them, through masking, or pretending things may not really be happening, or that they are feeling the way they are. These moments are when autistic children tend to shut down and become unreachable.

We had a young person who was frustrated because another child had popped a balloon near them during a session. She was visibly angry and upset with the other child, shouting for them to go away. We supported her by accepting her frustration and by asking the other child, who was oblivious to what they had done, to go into the other room for a moment. We validated how she was feeling, and she felt safe enough to express her frustrations. If we had said to her, "Stop being silly, it's just a balloon popping!" this response would have put her on the defensive, thinking her feelings were not important or accepted. She would have hidden her feelings, which would have then manifested into more stressful behaviours, and shut down. As a result of the adults accepting her frustrations, she was able to move on almost immediately. After expressing her annoyance with the balloon, she continued the session and moved on.

## Summary

As a professional, I find that humanistic principles help autistic children engage more effectively with support when they know they can feel safe and accepted. They begin to be who they really are, knowing it's OK to do so, and when this happens, the opportunities are endless. They begin to learn that they are free to be themselves without condition or the need to comply.

My aim in this chapter was to show Roger's key ideas and share how we can apply his principles to support autistic children and young people. His thinking is embedded throughout the ideas in this book, and his principles have inspired and shaped the Accept Approach, which I introduce you to in Part Three. Rogers shows us the importance of developing relationships based on acceptance. In the next chapter, we discuss another humanistic thinker who has also profoundly shaped how I support autistic children and young people, Abraham Maslow.

## Notes

1 Rogers, C.R. (1961). *On Becoming a Person: A Therapist's View of Psychotherapy*. Houghton Mifflin.
2 Rogers, C., Lyon, H.C. & Tausch, R. (2013). *On Becoming an Effective Teacher: Person Centered Teaching, Psychology, Philosophy, and Dialogues with Carl R. Rogers and Harold Lyon*. Routledge.
3 Kirschenbaum, H. & Jourdan, A. (2005). The Current Status of Carl Rogers and the Person Centered Approach. *Psychotherapy: Theory, Research, Practice, Training*, 42(1), pp. 37–51.
4 Rogers, C.R. (1961). *On Becoming a Person: A Therapist's View of Psychotherapy*. Houghton Mifflin.
5 Rogers, C.R. (1961). *On Becoming a Person: A Therapist's View of Psychotherapy*. Houghton Mifflin.

6 Rogers, C.R. (1980). *A Way of Being*. Boston, MA: Houghton Mifflin.
7 Rogers, C.R. (1980). *A Way of Being*. Boston, MA: Houghton Mifflin.
8 Rogers, C.R. (1957). The Necessary and Sufficient Conditions of Therapeutic Personality Change. *Journal of Consulting Psychology*, 21(2), pp. 95–103. https://doi.org/10.1037/h0045357
9 Rogers, C.R. (1959). A Theory of Therapy, Personality and Interpersonal Relationships as Developed in the Client-Centered Framework. In S. Koch (Ed.), *Psychology: A Study of a Science. Volume 3: Formulations of the Person and the Social Context* (pp. 184–256). New York: McGraw-Hill (Accessed January 2026). https://www.beeleaf.com/wp-content/uploads/2017/09/rogers_chapter_in_koch-1.pdf

Chapter 11

# Beyond the Pyramid

Abraham Maslow was a humanistic psychologist who believed that the roles of the teacher, therapist, and parent should be those of a *horticulturist*, concentrating on supporting people's development in their own way. Much like helping a rose to be the best rose it can be, instead of trying to make it into a Lily.[1] Maslow also regarded psychological safety as vital for human growth and well-being. He argued that if society can create conditions to fulfil basic needs, such as allowing the freedom to speak honestly and openly, and to develop and own their natural abilities and passions, then the best qualities in humanity would naturally emerge.[2] In this chapter, we examine Maslow's ideas and concepts and explore how they can be utilised to support autistic children and young people. To achieve this, we must first address misconceptions about Maslow and his work, such as the idea that he created a pyramid diagram to illustrate his hierarchy of needs. He did not.

## Addressing the Pyramid

The first misconception to address is the idea that Maslow created a pyramid diagram to represent his ideas, when in fact he never did;[3] no such diagram was published in any of his writings.[4] Most believe the pyramid was developed by Maslow because it is consistently found in psychological and management textbooks and in online searches. The truth is more likely that a management consultant in the 1960s created the pyramid, quickly evolving into the popular representation of his ideas.[5] It is documented that the continuation of the pyramid in management textbooks reduced Maslow's ideas to a "parody", betraying the actual spirit of Maslow's notion of self-actualisation and the realisation of one's potential.[6]

When considering why, in his research, Maslow never directly challenged the diagram, there is suggestion in his personal diaries that he needed to stay relevant due to ill health and financial difficulties, and the management community, which used the pyramid diagram effectively, gave him much needed recognition especially as he felt so underappreciated in psychology, due to the dominance of experimental studies.[7]

DOI: 10.4324/9781003686064-14

## Levels of Need

Another misconception of Maslow's work is that his hierarchy of needs is often misinterpreted as a *fixed* set of levels or stages in which each must be completed *before* moving on to the next. Scott Barry Kaufman, in his book *Transcend*, likened this misconception to a video game: where a person completes the safety level and is then congratulated for unlocking the belonging level,[8] which, as Kaufman states, is an incorrect assumption about how the hierarchy of needs actually works.

Maslow also predicted this would be a common misconception and explained himself in his first major publication, *A Theory of Human Motivation*,[9] that for some people, these needs are *not* fixed. For example, some individuals seem inherently motivated to be creative, even if their basic needs are not yet completely satisfied. He suggested that, for these people, creativity, for example, does not emerge only once they have achieved comfort and security. Instead, it appears *despite* any of the other unmet needs. This implies that creative motivation is more important to them. He goes on to explain,

> *A more realistic description of the hierarchy would be in terms of decreasing percentages of satisfaction as we go up the hierarchy of prepotency, For instance, if I may assign arbitrary figures for the sake of illustration, it is as if the average citizen is satisfied perhaps 85 per cent in his physiological needs, 70 per cent in his safety needs, 50 per cent in his love needs, 40 per cent in his self-esteem needs, and 10 per cent in his self-actualisation needs.*[10]

For Maslow, life was not about climbing a pyramid of levels and achieving each stage before reaching the top. He did not see human growth as a *reward system*; he saw self-actualisation as the process of living life to the full, moment by moment, finding meaning and purpose.

## Maslow's Starting Point

We will now consider how Maslow's Hierarchy of Needs can inform professionals' and parents' support for their autistic children and young people. Maslow developed his ideas, as Rogers did, during a time when psychology was dominated by two strong traditions, behaviourism, and psychoanalysis. He believed that both principles ignored what gives a person *meaning* in life and became one of the earliest and most influential thinkers in *humanistic psychology*. His work drew much attention and support, and in 1961, alongside Anthony Sutich, he founded the *Journal of Humanistic Psychology*.[11]

Maslow introduced to the world the idea of *self-actualisation*, proposing that human beings are naturally driven to grow throughout their lifespans. In studying self-actualising individuals, he found that those who achieved their full potential often showed traits such as altruism, creativity, openness, authenticity, acceptance, and independence. However, he did not think we needed all these traits to achieve self-actualisation. Instead, he believed that the most effective way to help people reach self-actualisation was for society to meet their basic needs, after which the qualities that represent the best of humanity would emerge.[12]

## Maslow's Hierarchy of Needs

More than 80 years have passed since Maslow proposed that human motivation is formed as a hierarchy of basic needs. His ideas have had a lasting impact on psychology, influencing the study of personality, social psychology, developmental psychology, psychopathology, and organisational behaviour.[13] We will now examine each need and explore its specific meaning.

### 1. Physiological Needs

Maslow believed there are at least five basic needs. He listed them as physiological, safety, love/belonging, esteem, and self-actualisation. He saw that these needs are interrelated, with *physiological needs* being the most fundamental and critical for human development. He stated that if a person lacks all the basic needs, including food, safety, love, and esteem, they would most likely desire *food* above all else. He said that for a man who is extremely and dangerously hungry, nothing else matters but food:

> *No other interests exist but food. He dreams food, he remembers food, he thinks about food, he emotes only about food, he perceives only food, and he wants only food.*[14]

**Reflection**

An autistic child who feels exhausted, hungry, and overwhelmed will not be able to engage in any kind of learning or be able to process demands/expectations place on them. There have been many occasions where I have supported a child or young person, who is overwhelmed in the morning, and a nice cup of tea, some toast, or a favourite snack has completely changed how they feel.

### 2. Safety Needs

When physiological needs are met to a reasonable level, Maslow suggested that a person's attention will shift towards ***safety needs***, and as with physiological needs, they will be dominated by seeking out ways to feel safe. He suggested that for children to feel safe, they naturally prefer orderly, predictable, organised worlds they can count on. Whereas for adults, they will notice safety needs the most when they are *missing*, much like people living in constant anxiety, instability, or social exclusion.

Safety needs, according to Maslow, are reached when a person can live in a mostly predictable, stable, and harm-free life, where they experience emotional security, health, financial stability, and a sense that life is generally OK. Maslow believed that safety needs develop alongside family, community, and social systems, such as healthcare and legal frameworks. However, when these sources are unavailable, individuals will often seek alternative ways to find safety. Maslow said:

> *Other broader aspects of the attempt to seek safety and stability in the world are seen in the very common preference for familiar rather than unfamiliar things, or for the known rather than the unknown.*[15]

Many autistic children and young people tell us that they do not feel safe in school. Sometimes this is easily recognised, but other times it can be hidden, due to masking or camouflaging. Children often hide their true feelings because they may fear being singled out, and don't want any attention drawn to them. Other children might not feel safe and may be unaware of their own experiences, which can often show up as behavioural issues.

Maslow described how children may appear when not feeling safe,

> *Infants will react in a total fashion and as if they were endangered, if they are disturbed or dropped suddenly, startled by loud noises, flashing light, or other unusual sensory stimulation, by rough handling, by general loss of support in the mother's arms, or by inadequate support.*

### Reflection

Before any learning or support can be effective, a lot of autistic children and young people need to feel safe. However, it is vital that when a child is struggling in any environment, to look first at how safe *they* feel, not how safe they may appear.

### 3. *Love and Belonging Needs*

This brings us to the next most important need: ***love and belonging needs***. Maslow said that if both physiological and safety needs are mostly met, then the desire for love, affection, and belonging will emerge. A person will seek out love so much that Maslow said he may even forget how, when he was hungry, he did not even *consider* the idea of love. He also said the critical aspect of this need is that it must involve both giving *and* receiving of love.

The need to feel as though a person belongs is also crucial to human development. Maslow argued that a person is motivated to belong *before* being motivated to achieve. He also pointed out that acceptance of others is key to this development, embedded in relationships with friends and family, being loved and valued without conditions. When a person does not feel they belong or are loved, they withdraw, put on a mask, and resist because they don't feel safe or accepted; they are protecting themselves.

**Reflection**

Much like Carl Rogers idea of unconditional positive regard, Maslow also saw the importance of being accepted by others, *without* conditions. This is why whenever an autistic child is showing signs of extreme distress or overwhelm, it is vital that I can show they are *completely* accepted by me in any given moment. This in turn, helps them to see me as an adult who accepts them no matter what is going in school, or at home.

### 4. *Esteem Needs*

After love and belonging, the next important need is ***esteem needs***. Maslow identified two types of esteem needs: inner and external. Inner esteem needs were necessary for confidence, independence, and freedom. Then, external esteem needs included the desire for recognition, respect, and approval from others. Maslow argued that esteem needs are vital because they help a person feel self-confident and worthy and find meaning and importance in the world. When discussing esteem needs, he said,

> *All people in our society (with a few pathological exceptions) have a need or desire for a stable, firmly based, (usually) high evaluation of themselves, for self-respect, or self-esteem, and for the esteem of others.*[16]

**Reflection**

When looking at esteem needs in autistic children and young people, I often observe that they are driven more by internal motivations than external rewards. For instance, if a child shows no interest in participating in a lesson activity, offering a reward or praise from an adult usually proves ineffective because they do not perceive any worth in doing something they are not interested in.

When a child completes a task, they are engaged in through their own choice, they don't look for an external reward, they already feel accomplishment *inside*. They don't really need recognition from others. Although of course it is nice to receive a compliment from someone, I just don't think that is what drives a child to complete the task.

When looking at esteem needs in autistic children and young people, I often observe that they are driven more by internal motivations than external rewards. For instance, if a child shows no interest in participating in a lesson activity, offering a reward or praise from an adult usually proves ineffective because they do not perceive any worth in doing something they dislike.

### 5. *Self-Actualisation*

Then, finally, there is the need for ***self-actualisation***. Maslow believed that even when all other needs are met to a reasonable level, a person still needs to feel they are doing what they are *meant* to do. The concept of self-actualisation, initially introduced by Kurt Goldstein in his book *The Organism,*[17] is referred to by Maslow as the desire for self-fulfilment, in which a person reaches their *potential*. He believed that a person reaching self-actualisation rests upon having their physiological, safety, love, and esteem needs met. As discussed, it is essential to note that we must not be caught up in the misconception that self-actualisation can be achieved only when others' needs are met, as these needs overlap and change throughout a person's life. Maslow best described self-actualisation when he wrote,

> *A musician must make music, an artist must paint, a poet must write, if he is to be ultimately happy.*[18]

**Reflection**

I find that the idea of self-actualisation fascinating but also somewhat difficult to understand. For example, I have not yet met anyone who has reached their "full" human potential, however I do know people who are grounded and happy doing what they love to do.

I think that for autistic people, Maslow's ideas help me to understand the importance for placing value on a child's interests and passions. I often see children and young people self-actualising when they are fixated on their special interest whether this is a game, drawing a picture, or walking for hours looking for a rare bird. It is in those moments; I see them self-actualise.

Maslow's hierarchy of needs offers us a way to understand how to help someone become their whole self. When considering autistic people, Maslow never discussed the condition as it was not fully recognised when he developed his ideas. However, I believe the key takeaway from his ideas on motivation is to use them to recognise unmet needs when an autistic child or young person is having difficulty coping. Knowing that children need to feel a sense of belonging, to feel safe and accepted, and to know that their interests and passions are validated are all important factors to consider when supporting them in both education and mental health systems.

**Real-Life Experience 9**

We supported a young autistic adult who was not coping with life, and nothing that had been tried up to the point of our support had worked for her. When we first began supporting her, we identified that some of her basic needs were not being met, and she found it extremely difficult to exist in her world as a result of this. She lived with her family, and her basic psychological needs were met. She was housed, fed, and loved by her family, but she didn't feel *safe* in her education experiences. Every school she had attended broke down, even with one setting banning her from ever returning to the site. She was made to feel that all the problems were her fault and that she needed to change her ways. She was constantly in trouble with the local police and was often found walking the streets late at night and sometimes found unconscious on the roadside after failed attempts to end her life.

I recognised that she didn't feel safe, and that providing safety was the most important thing we could do to support her. Safety is vital because it offers stability, certainty, predictability, and coherence, fostering trust in the environment the young person is in. It forms the foundation upon which all other needs are built. The need for safety is linked to the struggle to make sense of experiences and serves as motivation to regain control over past traumatic events.

We applied the foundations of acceptance by *removing* anything that made her anxious or stressed, *reminding* her that it is not her fault she was finding things difficult, and *reassuring* her that it's going to be OK; we will help her find a way. We also *reaffirmed* that we are not going anywhere and would stand by her side, unconditionally accepting her for exactly who she is.

At first, she found our support somewhat difficult to accept. This young person had never really been accepted exactly as she was, and she found this a little strange at first. As the weeks went by, she began to embrace the rules of our sessions, knowing first that she is the boss of what we do, and second that she doesn't have to do anything she doesn't want to. For example, during the early days of support, there were some members of staff she did not like to work with because she could not connect with them. This was totally fine with us, and we changed the staff to find people she could connect with. We never pushed her or expected her to change. We adapted when she needed us to, to the best of our ability.

After a few months, we noticed she was beginning to respond positively to acceptance-based support. She was attending more sessions and visiting our learning centre regularly. Her safety needs were slowly being established, and we could see this because she was engaging more and wanted to do learning activities, which was something she had not done in a while. She was also no longer getting in trouble with the police, her mental health was improving, and she did not feel suicidal anymore. She still had her difficult days, but we helped her to get through them as best we could, through unconditional acceptance.

This young person has overcome obstacles that most of us will ever experience. Throughout her life, her learning journey was marked by rejection and blame for behaviours beyond her control. However, within our team, she was accepted unconditionally and has shared with us now that she finally feels safe and valued. Recently, I arrived at our learning centre (discussed in Chapter 21), and she was sitting in the corner, as she now usually is, independently writing and studying her chosen topic. I recalled our first meeting, when I met her at her home, sitting with her legs shaking, head down, overwhelmed. Feeling unsafe. Six months on, I could never have imagined such a level of engagement would be possible. However, that was not the most impactful moment of that day.

In the afternoon, we were interviewing potential tutors and asked whether she would like to join the interview panel. Meeting people she did not know was not easy for this young person; we were not sure what her reaction would be. She jumped at the chance and enjoyed the experience. Staff later reflected on how confident she was and on the thoughtfulness of her questions to the candidates. They were so proud of her for confidently asking questions and having a dialogue with someone she did not know. Towards the end of the interview, a candidate asked her why this support had worked for her above all else. She replied,

> *I can be myself with them. I can get up and walk out whenever I need to. I can learn what I want to, and they let me do what interests me. I like being here. I feel safe.*

In my experience, autistic children and young people who have not been able to engage in traditional education or mental health models of support do not feel *safe*. This is fundamental if we as professionals are to help children find ways to cope in life. They need to feel safe first and foremost before we can even consider supporting them effectively in any other way. There is no point in doing a six-week therapy course or finding them a school placement if they don't feel safe enough to *engage*.

Maslow said people move towards growth when their needs are met, not when they are controlled or constrained to be someone, they are not. This is particularly relevant to autistic children, especially those in schools. Those children who are constantly outside the head teacher's office, banned from playgrounds, or unable to cope with a whole day without a meltdown. These children require professionals, teachers, and parents to focus on unmet needs rather than what the child must do to improve.

## Summary

Maslow's ideas can help us see what is *missing* when supporting an autistic child or young person, rather than thinking we need to teach them something to improve. His ideas can help us to remember that there is so much more to a child whose behaviour is deemed problematic or pathological. He reminds us that these children are, in fact, struggling with life and are not experiencing problems that require intervention or the development of emotional resilience. These children have unmet needs, and that is the *real* issue.

Maslow's ideas show that a child cannot move forward unless they feel loved and safe and have a healthy view of who they are as a *whole* person. His hierarchy of needs shows that until these needs are met, *nothing* else will work.

## Notes

1 Kaufman, S.B. (2020). *Transcend: The New Science of Self-Actualization.* London: Penguin.
2 Kaufman, S.B. (2020). *Transcend: The New Science of Self-Actualization.* London: Penguin.
3 Bridgman, T., Cummings, S. & Ballard, J. (2020). *Who Built Maslow's Pyramid? A History of the Creation of Management Studies' Most Famous Symbol and Its Implications for Management Education.* Victoria University of Wellington Library. https://doi.org/10.26686/wgtn.12735929.v1
4 Kaufman, S.B. (2019). Who Created Maslow's Iconic Pyramid? *Scientific American* (Beautiful Minds blog), 23 April (Accessed 19 December 2025). https://www.scientificamerican.com/blog/beautiful-minds/who-created-maslows-iconic-pyramid/
5 Bridgman, T., Cummings, S. & Ballard, J.A. (2019). Who Built Maslow's Pyramid? A History of the Creation of Management Studies' Most Famous Symbol and Its Implications for Management Education. *Academy of Management Learning and Education*, 18(1), pp. 81–98. https://doi.org/10.5465/amle.2017.0351
6 Mills, A.J., Simmons, T. & Helms Mills, J. (2005). *Reading Organization Theory: A Critical Approach to the Study of Organizational Behaviour and Structure*. 3rd edn. Toronto: University of Toronto Press.
7 Kaufman, S.B. (2019). Who Created Maslow's Iconic Pyramid? *Scientific American* (Beautiful Minds blog), 23 April (Accessed 19 December 2025). https://www.scientificamerican.com/blog/beautiful-minds/who-created-maslows-iconic-pyramid/
8 Kaufman, S.B. (2020). *Transcend: The New Science of Self-Actualization.* London: Penguin.
9 Maslow, A.H. (1943). A Theory of Human Motivation. *Psychological Review*, 50(4), pp. 370–396.
10 Maslow, A.H. (1943). A Theory of Human Motivation. *Psychological Review*, 50(4), pp. 370–396. (page 14).
11 The Journal of Humanistic Psychology. https://uk.sagepub.com/en-gb/eur/journal/journal-humanistic-psychology
12 Kaufman, S.B. (2020). *Transcend: The New Science of Self-Actualization.* London: Penguin.

13 Kenrick, D.T., Griskevicius, V., Neuberg, S.L. & Schaller, M. (2010). Renovating the Pyramid of Needs: Contemporary Extensions Built Upon Ancient Foundations. *Perspectives Psychological Science*, May, 5(3), pp. 292–314. https://doi.org/10.1177/1745691610369469. PMID: 21874133; PMCID: PMC3161123.
14 Maslow, A.H. (1943). A Theory of Human Motivation. *Psychological Review*, 50(4), pp. 370–396. (page 5).
15 Maslow, A.H. (1943). A Theory of Human Motivation. *Psychological Review*, 50(4), pp. 370–396. (page 8).
16 Maslow, A.H. (1943). A Theory of Human Motivation. *Psychological Review*, 50(4), pp. 370–396. (page 10).
17 Goldstein, K. (1934). *The Organism: A Holistic Approach to Biology Derived from Pathological Data in Man.* Hague: Nijhoff/Zone Books (English translation 1939/1995).
18 Maslow, A.H. (1943). A Theory of Human Motivation. *Psychological Review*, 50(4), pp. 370–396.

Chapter 12

# Thinking Differently

When an autistic child doesn't engage in learning, there are other creative ways we can support them. This chapter features key thinkers who question traditional education models, demonstrating that difference can be understood in alternative ways and from different perspectives. We will explore Ken Robinson's perspective on creativity and education, Mihaly Csikszentmihalyi's idea of flow, Peter Gray's ideas on the significance of play, and Ross Greene's alternative approach to understanding behaviour. Throughout, we will reflect on how their ideas could be used to better support autistic children and young people in their learning.

## The Importance of Creativity

When I first watched Sir Ken Robinson's TED Talk: *Do Schools Kill Creativity?*[1] I was instantly moved by his case for nurturing creativity rather than educating children out of it. In just 20 minutes, he laid bare all that is wrong with the education system today, such as how mistakes are viewed as the *worst* thing you can do, and that education steers creative people away from their natural abilities, with academic ability *wrongly* dominating our view of intelligence. Robinson exposing the blunt reality that as children become adults, "*We start to educate them progressively from the waist up, and then we focus on their heads and slightly to one side*".

Within the education system, Robinson argued, creative children are often met with the advice "*Don't do art, you won't be an artist. Don't do music, you're not going to make it as a musician*". Consequently, many talented children end up believing they are not, because their natural strengths are undervalued in school and often stigmatised.

During his talk, he shares a conversation he had with the choreographer Gillian Lynne, who, as a child, was referred by her school to a specialist for assessment because they believed she had a learning disorder. The school was concerned for her because she was easily distracted, constantly fidgeting during lessons, and disturbing others. During the assessment, Gillian said she recalled sitting on her hands for 20 minutes while the doctor spoke with her mother about the problems she was having in school. The doctor came over to sit next to Gillian and asked if it would be OK to speak to her mother privately outside the room. Just as he left the room,

DOI: 10.4324/9781003686064-15

he turned on the radio. He then asked her mother to watch for a moment to see what she did. As soon as they left, Gillian said she was up on her feet, moving around to the music. The doctor turned to her mother and said,

> *Gillian isn't sick. She's a dancer. Take her to a dance school.*

That was precisely what her mother did. Gillian recalled that when she first walked into the school, she saw children *just like her* – children who couldn't sit still, children who needed to move to think. She had found her place. Gillian Lynne graduated from the Royal Ballet and was responsible for some of the most successful musical theatre productions in history.

In 2013, she received a Special Award at the 2013 Olivier Awards,[2] and during her acceptance speech, she said,

> *It's difficult to believe that this is happening, I find it almost impossible to grasp because I've done nothing but follow my ideal life, which is to work with actors and singers and dancers and make theatre, and I don't want much more out of life.*

Where other schools would have focused on getting her to calm down and sit still in lessons, her mother *listened* to her needs and found her an education setting that focused on her natural abilities, rather than getting her to conform and comply with a set of standards she was never going to engage with.

**Reflection**

How many 8-year-old Gillian Lynnes are in schools today being told to calm down, to focus not on movement but on good sitting, and encouraged to concentrate instead of being allowed to freely be who they are? Lynne's story is just one example of why we must, as educators and mental health partitioners, nurture and view autistic children for who they are, not who society thinks they should be.

Ken Robinson's inspirational TED Talk argues against the norm of favouring academic achievement over creativity, in which children are no longer encouraged to take chances and embrace their natural talents. Children are discouraged from making mistakes, which, as Robinson argued, is why so many adults develop a fear of getting things wrong.

At the core of Robinson's ideas is the humanistic principle that people thrive when they are accepted for who they are. In *The Element*,[3] Robinson showed how the most impactful ways to learn are when a person connects with their personal interests and finds meaning in what they do. If what a person is learning matters to *them*, then engagement occurs naturally, without coercion or conformity. In *Creative Schools*,[4] he goes on further to argue that the main problem with our education system is that it is rooted in *control* and should instead be focused more on interest-led learning.

Sadly, Sir Ken Robinson passed away in 2020, but his thinking feels more urgent than ever. His ideas have reshaped how I view education and how to effectively support autistic children and young people, who, just like Gillian Lynne, do not "fit in". There are too many autistic children today who are misunderstood and wrongly viewed as problems to be fixed, and it is time we started listening to these great thinkers. Rogers, Maslow, and Robinson are just a dip in the ocean. They are not alone in their humanistic values, and in the rest of this chapter, I want to show that we do not have to remain stuck in these systems of failure. Autistic children and young people need us to *think differently*. All we need to do is have the courage to listen and stand up, making the changes that need to happen *now*.

## Flow Theory

Another way of thinking differently is to *value* a child's special interests and obsessions rather than ignoring them, and to even use them to *engage* a child in their learning, not as a motivator but as their main interest in learning. One of the most interesting things about many autistic children is their natural ability to fixate on something. Many have a gift for focusing on a subject of interest and, with ease, knowing everything there is to know, from the biggest to the smallest of details. An autistic child who loves trains, for example, will know all the routes, timetables, engine models, and even historical changes, and be able to recall them with accuracy. However, in education, having this type of passion and drive for just one subject is not considered enough; their special interest is often put aside, not valued and only used as a reward or an incentive to study other subjects.

My daughter has a special interest in Taylor Swift. She can name every song on every album, knows all the lyrics and everything about Taylor from what dresses she wore for each song on the Eras Tour, to the names of her cats Meredith, Olivia, and Benjamin. She will also spend hours editing video clips and creating amazing transitions, all self-taught, and has a TikTok channel with thousands of followers, with one of her clips reaching 1.7 million views. Sadly, in educational settings, this type of creativity is often unrecognised and undervalued when compared to core subjects like maths and English. Despite my daughter's best efforts, she remains unable to engage fully in a day-to-day educational setting, and she is not alone. She represents so many young people who just cannot cope in mainstream or specialist education. For these children and young people, there is not much on offer to *pursue* their special interests in their own time and in their own ways.

Within traditional education models in the UK, special interests are often viewed as obsessions that can negatively impact core learning, with teachers often struggling to decide whether to include them to engage an autistic child in learning or to remove them altogether.[5] Usually, it is the latter that many educators opt for, using a child's special interest as a *reward* they can have only if they do their schoolwork first. This, of course, can trigger many problems, especially if a child does not feel safe at school and their special interests are also undervalued.

What exactly is happening when an autistic child or young person is fixated on a special interest? Psychologist Mihaly Csikszentmihalyi would say in those moments that the child is in a state of *flow*. In his book *Flow: The Psychology of Optimal Experience*,[6] he describes flow as a state in which an individual becomes so fully immersed in what they are doing that nothing else matters. The activity is so naturally fulfilling that people engage in it mainly for the personal experience rather than external outcomes.

Autistic people who are "locked" into their special interests are said to have *hyperfocus*[7] or to be experiencing *monotropism,*[8] which is a theory associated with autism, explaining how a person can focus on a singular interest, often for hours at a time, with *unbreakable* attention.[9] Autistic people's experience of being in a hyperfocus state is often the same experience as people in states of flow. However, there appears to be little comparison of both autistic people's hyperfocus experiences and flow state in the research literature.[10]

In one study,[11] 24 autistic adults were interviewed and asked to describe how they feel when in hyperfocus. Many described becoming deeply absorbed in tasks and fully immersed. It was reported that they often lose track of time and find much joy and comfort in those moments. There was also some tension discussed about being so immersed in something can make it extremely hard to switch tasks or keep up with the demands of the day. Despite this the experience is itself positive and embraced. This is close to how people report being in a state of flow, suggesting that autistic hyperfocus is a state that can provide great potential value for the lives of autistic people.

In a state of flow, Csikszentmihalyi believed that time passes differently, anxieties are reduced, focus naturally increases, and learning happens *effortlessly.* After working with autistic children and young people for many years, I believe states of flow are of vital importance, and something we should prioritise in education. In school, for example, when a child can be completely absorbed in writing a story or drawing for hours but cannot tolerate a classroom environment for more than five minutes, there is a tendency to focus on what they *cannot* do. Why is this? Why is it that a child's inability to access a classroom is the primary concern, and a child's drawings or stories are viewed as a lesser activity?

Traditional education often dismisses special interests and states of flow as distractions and unhealthy obsessions. However, if we viewed them as Csikszentmihalyi did, we would reframe these as optimal learning experiences, and for an autistic child struggling in school, precisely what can make their life worth living.[12]

**Reflection**

In the context of autistic children who are not engaging in school, and are often dysregulated, I believe they are *not* the problem. With flow theory, we reconsider what learning actually looks like to an autistic child.

Flow theory asks what is more important? The constraints of teaching what we think a child should learn or allowing them to learn whatever they are interested in, and to pursue their interests instead.

How would autistic children and young people view education and learning in school if they were given complete autonomy to learn and study *only* what interests them? I am convinced there would not be so many avoiding school if this were the case.

## The Importance of Play

Peter Gray is a psychologist who thinks differently about education and learning. He is known for his work on the importance of self-directed learning and play in education. He argued that children are naturally driven to learn when they feel free to learn and not coerced. He believed that education is most effective for children when it aligns with how humans naturally evolved to learn: through play and exploration. He said,

> *Play is always voluntary. It is what one wants to do as opposed to what one is obliged to do. Players not only choose to play, but they also choose what and how to play.*[13]

Gray, like Csikszentmihalyi, found that play is something a child does with ease, because they *enjoy it,* not because of any outcome or reward they may receive at the end. Gray states that when someone is learning through play, the activity is what matters most, not the achievement of finishing it. The focus is on the *doing*, and not the *outcome*.

He goes on to suggest that outside of play, people usually only attempt to reach a goal if it is easy and quick. In play, however, goal setting is more about taking on challenges and doing things in different ways because the person wants to, *not* because they are directed to do so. Gray saw that this is why play, *at all ages*, is so essential to learning, as it supports curiosity, persistence, and creativity, all of which develop naturally in play without any pressure to conform.

Gray believed in self-directed learning where children and young people are given the freedom to choose what they want to learn, and how they learn. He believed adults should act as facilitators rather than control and dictate what the child learns.[14]

**Real-Life Experience 10**

An example of the importance of play was a case of a 6-year-old autistic boy who could no longer attend school. We were informed that he often experienced frustration and emotional dysregulation when in school and would drop to the floor, screaming or making loud vocalisations. We were told he was also prone to throwing items at peers and adults and would need constant support to help him regulate his emotions. He was also known to have anger outbursts, during which he would spit and display impulsive reactions when told "no" or when asked to wait for something he wanted.

When we began working with him, he first came to our learning centre. His mother was aware of our approach using acceptance-based support, and she prepared him beforehand to know the rules of our sessions, which were that (1) he was the boss of his learning and (2) we would only do whatever he wanted to, which she said he was OK with.

The setup was simple: he would arrive when he could and was free to explore our rooms, with games and activities set up for children to choose from. He took to this really well and often enjoyed moving from one table to another. During one session, he asked to go for a walk in the nearby forest. When on the walk, he started digging holes in the soil, saying, "*Let's look for diamonds!*" The staff members got involved and shared that he really enjoyed the activity, which sparked an idea for the next session.

The week after, before his arrival, the staff went outside and buried lots of costume jewellery diamonds throughout the forest floor. As soon as he arrived, we suggested going for a walk again, this time with another child. He loved the idea of looking for more treasure. He started digging again, and this time, with a little gentle guidance to particular areas on the ground, he began to find the diamonds. He was extremely happy and was fixated on gathering as many diamonds as he could. Loading them into his pocket, he said, "*Mummy will be rich now!*"

What stood out the most for me during this activity was how he invited the other child to explore with him. They shared ideas of where to dig next and worked together naturally without needing instruction or guidance. This same child, who was deemed problematic in school, often showing aggression toward other children, was happily playing, engaging, and connecting with another child, with no issues at all.

This is just one example of the importance of play. Here, the child was free to learn and explore what he chose, and the learning was natural rather than imposed. During all our sessions, we have never seen him get angry or throw anything. He doesn't throw himself on the floor, and when he asks for something, we give it to him. The impact has been transformative, and his mother has seen a real impact in our sessions. Here is some feedback she gave.

> *Previously, he was very attached to me and showed little interest in learning, as he hadn't been in education for the last six months. His sessions are the*

*highlight of his week, and he eagerly looks forward to them. He is happy to explore and participate, even without my presence.*

## Thinking Differently About Behaviour

When it comes to thinking differently about behaviour, Ross Greene stands out for his work on understanding challenging behaviours in children, exploring why they occur and how we can better support them. In his book *The Explosive Child,*[15] he stated that children will do well if they *can.* He argues that behaviours that are seen as challenging are not a choice but a sign that a child lacks the skills to cope with the demands placed on them. He suggests that the way forward is not to ask how to stop the behaviour, but instead to ask what is getting in the way for this child. What is their behaviour trying to tell us?

What I want to consider here is how this idea could work for autistic children who are viewed as demand-avoidant or too anxious to follow instructions. Could it be that these children are struggling because they cannot do something, rather than because they don't want to? I would say yes, this is exactly what is happening. In my years of experience, autistic children often deemed the most problematic are in fact the ones who are the most fragile and need the most support and help.

As Greene argues, "*If your kid could respond to problems and frustrations adaptively, he would*". Greene is saying here that children often labelled with behaviour issues are just frustrated by not being able to do something others think they can. Greene points out that the misleading view, which often dominates education today, is that *children do well if they want to,* suggesting that they have a *choice* in how they behave. Greene argues that this wrong thinking is why punishing unwanted behaviours and rewarding desired ones often do not work, because the child is struggling to understand and is being misunderstood as a result. Instead, Greene argues that *children do well if they can.*

How I approach behaviours deemed challenging is to remove anything that causes the problem in the first place, and then I see the behaviours do not occur. I believe that autistic children do react appropriately; it is just that their *appropriateness* is usually deemed *inappropriate* to the outside world. That is more about social acceptance than any lack of skill.

## Summary

For autistic children, we need to think differently about how they learn and engage with the world. Thinking differently requires a lot of courage, and sometimes this is what is most difficult for many professionals and educators supporting autistic children and young people. Thinking differently means questioning the "norm" and challenging practices that are considered effective, when we know they are not. Thinking differently helps us to reshape what education means for autistic children. It asks us to value creativity, explore special interests and states of flow, and to look more at the effectiveness of learning through play. All of these ideas offer us other ways to engage children who cannot engage with traditional methods of learning. Thinking differently means resisting the urge to correct unwanted behaviours and to fix perceived problems. Thinking differently calls us to stop fighting against children who say "no" and to start looking at how we can help them to say "yes".

## Notes

1 Ken Robinson TED Talk 'Do Schools Kill Creativity? https://www.ted.com/talks/sir_ken_robinson_do_schools_kill_creativity
2 Olivier Awards 2013. https://officiallondontheatre.com/olivier-awards/year/olivier-awards-2013/
3 Robinson, K. (2009). *The Element: How Finding Your Passion Changes Everything.* New York: Viking.
4 Robinson, K. & Aronica, L. (2015). *Creative Schools: The Grassroots Revolution That Is Transforming Education.* London: Penguin.
5 Gunn, K. & Delafield-Butt, J. (2015). Teaching Children with Autism Spectrum Disorder with Restricted Interests: A Review of Evidence for Best Practice. *Review of Educational Research.* https://doi.org/10.3102/0034654315604027. https://www.researchgate.net/publication/282441221_Teaching_Children_With_Autism_Spectrum_Disorder_With_Restricted_Interests_A_Review_of_Evidence_for_Best_Practice
6 Csikszentmihalyi, M. (1990). *Flow: The Psychology of Optimal Experience.* New York: Harper & Row.
7 Rapaport, H., Clapham, H., Adams, J., Lawson, W., Porayska-Pomsta, K. & Pellicano, E. (2024). "In a State of Flow": A Qualitative Examination of Autistic Adults' Phenomenological Experiences of Task Immersion. *Autism in Adulthood,* 6(3), pp. 362–373. https://doi.org/10.1089/aut.2023.0032
8 Murray, D., Lesser, M. & Lawson, W. (2005). Attention, Monotropism and the Diagnostic Criteria for Autism. *Autism,* 9(2), pp. 139–156.
9 Description of Monotropism. https://www.bera.ac.uk/blog/autism-the-benefits-of-monotropism-and-flow-states-and-its-applications-for-the-classroom
10 Rapaport, H., Clapham, H., Adams, J., Lawson, W., Porayska-Pomsta, K. & Pellicano, E. (2024). "In a State of Flow": A Qualitative Examination of Autistic Adults' Phenomenological Experiences of Task Immersion. *Autism in Adulthood,* 6(3), pp. 362–373. https://doi.org/10.1089/aut.2023.0032
11 Rapaport, H., Clapham, H., Adams, J., Lawson, W., Porayska-Pomsta, K. & Pellicano, E. (2024). "In a State of Flow": A Qualitative Examination of Autistic Adults' Phenomenological Experiences of Task Immersion. *Autism in Adulthood,* 6(3), pp. 362–373. https://doi.org/10.1089/aut.2023.0032
12 "What Makes a Life Worth Living?" a Statement Taken from His TED Talk: Flow, The Secret to Happiness. https://www.ted.com/talks/mihaly_csikszentmihalyi_flow_the_secret_to_happiness
13 Gray, P. (2017). What Exactly Is Play, and Why Is It Such a Powerful Vehicle for Learning? *Topics in Language Disorders,* 37(3), pp. 217–228.
14 Gray, P. (2013). *Free to Learn: Why Unleashing the Instinct to Play Will Make Our Children Happier, More Self Reliant, and Better Students for Life.* New York: Basic Books.
15 Greene, R.W. (2014). *The Explosive Child: A New Approach for Understanding and Parenting Easily Frustrated, Chronically Inflexible Children.* 5th edn. New York: Harper.

Chapter 13

# Where Is the Evidence?

In this concluding chapter of Part Two, before exploring the Accept Approach further in Part Three, it is important to consider what determines a good support model. To do so, we first explore what is meant by "evidence-based" in research. Given the many autism strategies accessible today,[1] it is essential that, as professionals, parents, policymakers, and stakeholders, we know how to identify effective approaches so that we can better support autistic children and young people. To achieve this, we will first consider what constitutes valid and reliable evidence, then look at the differences between quantitative and qualitative research, and the types of data they collect. Finally, as a researcher gathering evidence for this book, I explain why I selected qualitative methods as the most reliable way to demonstrate the impact of the Accept Approach. This chapter was initially inspired by a question I was recently asked, so we'll start there. Here's the question: "*What evidence do you have to support your approach?*"

A mental health professional posed this question to me during a meeting to discuss continuing support for an autistic young person and their family. Up to this point, the child had been responding positively to acceptance-based support, and the parents wanted to continue the provision while also involving the mental health team to see if they could offer additional help. However, the mental health practitioner sought evidence demonstrating that the support method being used was effective. I took this question very seriously because it is the *right* question to ask, and I responded with what I believed was the appropriate reply.

*What evidence are you referring to?*

Data and evidence can be collected primarily through two approaches: quantitative and qualitative.[2] Quantitative research focuses on collecting large amounts of measurable data from randomised controlled trials, standardised assessments and using statistics to test ideas, looking for patterns to make predictions. Qualitative research focuses on non-numeric information to gather evidence through real-life experiences and perspectives. This can be collected through interviews, observations, case studies, and conversations to understand how people think, feel, and interpret their experiences.

DOI: 10.4324/9781003686064-16

In my experience, professionals often favour quantitative data because they presume it provides stronger evidence and larger sample sizes, whereas qualitative data is often treated as *anecdotal*, seen as less reliable because of small sample sizes, subjectivity, and biased evidence. Anecdotal evidence is often frowned upon in research, considered a *substitute* for proper evidence, and described as *fallacious.*[3] For example, Trudy Govier, in her book *A Practical Study of Argument*, writes, "*Anecdotal arguments are based on stories, typically drawn from the personal experience of the person making the argument*".[4]

When asking the question "*What evidence are you referring to?*" I was attempting to address a common misconception: that quantitative and qualitative data are opposites. In fact, both are valid *and* important ways to gather evidence on whether an autism approach is effective. However, quantitative data is still viewed as more scientific and more reliable, which leads to a recurring problem within autism research.

The director of the Autism Centre for Education and Research, Karen Gulberg,[5] highlights this problem, stating, "*The dominance of experimental designs leads to a schism between research and practice in this field*".[6] Guldberg argues that autism research becomes limited when only one type of evidence is given greater weight. Effective autism research, according to Gulberg, needs to be grounded in the real-world experiences of autistic people, their families, and the professionals supporting them. For example, in educational practice, educators cannot rely solely on data and must also consider the complexities of autistic experiences.

When asking "*What evidence supports this approach?*" we need to be able to make a judgement by combining experimental research with lived experiences and professional judgement, so that research and real-life practice can work together to find more meaning in answering the question. This is why I believe we cannot ignore feedback from those who have experienced a support model first-hand.

## Relying on Evidence-Based Support

As professionals, we are often trained to use evidence-based support and to avoid methods without substantial evidence. This means that professionals will use only evidence-based support deemed credible *and* trustworthy. Although I completely agree that this is the right approach, I think a problem lies in how evidence is *perceived.* What is clear is that there are no support models, no matter how much evidence-based support they may have, that work for *all* autistic children and young people;[7] therefore, not all evidence-based support works, and it is not possible to suggest one strategy can work for every autistic child.[8]

While working as an autism advisor in schools for a local authority, I often observed the same set of autism strategies displayed on classroom walls during visits. It was always viewed as good practice, for example, for structured timetables, visual schedules, zones of regulation, social stories, and behaviour prompts, such as good sitting, good listening, and good looking, placed on walls as visible proof of effective autism support. It always seemed that these were treated as non-negotiables and that their presence was evidence that autistic children were being supported the right way, even when they had little relevance to the child I was actually observing on the day.

I recall a situation at a school where an autistic child was constantly running out of class in a distressed state, and despite trying the traditional autism strategies, staff couldn't keep the child in the classroom. I remember the teacher saying, "*Look, I've even stuck an emotional scale on his desk for him to show me how he is feeling, and even that isn't working!*" The teacher here was not questioning whether the emotional scale strategy was effective for the child; instead, they believed that if the child just accessed the strategy, everything would be fine. The assumption was never challenged. The focus was on the child's behaviour, rather than on the effectiveness of the strategy itself or on the possibility that this approach may not suit the child's needs.

In another example, I was asked to support a child who was actually happy to stay in class but could not sit on a chair and found it especially difficult to remain still during circle time. This was seen as problematic behaviour, and the teacher asked for my advice on how to get him to sit. She told me they had tried a wobble cushion and placed a spot on the floor to help him focus, but neither was working. Because these were ineffective, the *child* was viewed as the problem, not the strategies.

This is where traditional autism strategies fail. They are often treated as solid solutions that, if used correctly, will work. Teachers will place too much confidence in a strategy and, when it doesn't work, will look to the child as the source of the problem. When autism strategies are used as the solution, and a child doesn't respond, it is then the child who is repeatedly let down. The real issue is then dismissed, with no one questioning autism strategies because they are often displayed around rooms as solid evidence-based approaches that will work for autistic children. When the truth is more likely, yes, they will work for many, but there will always be one child where they don't work, and that child is not the problem; the belief in the unwavering strategies is. This is why evidence cannot be reduced to one single fixed model that works without questioning it. Another way to explain this is the black swan problem.

## The Black Swan Problem

In the 1600s, Europeans believed that only white swans existed, and this was never questioned and accepted as fact because nobody knew any better or had seen anything different. That was until 1697, when a black swan was discovered in Western Australia, *instantly* disproving the theory that all swans were white.[9]

Karl Popper used this example in his work to highlight a fundamental issue in scientific knowledge.[10] He argued that the claim that "all swans are white" can never be conclusively proven, because it is impossible to observe *every* swan in the world. No matter how many white swans are observed, you cannot conclusively prove that all swans are white, because finding just one black swan is enough to *disprove* the theory. This reveals the concept of falsification. Popper argued that a theory's strength lies not in the amount of supporting evidence but in its testability and potential for falsification. Hence, good science is focused on actively testing ideas to see if they can be refuted, rather than just seeking confirmation. This willingness to be proven wrong is what gives scientific explanations their strength.

I believe the black swan problem shows us that what really matters is not proving that there are only white or black swans, but considering *all* swans. In schools, educators will stand firm in their belief that autism strategies are the only tools to use. Therefore, when an autistic child is not coping with their emotions and is running out of class, they need an emotional scale chart to cope. If a child cannot sit still during lessons, they need a wobble cushion or a red spot to stay seated. There is an unwavering belief that this works, until that is completely disproven by the one child who doesn't use the emotional scale, and still cannot sit still, even when brought the best, most expensive wobble cushion.

### Is the Accept Approach Evidence-Based?

When I first developed the Accept Approach, it was just an idea I had been playing with in my teaching and my advisory roles. I had seen a few children who had a transformative response to acceptance-based support so much that I explored more research in this area, producing journal articles of my findings, and eventually setting up Accepting Behaviour in 2021, and now at the time of writing this, we have a 25-strong team of specialists supporting hundreds of children across the West Midlands. This has given me enough data to produce this book, and to share experiences of children and young people responding to humanistic, acceptance-based support, particularly the Accept Approach.

I decided to use qualitative methods to gather data and share the findings in this book because of the nature of the children and young people I was supporting. Fundamentally, I began with asking one key question, which has been the foundation of my research:

> *How is the Accept Approach experienced in practice, and what impact does it have on autistic children and their learning over time?*

Quantitative methods can show us certain data, such as how many autistic children are out of school,[11] but they cannot tell us *why*. I believe that asking this question focuses well on lived experiences and perceived impact. By also exploring changes over time in real-life contexts, this helps to explore autistic lives and produce evidence from real-life situations.

I am confident my research and findings will help to bridge the recognised gap between research and everyday support. For example, quantitative data can't explain *why* a child stops attending school, but the type of qualitative data I am gathering can, as it enables us to ask deeper questions and explore issues more thoroughly. This approach will help to reveal a complex world that isn't as straightforward as it might seem in large datasets.[12]

## Triangulation

Returning to the question I was asked at the beginning of this chapter. What I was trying to show is that, through the lived experiences and feedback from myself, the parents, and the child, there was more than enough evidence to demonstrate impact and determine the effectiveness of the acceptance-based support being questioned. As the observer, I noted that he attended every session and engaged well throughout. His parents also reported that he felt safe in the sessions and was keen to attend. They said he was happier at home and even asked if he could have more sessions. One particular point they mentioned was how well he responded to knowing "he is the boss of his learning". They said he really took to that message well. Finally, the young person also gave feedback through conversations with his social worker and me. He said he enjoyed the sessions and wanted the support to continue.

In qualitative research, these three real-life experiences are considered important when examined through *triangulation*,[13] which demonstrates that similar conclusions have been reached across different sources. Rather than relying on a single account, triangulation brings together multiple perspectives[14] and reviews how effective the support was, which is *not* dependent on a single perspective or a single source of bias; instead, it is supported by independent viewpoints. This data is considered evidence-based in qualitative research and allows the conclusion that this acceptance-based support in this case *was* effective for this child.

Throughout this book, I have presented evidence of the Accept Approach by including real-life experiences and feedback gathered from observations and anonymous surveys. Consequently, all data-gathering methods are qualitative. The decision to collect evidence through qualitative research was made based on the nature of the children and young people supported.[15] All children and young people discussed are real-life experiences of those who have not been able to access traditional support and have been failed by the mental health and education systems, and through qualitative methods, I can explore autistic children's *subjective* realities, capturing the complexities and meanings behind their actions and decisions, something I do not believe quantitative methods could achieve as effectively.

I also acknowledge that, in recent years, we have seen significant steps toward developing more effective methods for listening to and understanding the perspectives of autistic children and young people.[16] I want to contribute to this progress, as it is an effective way to demonstrate the direct impact of acceptance. I will now share two real-life examples to illustrate why I believe this.

**Real-Life Experience 11**

I was asked to support a young autistic person who had completely shut down at school and could no longer attend. His parents informed me he was "exhausted" by the demands of his mainstream school and had developed an intense anxiety and was now unable to leave his house at all. They also reported that all the extracurricular activities he once enjoyed outside of school ceased.

Within a few weeks of support, however, he began leaving the house with supporting adults, and gradually, his parents said they could see his confidence was returning. His anxiety also reduced significantly, and he began to return to his favourite activities, leaving his home more, no longer confined as he was.

This shift was not driven by pressure for him to face his anxieties or build emotional resilience; instead, the approach was to follow the Four Foundations of Acceptance, which were to *remove* anything that made him anxious, *remind* him it is not his fault he is struggling, *reassure* him that things are going to be OK, and *reaffirm* that we accept him unconditionally.

### Feedback Cádiz

> *Before beginning sessions, he had left mainstream school because he was burnt out. He was dealing with poor mental health, such as severe anxiety, and showed little interest in leaving the house or participating in activities he previously enjoyed. This support has helped him rebuild his confidence; he now comfortably leaves the house with the staff, manages his anxiety more effectively, has re-engaged with old hobbies, and even tried a new activity.*
>
> *The positive changes include his increased self-esteem; e.g. after 15 months of not opening a book or allowing anyone to read to him, he asked if he could read a page from a souvenir booklet bought after visiting a place of interest during one of his sessions.*

When considering the impact of the support here, qualitative data captured the *whole* picture. I do not believe quantitative methods would have been as effective in capturing this. For example, there may have been some effectiveness in logging how many times he left the house or how many activities he re-engaged in each week. However, this method may not fully capture the depth of meaning and the positive reactions to acceptance-based support that qualitative data reveal revealed. This is why qualitative methods are the preferred means of gathering data: they can capture emotions and lived experiences more effectively than statistics can.

**Real-Life Experience 12**

In another example, we were supporting a child who had disengaged from all support, both education and mental health. She was not able to cope with any demands or expectations and was having extreme difficulties at home and in school. Her school asked us to support her because things had gotten so bad that she could no longer attend school and was also unable to leave her house.

When we began supporting her, we had to take things slowly, as she could tolerate only so much and was unable to engage in any learning. Over time, through our consistent acceptance-based approach and the message that "she is in control of her learning", she began to connect positively with one of our specialist teachers.

She started to re-engage at her own pace, and now consistently participates in full sessions, taking part in learning activities, both inside and outside the home, without her parent present, which, as her mother reported, had been a milestone for her. She now consistently communicates her feelings, and whenever things are too much for her, she will tell her teacher. This was something she could *not* do before. She no longer has the daily meltdowns she used to have. She has gained confidence in writing and asking for help, which she could not do before.

### Parent Feedback

> *She had been out of school for nearly a year and was very burnt out. She was restricted about what she was able to do and would sit and watch TV most days, as her capacity was very low. She was untrusting of other adults, unable to leave the house without me present, and unable to visit family members' houses. Any mention of school or learning, and she would melt down. She wouldn't pick up a pen or pencil, wouldn't touch a book. She was very anxious.*
>
> *Over the past year, I've observed a noticeable positive shift. She now actively participates in her sessions and feels secure enough to express her emotions. She chooses her own activities and has become much more verbal. She's started engaging in activities at home and outside without my presence, something I never expected. She can articulate when she has had enough and appears more confident in her abilities.*
>
> *She now asks for help with spelling and other tasks without feeling anxious. She can detach from me to join activities, looks forward to her sessions, and demonstrates a significantly greater capacity. She can say no or share her thoughts without feeling overwhelmed, and overall, she is happier, more confident, and enthusiastic about her activities.*

Again, quantitative methods could not capture *why* she now copes better with acceptance-based support. Removing anxieties and giving her complete control over what she learns and how she learns is not something statistics can truly capture. Yes, they could tell how many sessions she engages in and how many new activities she is trying, but they cannot explain why or how she got there. Whereas qualitative data clearly shows the impact and positive response to our support, even when nothing else worked for her.

## Summary

What I have tried to show in this chapter is that those involved with supporting autistic children and young people can often become too reliant on what is perceived as evidence-based and effective models of support but are often not. When a child is struggling, the norm is to reach for a social story, create some form of structure, or use behaviour modification strategies, assuming that these will work; if they don't, the view is there must be something wrong with the child. Yes, these strategies can work, but not for everyone, and when they don't work, we need to not think it is the child who is the problem. These children are the black swans, the children who come to show us that traditional approaches do not always work, and we have to stop relying on the idea that they do. As professionals, parents, policymakers, and service providers, we need to stop relying on evidence-based models and look to the children in front of us. Ask them what works best. Ask the parents what works best. And then develop models of support that fit *their* needs, not the needs of systems, services, or conditions imposed on them by others.

The children who need something different help us not to ignore what we already have, but to widen our options for support. To consider other ways, such as the Accept Approach, as effective forms of support because what the evidence shows is that these children, the ones who have not responded to anything else, have responded to being accepted, completely as they are, without conditions or expectations for them to be anyone else other than exactly who they are.

Before moving to Part Three, I want to share a message from a specialist teacher who used the Accept Approach with a young adult. Initially, no one was willing to support this person. They were considered uneducable, excluded from their old schools, known to the police, labelled a teenage delinquent, and seen as problematic and defiant. Before receiving support, this young person had attempted suicide and didn't want to live.

After six months of acceptance-based support, she independently sent this message to her supporting teacher:

> *I just wanna tell you thank you for coming into my life, thank you for actually making me smile and laugh, thank you for being so understanding. Thank you for being my biggest supporter. Thank you for caring about me. I really appreciate you so much.*

We previously met this young person in Chapter 4. She was the person who was restrained in the hospital for being denied the right to pace. She no longer attends the hospital. Despite a few difficult days, she smiles more, participates actively in her sessions, and tells us she feels safe with our staff. She also no longer wants to end her life. This young person now feels that her life matters. The Accept Approach helped her get to a better place. Let's now dive deeper into this approach and see how it works.

## Notes

1 National Autistic Society – Strategies and Interventions. https://www.autism.org.uk/advice-and-guidance/topics/strategies-and-interventions

2 Mcleod, S.M (2025). Qualitative vs Quantitative Research: What's the Difference? https://www.simplypsychology.org/qualitative-quantitative.htm
3 Govier, T. (2009). *A Practical Study of Argument*. 7th edn. Belmont, CA: Cengage Learning.
4 Govier, T. (2009). *A Practical Study of Argument*. 7th edn. Belmont, CA: Cengage Learning.
5 Karen Gulberg Profile. https://www.birmingham.ac.uk/staff/profiles/education/guldberg-karen
6 Guldberg, K. (2017). Evidence-Based practice in Autism Educational Research: Can We Bridge the Research and Practice Gap? *Oxford Review of Education*, 43(2), pp. 149–161. https://doi.org/10.1080/03054985.2016.1248818
7 Guldberg, K. (2017). Evidence-Based Practice in Autism Educational Research: Can We Bridge the Research and Practice Gap? *Oxford Review of Education*, 43(2), pp. 149–161.
8 Guldberg, K. (2017). Evidence-Based Practice in Autism Educational Research: Can We Bridge the Research and Practice Gap? *Oxford Review of Education*, 43(2), pp. 149–161.
9 University of Melbourne Information About Black Swans. https://myswan.science.unimelb.edu.au/black-swans/
10 Popper, K.R. (1959). *The Logic of Scientific Discovery*. London: Routledge. Original work published 1934 as *Logik der Forschung*. This is Popper's foundational text where he explains the problem of induction and argues that universal statements such as "all swans are white" cannot be verified by observation but can be falsified by a single counterexample. The black swan example is used to illustrate the logical asymmetry between verification and falsification.
11 Pupil Attendance UK Government Statistics. https://www.gov.uk/government/statistics/pupil-attendance-in-schools
12 Toye, F. (2015). Not Everything That Can Be Counted Counts and Not Everything That Counts Can Be Counted (Attributed to Albert Einstein). *British Journal of Pain*, February, 9(1), p. 7. https://doi.org/10.1177/2049463714565569. PMID: 26516551; PMCID: PMC4616986.
13 Carter, N., Bryant-Lukosius, D., DiCenso, A., Blythe, J. & Neville, A.J. (2014). The Use of Triangulation in Qualitative Research. *Oncology Nursing Forum*, September, 41(5), pp. 545–547. https://doi.org/10.1188/14.ONF.545-547. PMID: 25158659.
14 Decrop, A. (1999). Triangulation in Qualitative Tourism Research. *Tourism Management*, 20(1), pp. 157–161. https://doi.org/10.1016/S0261-5177(98)00102-2
15 Information about Accepting Behaviour Ltd. www.Acceptingbehaviour.com
16 Scott-Barrett, J., Cebula, K. & Florian, L. (2023). The Experiences and Views of Autistic Children Participating in Multimodal View-Seeking Research. *International Journal of Research & Method in Education*, 46(4), pp. 342–373. https://doi.org/10.1080/1743727X.2022.2149728

## Part Three

# To Be Accepted

With acceptance,
you are enough, exactly as you are.
You are not a problem needing to be solved.

DOI: 10.4324/9781003686064-17

Chapter 14

# The Accept Approach™

After 20 years of professional experience, I developed the Accept Approach in 2019,[1] in response to the lack of effective support for autistic children and young people who did not respond to traditional approaches. Although defined as an approach, it is so much more. It is a way of *being*, grounded in the principles of humanistic psychology, that views a person as a whole human with lived experiences and the need to feel accepted and psychologically safe. The Accept Approach can be applied by anyone, regardless of their background or identity. You do not need extensive knowledge of autism or a degree to practice the principles. You do not need to be a specialist teacher, medical professional, or experienced parent. All that is required is to accept a child *exactly* as they are, unconditionally, without any expectation for them to be anything more.

I define the Accept Approach as a framework grounded in the principle that whatever problem or issue a child/young person is experiencing, you accept them exactly as they are, without condition or judgement.

## A New Paradigm Shift in Autism Support

So far, in the book, I have addressed the problems we face and given reasons as to why I think autistic children and young people are being failed. In Part One, I presented evidence of systemic failures in the mental health and education systems, showing that the situation in the UK is worse than ever. In Part Two, I moved the focus from problems and issues to presenting a solution through humanistic perspectives. Now, in Part Three, I am taking this further and introducing a new paradigm shift in autism support grounded in the principles of acceptance.

The Accept Approach is specifically designed to support autistic children and young people within both educational and mental health services. I am presenting it as a *new* development in autism support, positioned as a humanistic, acceptance-based model developed for autistic children and young people who have not responded to traditional autism strategies. Inspired by the principles of humanistic psychology, the Accept Approach follows in the footsteps of Carl Rogers, Abraham Maslow, James Bugental, Rollo May, and other humanistic thinkers, following the

DOI: 10.4324/9781003686064-18

belief that people are *whole* human beings who can grow when they feel safe, are given meaning and purpose, and accepted exactly as they are, without conditions.

### The Five Guiding Principles of the Accept Approach

We begin by first becoming familiar with the *Five Guiding Principles.* These principles provide the foundations and serve as the message you communicate when supporting an autistic child or young person. They are as follows:

1. You are enough exactly as you are.
2. You are not a problem to be solved.
3. You do not lack social communication skills.
4. You do not need to build emotional resilience.
5. You will find your own way, in your own time.

By following these principles, you begin to offer support specifically designed to show the child or young person that you accept them *completely*, without conditions, or any expectation that they need to be better or to do better. The child begins to believe that they are not broken and do not need to be fixed; they are OK just as they are, completely and unconditionally.

### The Lens of Acceptance

When applied, the principles help you see problems/issues differently through the lens of acceptance. Take, for example, an autistic teenager refusing to go to school, or a child who is hitting other children at playtime. Whatever issue you are supporting, through this lens you don't see problems needing to be *dealt* with; instead, you recognise them as signs of a child fighting to *protect* themselves from perceived and real danger.

Through the lens of acceptance, you ask *why* the young person cannot attend school and why the child is hitting other children during playtime. What is it about these situations that makes them feel unsafe? Are these behaviours communicating an unmet need? Through the lens of acceptance, the behaviour is not the focus; the main aim is to show the child or young person that you accept them unconditionally and are there to help them begin to feel psychologically safe. We will now consider each guiding principle in detail.

#### 1. *You Are Enough Exactly as You Are*

This first principle follows the humanistic psychological concept of *unconditional positive regard*: accepting and valuing a person exactly as they are. Telling a child or young person they are enough creates space for them to develop their own self-worth and speaks directly to what James Bugental defines as the "*inherent potential of being human*".[2] Telling a child that they are OK just as they are. Applying unconditional acceptance is a transformative act which has been shown to help relieve depression and lower anxiety.[3]

**Reflection**

Unconditional positive regard is exactly that. *Unconditional.* You are not accepting the child because of what they do, not how well they behave. You are accepting them just as they are in the moment. This principle is one of the most important parts of the Accept Approach methodology and is non-negotiable.

### 2. *You Are Not a Problem to Be Solved*

So many autistic children and young people we support tell us that they often feel as though they are a problem to themselves and to others. This is not unique and is an occurring theme that children and young people report experiencing in education[4] and in mental health[5] systems.

Feeling like you are a problem can lead someone to think they must meet certain standards to be accepted by others, which they find impossible to achieve.[6]

To help an autistic child or young person not feel as though they are a problem, we need to create for them what Carl Rogers called *psychological freedom.* This freedom is established when a teacher, parent, therapist, or other person supporting the child shows the child that, no matter what has happened, they still have worth and are not a problem to be fixed. Rogers defined the process of psychological freedom being:

> *When a teacher parent therapist, or other, facilitating person permits the individual a complete freedom of symbolic expression, creativity is fostered this permissiveness gives the individual complete freedom to think to feel to be whatever is most inward within himself.*[7]

**Reflection**

Psychological freedom *does not mean* you are just letting children do whatever they want. It is so much more than that. You are showing the child that with you, they can be safe and free to be who they are. Free to make mistakes, and to be responsible for them. With you as the adult, a child learns they are free to experience the consequences of both their achievements as well as their mistakes, knowing you will always unconditionally accept them and never judge them.

### 3. *You Do Not Lack Social Communication Skills*

I believe one of the biggest *misconceptions* about autism is the view that autistic children lack the ability to communicate socially. The assumption is that from a very early age, autistic children need to learn a set of skills and must be taught how to *be* social. With the Accept Approach, you view social communication differently, focusing on how a child *chooses* to be social.

The idea here is that when a child begins to feel they can be their true selves, knowing they are unconditionally accepted, they will show their *natural communication skills*, which we will discuss more as a concept in Chapter 19. In short, I believe autistic children already have natural and preferred communication skills, and to see them, we need to step away from the perceived idea that there is a right way to be social. There isn't. Studies have shown that what often occurs with autistic people is that they will hide their natural communication style in order to try and meet the expectations of neurotypical people, which sadly usually leads to stress, anxiety, and burnout.[8]

Take, for example, an autistic child who does not want to be around other children, preferring their own company. This is often viewed as a problem and unhealthy for them. Parents can feel their child is missing out on friendships; teachers fear that being alone may lead to isolation; and professionals see this as a deficit, interpreted as avoidance or as a social impairment in need of correction. In this instance, the child is often encouraged to make friends, join a social group, work with others in class, and spend more time with family members at home. All seen as positive steps until the child begins to withdraw further, developing more anxiety, leaving adults wondering what they did wrong.

With this guiding principle, you see the child's preference not as a problem, but as a valid expression of safety and autonomy. You view their request to be alone as a social skill in itself, accepting that they prefer their own company and that this is totally fine for *them*. However, in certain situations, such as the school playground or in the classroom, this social preference does not fit the norm of what is viewed as being socially skilled, and in that situation the child is not the one with the problem the *expectation* placed on them is.

Damien Milton explained this well through the *double empathy problem*, where autistic and non-autistic people experience and express social cues differently, *not* because autistic people lack any ability.[9] When applying these principles and setting up environments that offer unconditional acceptance, autistic children will often unmask and show a wider range of social skills that would previously have gone unnoticed, buried in their coping strategies.[10]

### 4. *You Do Not Need to Build Emotional Resilience*

Another misconception in autism support is that children need to develop emotional resilience. This guiding principle reminds us that this is so far from the truth; in fact, studies in trauma-informed practice show that removing triggers and validating their experiences enhances long-term well-being,[11] with humanistic psychologists emphasising that a person doesn't have to build emotional resilience; instead, the focus needs to be on creating safe conditions for growth rather than demanding exposure to distress.[12]

**Real-Life Experience 13**

I was asked to advise a school on supporting an autistic child who couldn't sit and eat in the hall during dinnertime. The school had tried various strategies, including allowing her to sit with her friends and use ear defenders. They had also tried to break up her time to reduce demand. Another strategy the teacher mentioned was to encourage her to eat just one piece of food and to then allow her to leave the hall. The next day, they encouraged her to eat two pieces before leaving. The following day, they encouraged her to eat half of her plate before she could go. And so on. The idea was to help build up her emotional resilience to coping in the dinner hall. However, none of these strategies were effective, and her anxiety during dinner kept increasing, leading her to often run out in distress.

The concern from the school staff was that, unless she developed emotional resilience, she would never learn to cope with others and to eat in social situations.

What they failed to see was that she was *already* showing emotional resilience. This young person knew her limits and was developing ways of adapting to them. She knew the dinner hall environment was too much for her, so to protect herself and feel safe, she expressed a need to eat on her own in a quieter place, away from the dinner hall. Through an acceptance lens, this is viewed as healthy self-awareness rather than a weakness. All she needed to feel safe and OK was to eat somewhere else. The issue only continued because adults supporting her viewed her distress as a problem and, in turn, placed an unrealistic expectation on her to eat in the dining hall, because *they* felt it was good for her to eat with others.

**Reflection**

We can easily mistake an autistic child who is trying to protect themselves in order to cope, as lacking emotional resilience. In my experience autistic children and young people are the most resilient people. They have to cope with so many obstacles on a daily basis.

All we need to do is shift the way we view emotional resilience, and look at it for what it is, a way of helping a person cope in life with things that make them uncomfortable. This is a skill autistic child *already* have in abundance.

*5. You Will Find Your Own Way, in Your Own Time*

Finally, the last principle applies the concept of self-actualisation, which holds that a person can be their authentic self, feeling safe doing so, and finding purpose by growing in ways that are meaningful to them. Abraham Maslow said the idea of growth is an internal process guided by individual needs.[13] Research on self-actualisation also shows us that environments which support autonomy and safety can lead to more effective learning and improved psychological well-being.[14]

With this principle, you focus on creating environments where a child can find their own way, in their own time, when they are ready, and respecting a child's right to say "no", aligning with the emphasis on autonomy and personal agency.[15] The word "no" is seen here as a healthy, positive act of self-protection, especially when feeling stressed or anxious. Respecting a child's right to say no fosters the development of stronger internal motivation and emotional well-being.[16]

## An Overview of the Accept Approach

Now that we have discussed the Five Guiding Principles of the Accept Approach, we will examine the approach as a whole. The primary objective of the Accept Approach is not to view a problem or issue as a *deficit*, but rather to focus on ways the child can learn to accept themselves and then naturally move beyond an issue they may be experiencing. The approach comprises of four main components, as illustrated in Figure 14.1.

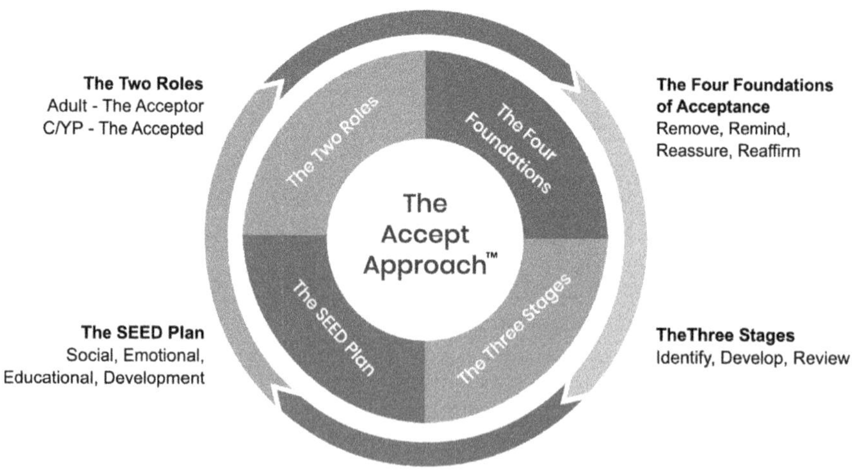


*Figure 14.1* The Four Components of the Accept Approach

### 1. *The Two Roles*

When supporting an autistic child, there are two roles fundamental to the delivery of the approach. The adult providing support is identified as the *acceptor*, and the child receiving support is identified as the *accepted.*

#### *The Acceptor*

The role of the adult, whether a parent, teacher, or supporting professional, is to practically apply unconditional acceptance through following the Five Guiding Principles and implementing the Four Foundations of Acceptance (discussed further here). The four foundations guide the adult to ensure they meet the child with unconditional positive regard, removing all conditions or judgements.

#### *The Accepted*

Then, by receiving unconditional acceptance from the adult, the child begins to grow *within* that support, experiencing unconditional positive regard and gradually learning that they are accepted exactly as they are, without any pressure to change or conform. Gradually, the child begins to develop self-acceptance as they begin to accept their experiences as they gain more control within the psychological safety of the support offered.

The idea behind the two roles is that the interaction between the adult and the child is centred on acceptance, rather than the adult focusing on changing behaviours and the child thinking they are the problem needing to be fixed.

**Reflection**

Within the Accept Approach, the adult's role is to accept the child *unconditionally*, without judging their behaviour or emotional state. The child's role is to *experience* acceptance from the adult, without any conditions or expectations for them to change.

### 2. *The Three Stages*

The next component is the three stages that the *acceptor* and the *accepted* go through. The first stage is for the adult to *identify* the issue or problem the child is experiencing. The second stage is to *develop* support by applying the Four Foundations of Acceptance. The third and final stage involves *problem-solving* anything that needs support, which is an ongoing process in which the adult and the child can re-evaluate and reflect on what help the child needs.

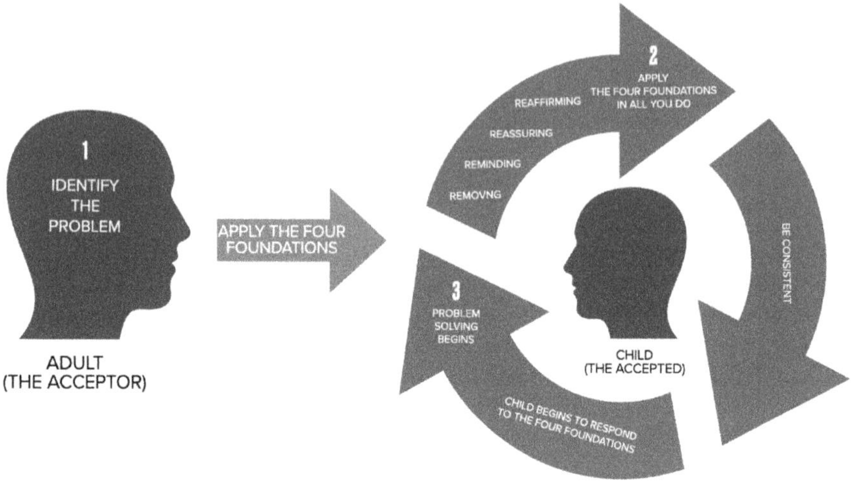


*Figure 14.2* The Three Stages

These stages continue in a cycle during the support process, as the adult and child engage with each other, building a relationship on acceptance, where they can face issues or problems together in a safe way. This is explained in Figure 14.2 here.

## 3. *The Four Foundations of Acceptance*

We now move to the third and most crucial component of the Accept Approach: the Four Foundations of Acceptance. These foundations are the specific steps for applying acceptance in any situation, grounded in the Five Guiding Principles discussed earlier. They are as follows: (1) remove, (2) remind, (3) reassure, and (4) reaffirm.

> ***The foundations of acceptance are discussed in greater detail in the following chapters, as each one serves a specific purpose within the model and requires in-depth explanation.*

### Remove

The *remove* foundation is where the adult removes whatever is causing the child anxiety or stress. The idea of removing is inspired by Maslow's principle of *safety needs.*[17] Maslow argued that when a child feels unsafe, they are unable to deal with other aspects of their life and will do whatever they can to feel safe, often seeking predictable, orderly patterns in order to cope with their feelings.

Maslow said that when someone feels unsafe or lacks control of their life, their safety needs must be met before they can begin to grow, learn, or develop a positive sense of well-being. If safety needs are left unmet, then a child will often stay in survival mode, and everything else deteriorates. The aim of the *remove* foundation is to restore the basic need for safety by helping the autistic child or young person regain control of their lives.

### *Remind*

The next foundation is *remind.* Here you remind the child or young person that *it is not their fault* they are struggling with an issue. This foundation is designed to address the problem of what Carl Rogers called *incongruence.* Rogers proposed that when individuals encounter difficulties with self-acceptance, they experience incongruence, a term that refers to the gap between their self-perception and their true feelings or experiences.

Rogers argued a person cannot thrive unless they are accepted for *exactly* who they are, not as what they think is expected of them. By reminding a child that it is not their fault, you are showing them that it is OK to accept themselves for exactly who they are, not who they think they should be.

The second part of the *remind* foundation is to continue applying *unconditional positive regard.* Many autistic children and young people feel that most of their issues are their fault, because often they are told this is so. For example, a child will struggle to accept themselves, especially when they are always being sent out of class, or constantly being banned from playtimes, or put on behavioural reports. These sanctions and many others convey the message "it *is* their fault", which the child will often internalise and develop a false view of who they really are.

When you remind a child that it is *not* their fault, you communicate that they are not broken, by directly challenging self-blame, as you accept them through the act of unconditional positive regard. This also supports Maslow's idea that people need to feel that they belong. When a child is constantly told to be better, to do better, they don't feel like they belong, and this will cause them to retreat, to refuse, to mask because they are trying to protect themselves in environments where they don't feel safe or that they belong there.

### *Reassure*

The third foundation is *reassure.* Here you reassure the child or young person that whatever is going on, whatever they are experiencing, *it's going to be OK.* This foundation is embedded in the humanistic principle of hope, characterised by Rollo May as a state of ongoing growth: an openness to discovering new possibilities within oneself and the world.[18] May viewed hope not as a mere fingers-crossed attitude, but as a mindset we can learn to adopt by remaining open to the possibility that everything will be fine, *regardless* of the situation.

In addition to hope, Maslow believed that we all have *esteem needs* that need to be met. He argued all people have a need or desire for self-respect, self-esteem, and the esteem of others. When you apply the *reassure* foundation, you are telling a child that things are going to be OK, because *they* are OK.

### *Reaffirm*

The *reaffirm* foundation is the basis of acceptance: the idea that no matter what is happening, you, as the acceptor, will *always* be on their side, accepting them unconditionally. Standing by them, *whatever* is going on. Grounded further in the humanistic principles of *unconditional positive regard* and *psychological freedom*, here you are supporting the child or young person in knowing that you are on their side. That you accept them unconditionally, without limitations or conditions.

The reaffirm foundation shows autistic children and young people, who have often faced rejection and exclusion, that they are not alone in this and that you will stand by them, and face whatever happens *together*.

### *Applying the Foundations in Order*

The Four Foundations of Acceptance work much like a combination to a lock. It is vital that each one is used in order for the approach to work effectively. Much like a combination lock, if the numbers are not in the correct order, the door will not open. If a child is told "It's not your fault" or "It's going to be OK" *without* removing whatever is making them anxious, then they will remain in a state of incongruence and will not feel psychologically safe. It is vital that you remove what is making them anxious/stressed *first*, before applying the other foundations.

Furthermore, reassuring them will not work if the very source of their distress remains, and offering unconditional acceptance will not help the child if they still feel that nobody is listening to them. By first removing what makes them anxious, you create the right environment for them to begin to feel psychologically safe. Only then can you remind them that it's not their fault, reassure them it is going to be OK, and only then will they believe you accept them unconditionally. The Four Foundations of Acceptance guide you in supporting autistic children and young people by viewing them as whole individuals rather than problems to solve.

## ***4. The SEED Plan (Social, Emotional, Educational, Development)***

The final component of the Accept Approach is the SEED Plan. This is a *reflective* document used to record observations in journal/diary form. We will discuss the SEED Plan in more detail in Chapter 20, with real-life examples of how it is applied. For context, here is a brief overview.

The SEED Plan has four focus areas: social, emotional, Educational, and development. It helps the adult to identify the most *crucial* areas of need first. These are the social and emotional aspects, which are always considered *before* the education and development areas. The idea is that if a child is not coping within these first two areas, then they will *not* be able to engage with education. The idea of the Accept Approach is to focus *first* on applying acceptance in the social and emotional areas, and then, once the child begins to engage with this process and feels safe, they will be ready to explore the aims of their education and learning.

The final part of the SEED Plan, the *development focus*, is set up as a section within the document where the child or their family can add their feelings about the support, whether everything is going well or if anything needs to be adapted. The information is then fed back into the SEED Plan and reviewed by all involved.

The most important thing to know about the SEED Plan is that it is an *active* document accessed by anyone supporting the child. This will include, firstly, the adult who sets up the plan and then shares it with the child, their family, teachers, local authority, service providers, mental health professionals, or anyone relevant to supporting the child. Here is an overview of the SEED Plan in Figure 14.3.

## The Accept Approach in Practice

**Real-Life Experience 14**

We will now look at a real-life example of how the Accept Approach is applied. The Pyjama Kid attended school without issues until he suddenly stopped going without any warning. He went from being a quiet, engaged, focused 8-year-old to one having an acute state of anxiety that was so severe he was unable to engage in anything school-related and became housebound.

Stuck at home, he could only eat specific food, wear pyjamas, and play online games. These were the only ways he could feel safe when everything else around him was falling apart. He also found it impossible to leave his mother's side, especially at night, where the only way he could feel safe was to sleep in his parents' room. Most nights, he slept in their bed, while his parents slept on the floor.

### *Mental Health Advice*

His parents were in desperate need of support, so they reached out to the school and the mental health team for help. This was the advice received from the mental health team:

1. The mental health team advised parents to be consistent about his school attendance. No matter how he responded, the advice was that they *must* get him into school.

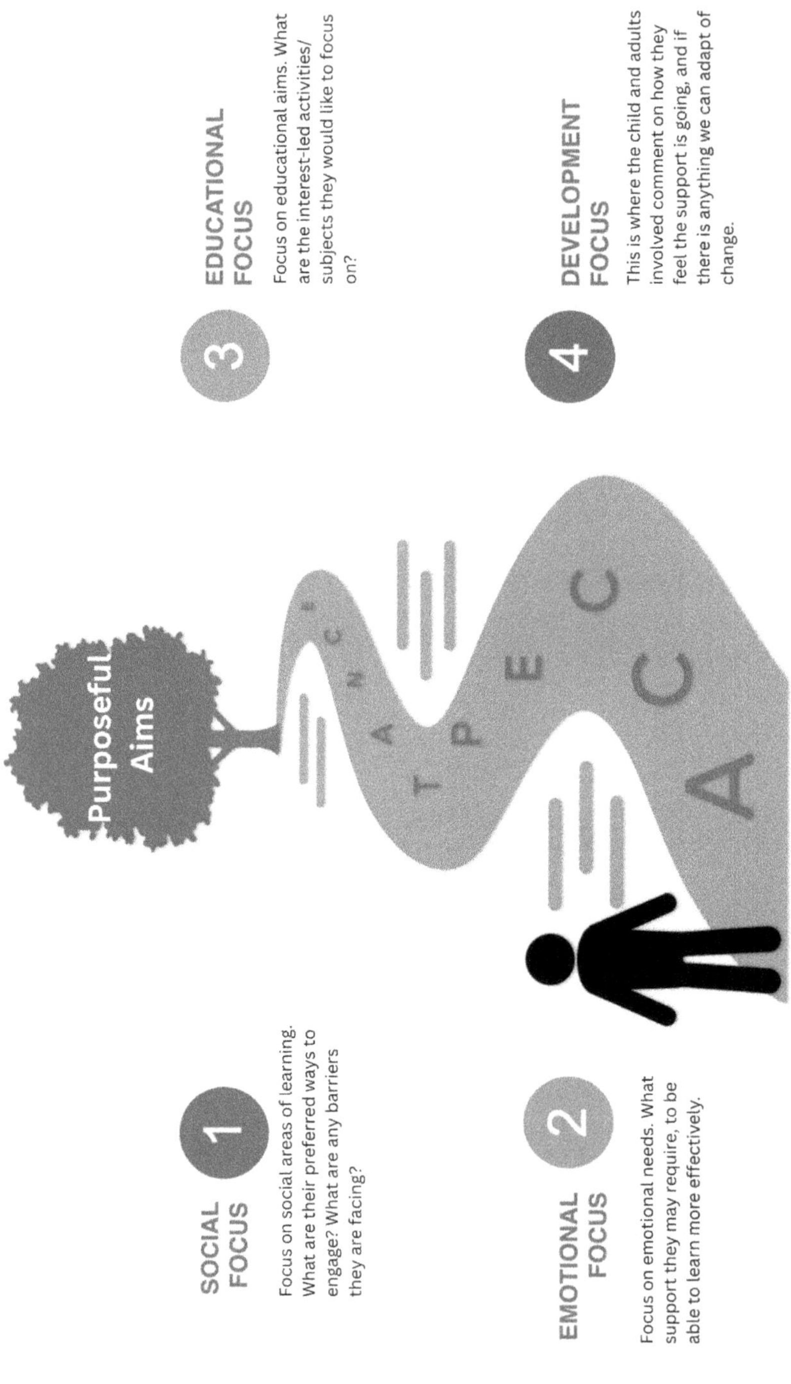


*Figure 14.3* The SEED Plan

2. On the days he really couldn't go, parents were advised to get him up and dressed in his uniform and to sit in the living room without any TV, or entertainment. And under no circumstances was he allowed to sit around in his pyjamas. The idea behind this advice was that if he felt uncomfortable at home during the day, he would then want to return to school.

### *Advice from the School*

The school also instructed parents to get him to school. What made it difficult for the staff was that they saw a completely *different* child from the one that his parents experienced at home. They said he was fine once inside the building and saw his problems as a transition issue from home to school, not an issue with being in school.

Despite the advice and support, the situation worsened, and he withdrew even further, no longer able to leave his house or walk to school. In a desperate last attempt, the parents would book a taxi to take him, even though they lived only half a mile from the school. But this, too, just made things worse. His father told me he had to physically carry him into the taxi, while his son cried out, "*Dad, why are you doing this to me?*" Upon arriving at school, a staff member would then have to pry him away from his dad and then also carry him into school. His dad said they had to stop this because he couldn't cope with the distress it caused him and his son.

### *Applying the Accept Approach*

After an initial meeting with the school, it was agreed that I could work with the boy in his home for a few weeks and that they would remove the pressure on him to attend, giving me time to see if I could help.

During my first session, I only managed to meet with his parents because the boy was hiding upstairs, fearing, his mother told me, that I was going to make him go to school. My aim here was to apply the first foundation of acceptance and *remove* whatever was making him anxious. In this moment, there were two things making him anxious: (1) the fear that he would be made to go to school and (2) the pressure to speak to me.

#### Remove

I needed to remove the anxiety *first*. So, to begin applying this foundation, just before I left, I called upstairs and told him that he "never has to go back to school if he doesn't want to" and that he "does not have to speak to me at all". I also told him that I was not part of the school and that if he wanted to have a session with me next time, we would do whatever he wanted. I said we could maybe play a game or just talk. I also informed him that during the sessions, "*He would be the boss, not me*".

When I returned a few days later, his mother opened the door smiling. She informed me that her son said he would like to speak to me and was sitting downstairs in his pyjamas. During this session, we talked about all the things he liked, his favourite games, his favourite food, and what he loved to do the most, which was to spend *all day* in his pyjamas. This moment was transformative for me because it demonstrated that he believed I had removed the anxiety that was causing him the issues in the first place: the pressure to go to school. As a result, he felt *safe* enough to step out of his room and come downstairs to meet me.

### *Remind*

The second foundation was to remind him that what he was going through was *not his fault*. During my sessions with him, I would mention that what he was struggling with was not his fault. We would talk about autism and how his brain works differently from other people, and that is not his fault. In addition, his parents repeated this message whenever he was sad, upset, or anxious. He seemed to respond well to this, and his mother reported that he was eating more and was less anxious now that he knew he didn't have to go to school and that he wasn't to blame.

### *Reassure*

The third foundation was to show him that *it is going to be OK*. To achieve this, I used affirmations during conversations and reassured him whenever I could see he was feeling anxious about school or about being made to go back. I would repeat that it's going to be OK and that he *never* had to go back to school if he couldn't. I repeated this message as many times as he needed to hear it. Applying acceptance here is all about using reassurance to help a child rebuild their confidence by making them feel safe and accepted. The message to give here is that it's going to be OK, whatever happens.

### *Reaffirm*

This foundation was about ensuring he knew I was on his side and accepting him *unconditionally*. To achieve this, I told him he could wear his pyjamas all day and play his games as much as he needed to. I acknowledged that I understood playing his games was his way of de-stressing, and wearing his pyjamas made him feel comfortable and calm. I also made it clear that my role was to follow what he wanted to do, and in every session, I ensured that everything was centred on what he wanted to engage with. Applying acceptance here is showing the child you are standing by them in a non-judgemental way. You are not there to tell them what to do or what to improve.

I also found that he responded really well to being given the message "*He is the boss of his learning*". His mother told me this is what really helped him engage and significantly reduced his anxieties.

**Reflection**

This young person responded so well to knowing he was the boss of his learning, that I continued to apply this thinking to other children and young people, leading to the development of to the Two Rules of Learning, which are discussed further in Part Three.

### *His Response to the Support*

After only a few sessions, he expressed a desire to *return* to school. He still could not go into lessons, but the school said he could go to their dinner club, so he could see some of his friends. His mother explained that this was only possible because he held onto the idea that it wasn't his fault and that he didn't have to go back to school if he didn't want to.

His mother mentioned that he kept saying, "*I am the boss, aren't I, mummy?*" which seemed to significantly affect his mindset in a positive way. His mother also noted that his anxiety at home had almost completely disappeared, and she attributed this improvement to the freedom he had to wear his pyjamas and play his games whenever he *needed* to.

I stopped supporting after a few months, as he was now in the process of finding a different specialist setting more suitable for him. After around six months, his mother contacted me and told me that he was now attending full-time in his new school and happily attends without any anxiety issues. She said he goes almost every day, which is something they never thought would happen. She also told me that on the days he is anxious about doing something, we tell him he doesn't have to do it, and it's OK. She said that knowing *he is the boss* has changed everything for him.

### *The Reason He Stopped Going to School*

The most interesting aspect of this case was that, until our support began, none of the professionals had been able to determine *why* he stopped attending school. It baffled everyone how he went from a shy, withdrawn child to an outwardly anxious, demand-avoidant one.

I found out why during one of our conversations in his living room. Sitting in his pyjamas, one day, he began to tell me that he had stopped going because there had been a lesson about demolition. And suddenly, out of nowhere, he had this intrusive thought: "*What if the school building collapses when I am inside, and we all die?*"

This thought did not leave him, and every morning he *believed* it would really happen if he went to school. All those times, he was crying and begging not to go to school, inside, he actually believed that the building was going to collapse on him. I can only imagine how that must have felt for him, especially when he kept being told that school was the best place and he just needed to try harder to attend. Without acceptance, he would not have felt safe enough to tell me how he really felt. Acceptance not only helped him find his way back to education in his own time but also gave him his voice back and enabled him to regain control of his life.

## Summary

In this chapter, I have introduced you to the Accept Approach and explained how each part works together to support autistic children in ways that apply the principles of humanistic thinking, specifically unconditional acceptance and psychological safety. We have explored the Five Guiding Principles and discussed the Four Foundations of Acceptance. In the following chapters, we delve deeper into the four foundations to better understand each and how they can be applied.

We will begin in the next chapter with the *remove* foundation.

## Notes

1 Yorke, A. (2021). A Case Study of Two Autistic Children Supported by the Accept Approach: A New Acceptance-Based Strategy. *Good Autism Practice*, 22(2).
2 Bugental, J.F.T. (1964). The Third Force in Psychology. *Journal of Humanistic Psychology*, 4, pp. 19–25.
3 Yadavaia, J.E., Hayes, S.C. & Vilardaga, R. (2014). Using Acceptance and Commitment Therapy to Increase Self-Compassion: A Randomized Controlled Trial. Journal of Contextual Behavioral Science, October 1, 3(4), pp. 248–257. https://doi.org/10.1016/j.jcbs.2014.09.002. PMID: 25506545; PMCID: PMC4260406.
4 Goodall, C. (2018). I Felt Closed in and Like I Could Not Breathe: A Qualitative Study Exploring the Mainstream Educational Experiences of Autistic Young People. *Autism and Developmental Language Impairments*, 3, pp. 1–16. https://doi.org/10.1177/2396941518804407
5 Riebel, M., Bureau, R., Rohmer, O., Clément, C. & Weiner, L. (2025). Self-Compassion as an Antidote to Self-Stigma and Shame in Autistic Adults. *Autism*, June, 29(6), pp. 1569–1584. https://doi.org/10.1177/13623613251316965. Epub 2025 February 17. PMID: 39959965.
6 Rogers, C. (1961). *On Becoming a Person*. Boston: Houghton Mifflin.
7 Direct quote form Rogers, in his book *On becoming a person* (page 384).
8 Hull, L. et al. (2017). "Putting on My Best Normal": Social Camouflaging in Adults with Autism Spectrum Conditions. *Journal of Autism and Developmental Disorders*, 47(8), pp. 2519–2534.
9 Milton, D. (2012). On the Ontological Status of Autism: The "Double Empathy Problem". *Disability & Society*, 27(6), pp. 883–887.
10 Cook, J., Hull, L., Crane, L. & Mandy, W. (2021). Camouflaging in Autism: A Systematic Review. *Autism*, 25(8), pp. 2243–2257.
11 Porges, S.W. (2011). *The Polyvagal Theory: Neurophysiological Foundations of Emotions, Attachment, Communication, and Self-Regulation*. Norton.
12 Rogers, C. (1961). *On Becoming a Person*. Boston: Houghton Mifflin.
13 Maslow, A.H. (1970). *Motivation and Personality*. 2nd edn. Harper & Row.
14 Ryan, R.M. & Deci, E.L. (2017). *Self-Determination Theory: Basic Psychological Needs in Motivation, Development, and Wellness*. Guilford Press.

15 Ryan, R.M. & Deci, E.L. (2017). *Self-Determination Theory: Basic Psychological Needs in Motivation, Development, and Wellness*. Guilford Press.
16 Deci, E.L. & Ryan, R.M. (2000). The "What" and "Why" of Goal Pursuits: Human Needs and the Self-Determination of Behavior. *Psychological Inquiry*, 11(4), pp. 227–268.
17 Maslow, A.H. (1970). *Motivation and Personality*. 2nd edn. Harper & Row.
18 May, R. (1953). *Man's Search for Himself*. New York: W. W. Norton.

# Chapter 15

# Remove

*Remove whatever is making the child anxious.*

Anxiety is fast becoming one of the defining mental illnesses of young people,[1] with autistic individuals twice as likely to develop anxiety disorders as their neurotypical peers.[2] Although we often relate anxiety to fear, they are not the same. Fear is much like a *warning* alarm, defined as an emotional response to a real or perceived imminent threat.[3] A sudden noise, a dog barking, or a person screaming all trigger fear responses. Anxiety, however, is more the *anticipation* of a future worry, such as a child who can't get ready for school, because they are anticipating how bad it will be when they get there, or after watching a horror movie, the rest of your night is spent worrying about whether the zombie, flesh-eating killer humans could actually one day become real.

## The First Step

Before anything else can happen, you have to start with Remove. This foundation comes first. If a child is anxious, distressed, or overwhelmed, nothing you say will help if the reason they are feeling anxious is still there. You cannot reassure a child that it is going to be OK if the thing hurting them has not been taken away. You cannot remind them it is not their fault while they are still in the situation causing the stress. Therefore, the first step to applying the Accept Approach is to identify what is causing the anxiety and remove it. In this chapter, we will look at why this is the most important foundation, and why it must be applied first. To do this we first need to explore what anxiety is.

## Between Fear and Anxiety

Of all the human emotions, fear is the most researched,[4] and during recent years, there has been a rapid increase in the examination of what actually drives fear in the brain.[5] We know that anxiety is more of a worry feeling we can get thinking of a possible future or uncertain threat,[6] but fear is the body preparing itself to fight, flight or freeze

DOI: 10.4324/9781003686064-19

*instantly*. We also know that within the brain, the amygdala plays a key role in fear, sparking rapid survival responses. Whereas anxiety is triggered within the prefrontal cortex and hippocampus, where the brain engages in longer and more anticipatory states.[7] There are also differences in hormonal responses. Fear triggers a rapid release of adrenaline, which activates the sympathetic nervous system; however, anxiety is a slower process, releasing cortisol, helping to reduce stress within the body.[8]

There are six major anxiety disorders specified in the DSM-IV. Generalised anxiety disorder (GAD), panic disorder (PD), social anxiety disorder (SAD), posttraumatic stress disorder (PTSD), specific phobias, and obsessive-compulsive disorder (OCD). When considering fear, there are no specific disorders, apart from several conditions described as fear-based because of acute fear responses rather than anticipatory anxiety, as their main factor. This is where the line is blurred because some of the fear-based disorders would also be specific phobias, panic disorder, and post-traumatic stress disorder.[9]

## Is It Fear or Anxiety, or Both?

What do the differences between fear and anxiety mean for autistic children? What are they *actually* experiencing when in a state of stress/anxiety, and how do we know if it's fear or anxiety, or both? Take, for example, a teenager who has managed to get up early, has had some breakfast, but then suddenly disappears back to their room, to be found curled up on the floor, unable to move, frozen by thoughts of not being able to go to school. Is this a result of anxiety or fear of school? Or a mix of both?

The case study of Pyjama Kid in the previous Chapter is a clear example of a child who could no longer attend school because he *feared* an imminent threat yet also *anticipated* a future worry. He believed the school was going to collapse in on him. Although this would be considered an anxious thought, it was a real threat to him, so he was experiencing both anxiety *and* fear at the same time. The professionals recognised that he was avoiding school and concluded this was an anxiety issue, brought on by perceived worry. They believed his anxieties would go away if he just kept going to school. The idea was that he would build emotional resilience, and his anxiety would eventually go away, the more he faced it. When in fact for him, the more he tried to "face it", the worse things got.

The problem with this approach and why it didn't help him was that it did not address his fear response. Imagine for one moment that the building you are in right now starts to collapse. Would you sit there and wait for it to happen, or would you run out as fast as you could? Imagine, then, if you were told just before walking into the building that it might collapse today due to structural issues, but no one could be sure, would you still go in? That feeling of avoiding the building and running for your life is what Pyjama Kid and many autistic children feel in times of anxiety, where they don't feel safe. It is real for them, and it is often more than just anxiety; it is also genuine fear.

## The Lions Have Escaped!

Picture yourself visiting the local zoo with your family. All of a sudden, you hear a voice echoing through the Tannoy: "*Everybody, run for your life! The lions have escaped!*" You all scatter. Some run for the exits (flight), a few brave souls grab whatever they can to defend themselves (fight), while others find somewhere they can hide (freeze). These are all fear responses, used to keep us safe from being mauled to death by the lions. Now imagine, with everyone safely outside, the zoo-keeper says, "*The lions are still loose, but we think it would be best if you go back inside to overcome your anxious feelings and face your fear of the lions*". Would you do it? Of course not. The danger is still very real. The lions are still loose.

Yet this is exactly what is happening to many autistic children and young people when they feel they have to face a demand that is too much for them, whether it's going to school or being asked to attend a family party; whatever the expectation is, it can be too much for them in the moment. For these children, they are not just anxious; they are in a state of fear. Getting them to face something, or to expose them to what is making them anxious, even gradually, is the same as putting someone back in a zoo with the lions still on the loose. These children have a nervous system on high alert because they perceive the demand as a life-threatening danger. So, what is the best way to help? By *removing* what is causing the fear, anxiety, and stress. Whatever it is, see it as a perceived life-threatening danger, and remove it. Much like the feeling you would get knowing you have escaped the lions, and there is no expectation for you to return to the zoo. You feel safe again, protected, knowing you *never* have to go back.

## Have We Got It All Wrong?

Despite all the advances in understanding how the brain responds to fear and anxiety, many researchers suggest this knowledge has still not led us to any significant advances in how we can better support fear and anxiety disorders.[10] For example, some studies found that children with anxiety respond well during treatment, but do not stay well over time;[11] with other studies highlighting that we cannot see the real-world impact of anxiety support, because many reviews overlook key details, such as how many people fully recover, or how many symptoms return after treatment.[12]

Whatever autistic children and young people experience when in an anxious state, we cannot simply presume that things will improve with a few trips to the school gate, attending a six-week social skills group, or parents trying to offer incentives to attend a family party, or to come downstairs to see their grandma. So much more is going on, and we need to think differently about how to support them.

The conventional view of anxiety is that people will avoid situations or develop persistent worry in order to keep themselves *safe*. Therefore, many professionals expose people to things that make them anxious because they are concerned that avoiding them will leave them unable to recognise when their predictions are wrong.[13] The classic learning theory suggests that first, a person learns to fear something, such as a crowded place. Then they learn that if they stay away, they won't feel fearful or anxious, thereby rewarding the initial avoidant behaviour. This avoidance is seen as the primary cause of the anxiety because it strengthens both the avoidance and the belief that being in a crowd is dangerous, which keeps the anxiety cycle in motion.[14]

When considering the effectiveness of traditional approaches to supporting autistic children with anxiety, we find that they are rarely effective. If they were, we would not see poorer outcomes for autistic children with OCD,[15] mixed responses to CBT,[16] weak evidence of early behavioural intervention,[17] and also little to support the provision of intensive intervention.[18]

## A Different Kind of Anxiety

Another thing to consider here is whether autistic children experience a *different* kind of anxiety. We already know that autistic children are twice as likely to experience anxiety as neurotypical children,[19] and there is also a lack of understanding of early presentations of anxiety in young autistic children.[20] In one study, they found that 64% of preschool children diagnosed as autistic already met the criteria for at least one anxiety disorder, and a third met the criteria for more than one phobia. The research asked how connected autistic children are to the state of anxiety and also questioned whether early anxieties were being missed by standard assessments.[21] Could it be, therefore, that autism and anxiety are more connected than we realise?

I believe that anxiety is experienced differently by autistic children because often, when they are encouraged to face an anxiety or to do something that they don't want to, things tend not to improve, but to get worse. This is why, with the first foundation of acceptance, you *remove* what is causing the anxiety, fear, or stress. You remove *anything* that is negatively triggering a child or young person's nervous system. By doing so, anxiety is immediately reduced, pressure is lifted, and the child's nervous system can begin to find balance as they start to feel *safe* again. It is then in those moments of calm that a child can see more clearly and develop their own confidence in saying no to things they *can't* do.

For example, the child who cannot leave their room or get dressed for school is not simply anxious about what *might* happen; they are, in fact, living in fear of what they *know* will happen. They are in protective mode, and when parents attempt to encourage them to get dressed, the child experiences raised heart rate, tense muscles and their amygdala begins to experience real fear responses,[22] which can often be mistaken for refusal, arguments (fight), running away from the school gate (flight), or being unable to leave the car when arriving at school (freeze).

Autistic children who are in a state of anxiety/fear are not just picturing a distant possibility. Their body believes the threat is happening *now*. They exist between fear, a response to a *clear* threat, and anxiety, a response to an *unclear* threat. This is why removing anxiety plays such an important role, as it instantly alleviates their fear and enables them to find balance and a place of psychological safety, and then, in time, they will be able to accept how they are feeling instead of suppressing it. Removing anxiety does not make things worse. It is the start of acceptance, which makes things better.

## Doing What We Don't Want to Do

This leads me to a common misconception that removing whatever makes a child anxious does not build resilience to handle things they don't want to do. I often hear this when someone says, "*We all have to do things we don't want to do in life*". This is where the lines can blur between *choosing* to be anxious or being trapped by it.

Take, for example, a young person on the school's running team. A marathon is coming up, so he is in training. Every morning before school, he gets anxious because he doesn't want to get out of bed and hates putting on his running gear. Outside, it is cold, and he would much rather stay in the warmth of his bed. However, he *makes* himself do what he doesn't want to do because the end result is worth more than his present feelings of anxiety. He *wants* to run the marathon, so he will make himself get up, get dressed, and go for his run before school.

Now consider an autistic child who is also struggling with leaving the house in the morning because he doesn't want to go to school. But for different reasons, his anxiety is trying to *protect* him. Hiding under his bed covers, he is worried his parents will try to make him go, but he knows he just can't do it. This child's anxiety is not chosen and will not help him win a race. His nervous system is trying to protect him by staying away from what is causing the anxiety: the school. The other child's anxiety is also trying to protect them from going out in the cold, but that type of anxiety will go away, because the desire to run *overrides* it. The autistic child's anxiety, however, will not go away, no matter how many times they try to go to school; it will only go away if you *remove* what is causing the anxiety, the demand to go to school.

When the desire to accomplish something is stronger than the reluctance to do it, we are willing to face anxiety to reach our goal. Nonetheless, distinguishing between choosing and complying is crucial. Choosing often leads to the anxiety diminishing over time, while complying usually results in no positive outcome, only more trauma and anxiety. Next time you work with an anxious child, consider whether they are moving toward what they want or trying to avoid something they feel unable to handle.

## After the Anxiety Is Removed

The conventional "face your fear" strategies also don't work with many autistic children because what is actually happening is they are often trapped between the cycle of anticipation that something might happen, and also the fear of events *triggering* the fear response. If an autistic child is anxious or stressed about something, *remove the thing that is causing the anxiety*, rather than trying to get them to "face it". By doing this, you are accepting the anxiety instead of applying fight or flight strategies. Removing the very thing that makes a child anxious is a powerful way to help them move past their anxiety much more effectively than trying to face it.

**Real-Life Experience 15**

A mother who was attending a parent group sought advice because her 16-year-old autistic daughter suddenly started refusing to attend college, claiming she felt too anxious to go. The college recommended that she continue attending and advised the mother to insist that she do so. However, this approach only worsened the situation. The mother explained, "*I'm telling her she has to go to college, but it just upsets her more, and now she is withdrawing from me and refusing to leave her room*".

She showed me messages from her daughter on her phone that said, "*Why are you doing this to me? I hate that you are trying to make me go*".

My advice was to tell her daughter she doesn't have to go to college and to *remove* the expectation that she should attend. I could see that the very thing causing the anxiety was the expectation to go to college, which was the obstacle we needed to remove *before* we could help understand what was really causing the anxiety. I advised her to go home and tell her daughter she didn't have to go to college and to take a break for a few weeks.

I didn't see the mother for a few weeks until the next parent group. She came straight over to me, saying, "*Look at these messages, it's amazing!*" She showed me this time different texts from her daughter saying, "*Mum, I love you*" *and* "*Mum, you're amazing*". I asked what had made the change in her attitude. She said that after our chat, she told her daughter she didn't have to go to college if she didn't want to. The mother also called the college and said her daughter would be taking a break for a few weeks. During the break, she immediately noticed her daughter returning to her old self, and her anxiety about college started to fade. She then said, "*After only a few weeks, I could see a massive difference in her, but what is most amazing is that she has now gone back to college!*".

Her mom told me that when her daughter was given the autonomy to make her own decisions, everything changed. If she was feeling too anxious one day, she wouldn't go in, but the rest of the week she would be totally fine. Her mom said that was why she now feels she can go back to college: she knows she doesn't have to if she doesn't want to.

## Summary

The *remove* foundation is the most important part of the Accept Approach. Nothing else will work as effectively if this is not done *first*. By removing the anxiety, you are telling the autistic young person that it is OK, and if something is too much for them, then they *don't have to do it*. Creating psychological safety so someone can calm their nervous system will help them gain clarity about what they can do to move forward. This is exactly what humanistic psychologist Rollo May meant when he said that thinking constructively about anxiety propels a person toward growth, which occurs only in spaces where freedom and support exist.[23] By viewing anxiety in this way, you are listening to it, validating the feeling, naming it and adjusting to the demand, and as the psychologist Kirk Schneider said, "*being with anxiety*" allows it to become "*the guide rather than a tyrant*".[24]

I really do feel that sometimes an autistic person just needs to know that they don't have to do something if they don't want to. When a child's nervous system is calmer and threats have been removed, we can begin offering support by exploring the other foundations of the Accept Approach. In the next chapter, we add to this thinking by exploring the *remind* foundation.

## Notes

1 Haidt, J. (2024). *The Anxious Generation: How the Great Rewiring of Childhood Is Causing an Epidemic of Mental Illness*. London: Allen Lane.

2 Vasa, R.A., Keefer, A., McDonald, R.G., Hunsche, M.C. & Kerns, C.M. (2020). A Scoping Review of Anxiety in Young Children with Autism Spectrum Disorder. *Autism Research*, 13(12), pp. 2038–2057. https://doi.org/10.1002/aur.2395 [PubMed: 32978905].

3 Vasa, R.A., Keefer, A., McDonald, R.G., Hunsche, M.C. & Kerns, C.M. (2020). A Scoping Review of Anxiety in Young Children with Autism Spectrum Disorder. *Autism Research*, 13(12), pp. 2038–2057. https://doi.org/10.1002/aur.2395 [PubMed: 32978905].

4 LeDoux, J.E. (2014). Coming to Terms with Fear. *Proceedings of the National Academy of Sciences of the United States of America*, February 25, 111(8), pp. 2871–2878. https://doi.org/10.1073/pnas.1400335111. Epub 2014 February 5. PMID: 24501122; PMCID: PMC3939902.

5 LeDoux, J. (1998). Fear and the Brain: Where Have We Been, and Where Are We Going? *Biological Psychiatry*, December 15, 44(12), pp. 1229–1238. https://doi.org/10.1016/s0006-3223(98)00282-0. PMID: 9861466.

6 Grupe, D. & Nitschke, J. (2013). Uncertainty and Anticipation in Anxiety: An Integrated Neurobiological and Psychological Perspective. *Nature Reviews Neuroscience*, 14(7), pp. 488–501.

7 LeDoux, J. & Pine, D. (2016). Using Neuroscience to Help Understand Fear and Anxiety: A Two-System Framework. *American Journal of Psychiatry*, 173(11), pp. 1083–1093.

8 Grupe, D. & Nitschke, J. (2013). Uncertainty and Anticipation in Anxiety: An Integrated Neurobiological and Psychological Perspective. *Nature Reviews Neuroscience*, 14(7), pp. 488–501.

9 Substance Abuse and Mental Health Services Administration. (2016). *Impact of the DSM-IV to DSM-5 Changes on the National Survey on Drug Use and Health* [Internet]. Rockville, MD: Substance Abuse and Mental Health Services Administration (US), June. Table 3.30, DSM-IV to DSM-5 Acute Stress Disorder Comparison. https://www.ncbi.nlm.nih.gov/books/NBK519704/table/ch3.t30/

10 LeDoux, J. & Pine, D. (2016). Using Neuroscience to Help Understand Fear and Anxiety: A Two-System Framework. *American Journal of Psychiatry*, 173(11), pp. 1083–1093.

11 Ginsburg, G.S., Kendall, P.C., Sakolsky, D., Compton, S.N., Piacentini, J., Albano, A.M., Walkup, J.T., Sherrill, J., Coffey, K.A., Rynn, M.A., Keeton, C.P., McCracken, J.T., Bergman, L., Iyengar, S., Birmaher, B. & March, J. (2011). Remission after Acute Treatment in Children and Adolescents with Anxiety Disorders: Findings from the

CAMS. Journal of Consulting and Clinical Psychology, December, 79(6), pp. 806–813. https://doi.org/10.1037/a0025933. PMID: 22122292; PMCID: PMC3371083.

12 Johnco, C.J., Dickson, S.J. & Seaton, A. (2025). A Systematic Review and Meta-analysis of Diagnostic Remission, Treatment Response, Attrition and Relapse Following Cognitive Behavior Therapy (CBT), Other Psychological Therapies and Pharmacological Treatments for Anxiety Disorders in Older Adults. *The American Journal of Geriatric Psychiatry*, June 10, p. S1064-7481(25)00356-2. https://doi.org/10.1016/j.jagp.2025.05.010. Epub ahead of print. PMID: 40581526.

13 Borkovec, T.D., Hazlett-Stevens, H. & Diaz, M.L. (1999). The Role of Positive Beliefs About Worry in Generalized Anxiety Disorder and Its Treatment. *Clinical Psychology & Psychotherapy*, 6, pp. 126–138.

14 Grupe, D.W. & Nitschke, J.B. (2013). Uncertainty and Anticipation in Anxiety: An Integrated Neurobiological and Psychological Perspective. *Natture Reviews Neuroscience*, July, 14(7), pp. 488–501. https://doi.org/10.1038/nrn3524. PMID: 23783199; PMCID: PMC4276319.

15 Jassi, A.D., Vidal-Ribas, P., Krebs, G., Mataix-Cols, D. & Monzani, B. (2023). Examining Clinical Correlates, Treatment Outcomes and Mediators in Young People with Comorbid Obsessive-Compulsive Disorder and Autism Spectrum Disorder. *European Child & Adolescent Psychiatry*, July, 32(7), pp. 1201–1210. https://doi.org/10.1007/s00787-021-01921-4. Epub 2021 December 16. PMID: 34914003; PMCID: PMC10276061.

16 Sharma, S., Hucker, A., Matthews, T., Grohmann, D. & Laws, K.R. (2021). Cognitive Behavioural Therapy for Anxiety in Children and Young People on the Autism Spectrum: A Systematic Review and Meta-Analysis. *BMC Psychology*, October 1, 9(1), p. 151. https://doi.org/10.1186/s40359-021-00658-8. PMID: 34598734; PMCID: PMC8487131.

17 Cochrane Collaboration (2018). Early Intensive Behavioral Intervention for Young Children with Autism Spectrum Disorders. *Cochrane Database of Systematic Reviews*, CD009260. https://doi.org/10.1002/14651858.CD009260.pub3.

18 Sandbank, M., Pustejovsky, J.E., Bottema-Beutel, K., et al. (2024). Determining Associations Between Intervention Amount and Outcomes for Young Autistic Children: A Meta-Analysis. *JAMA Pediatrics*, 178(8), pp. 763–773. https://doi.org/10.1001/jamapediatrics.2024.1832

19 Klein, J., Kerns, C., Hills, K., Hogan, A., Matherly, S. & Roberts, J. (2025). Brief Report: Prevalence and Predictors of DSM-Specific and Distinct Anxiety in Cognitively Impaired Autistic Preschool Children. *Journal of Autism and Devlopmental Disorders*, May, 55(5), pp. 1923–1931. https://doi.org/10.1007/s10803-023-05978-9. Epub 2023 April 11. PMID: 37039980; PMCID: PMC11441628.

20 Klein, J., Kerns, C., Hills, K., Hogan, A., Matherly, S. & Roberts, J. (2025). Brief Report: Prevalence and Predictors of DSM-Specific and Distinct Anxiety in Cognitively Impaired Autistic Preschool Children. *Journal of Autism and Devlopmental Disorders*, May, 55(5), pp. 1923–1931. https://doi.org/10.1007/s10803-023-05978-9. Epub 2023 April 11. PMID: 37039980; PMCID: PMC11441628.

21 Klein, J., Kerns, C., Hills, K., Hogan, A., Matherly, S. & Roberts, J. (2025). Brief Report: Prevalence and Predictors of DSM-Specific and Distinct Anxiety in Cognitively Impaired Autistic Preschool Children. *Journal of Autism and Devlopmental Disorders*, May, 55(5), pp. 1923–1931. https://doi.org/10.1007/s10803-023-05978-9. Epub 2023 April 11. PMID: 37039980; PMCID: PMC11441628.

22 LeDoux, J. & Pine, D. (2016). Using Neuroscience to Help Understand Fear and Anxiety: A Two-System Framework. *American Journal of Psychiatry*, 173(11), pp. 1083–1093.

23 May, R. (1977). *The Meaning of Anxiety*. Rev. edn. New York: W. W. Norton.

24 Schneider, K. (2013). *The Polarized Mind: Why It's Killing Us and What We Can Do About It*. University Professors Press.

Chapter 16

# Remind

*Remind the child it is not their fault.*

In the 1997 film *Good Will Hunting*, there is a pivotal scene where the character Will meets with his therapist, Sean. Holding Will's case file, filled with records of childhood abuse and neglect, he tells Will, "*It's not your fault*". At first, Will ignores him, but Sean keeps repeating the words "*It's not your fault*", until Will finally collapses, crying as the weight of all his shame and guilt slowly begins to fade away.[1]

When I watched this scene. I deeply resonated with the feeling of locking things away from the past. As a teenager, I was written off, excluded from school at the age of 14, told I would never amount to anything, and just like Will in the film, I developed unhealthy ways to *protect* myself. I acted as if nothing mattered, and I reacted with "rebellion" toward myself for every mistake, every panic attack, and every foolish decision I had made.

As an adult, the self-guilt and shame continued as I blamed myself for having mental health issues, a failed marriage, not being able to hold down jobs, and for my intrusive thoughts, all of which I presumed were just a part of *who* I was. Until I was diagnosed as autistic with ADHD, when I was 30, it was then that I had to rethink and reframe all these long-held beliefs. All the belief systems I had created had to go. I had to start accepting, just like Will in the film, that the complex struggles I had as a child were *not my fault.*

## It Is Not Their Fault

This chapter presents the second foundation of acceptance: *remind.* At its core is the affirmation "*It's not your fault*". The purpose is to help autistic children or young people realise and accept that the challenges they encounter, whether at school, home, or in daily life, are *not their fault*. We know that autistic people often feel stigmatised and labelled by society, through being treated differently.[2] It is also widely reported that autistic people often have to deal with more difficult life experiences than neurotypical people, which can lead to problems with mental health,

DOI: 10.4324/9781003686064-20

relationships and employment, higher rates of stress, trauma, and social adversity[3] inhabiting a social world set up mainly for neurotypical people,[4] and they often experience daily discrimination and feel shame for being autistic.[5]

When you speak this truth to a child in a moment of struggle, you are planting the seed of acceptance, reminding them that what they are struggling with is *not* a result of anything they are doing wrong. This thinking replaces the stigma surrounding the child, challenging the adverse reactions and conditions they have usually picked up from others.

## The Development of the Self

To help autistic individuals overcome many of their challenges, research has identified two key contributors to developing more positive self-views. These are self-advocacy (speaking up for one's own needs and rights) and self-determination (making independent choices and decisions about one's own life).[6]

When applying the Four Foundations of Acceptance, autistic children and young people begin to develop their own *self-advocacy,* beginning with understanding that what they are going through is not their fault. A powerful example of this in practice is Charlie in Chapter 2. It was this specific foundation that changed everything for him. Being told that what he was struggling with and going through was *not his fault* helped him begin to accept what he can and cannot do, and to be OK with who he is.

**Real-Life Experience 16**

By reminding a child it's not their fault, you are helping them to meet their safety and belonging needs. One such case was when our team was asked to support an autistic teenager who was experiencing mental health issues in school. He was a high masker and struggled to attend lessons, often running out of school whenever he could. We began supporting him at home, as he was unable to leave the house and was avoiding school completely. When applying the *remove* foundation first, we identified that attending school was the main demand that caused him the most fear/anxiety. Once he received the message that he no longer had to go back to school, his parents noticed a significant reduction in his anxiety. He was still struggling but calmer, spending more time with them and less time in his room.

After a few weeks of our support, his mother told me about a secret box he had been keeping in his room. This box contained pills, razor blades, and some rope. He had been gathering anything he felt he would need to end his life if things got too much. I was taken aback by the box; I had no idea he had this. I was even more struck when his mother told me he came downstairs the other day holding the box, and gave it to her, saying:

> *I don't need this anymore. I now know this is not my fault.*

This moment represents just one of many stories where we have seen the impact of telling a child it is not their fault. The process is simple: you are not looking to fix or improve, or to get a child or young person to return to a place such as school, where the main issues lie. You are following the child, offering unconditional positive regard, and helping them find their own way in their own time. This boy now works with us every week and no longer gets as low. He has his off days, but he says that knowing it's not his fault has changed everything, because he never knew this before, constantly blaming himself for how he felt and for what he couldn't do.

## Discovering Self-Acceptance

Acceptance of self is not easy to find, and acceptance of autism is even harder, especially when you are aware of your issues and struggles. I recall sitting in a psychologist's office during the first few years of my diagnosis. He turned to me and said, "*The difficulty with you, Aaron, is that you are too aware of your struggles*". I didn't really understand what he said because I was not in a good place, recovering from a nervous breakdown, and trying to accept that being diagnosed autistic with ADHD meant that my childhood, teenage years, and early adulthood life was not my fault, but also struggling to accept this.

Returning to the opening dialogue from *Good Will Hunting*, it is important that when working with autistic children and young people, we tell them it isn't their fault, and that we also know this ourselves. Whether they have challenging behaviours or severe mental health issues, these are not their fault. This simple affirmation helps them avoid feeling more stressed and anxious in their surroundings. It is the process of separating the child or young person from the problems or issues they face, giving them space to grow and find their own way through what they are experiencing.

## Summary

In this chapter, I have introduced the *remind* foundation, grounded in the notion that being autistic is *not* a person's fault. This is grounded in decades of neuroscience and developmental research; we know without doubt that autism is a neurodevelopmental difference, not a product of bad parenting or down to the child's behaviour. We know the autistic brain develops and functions differently in the earliest stages of life and that these differences affect specific experiences of perception, sensory processing, and stress responses. When parents, teachers, and professionals begin to apply this foundation to the children they support, you will see its impact. Why not try the next time you are helping an autistic child to overcome something, to start by telling "*It's not your fault*" and then start to accept this yourself about the child in front of you. In the next chapter, we discuss the *reassure* foundation of acceptance.

## Notes

1 Good Will Hunting (1997). Directed by Gus Van Sant [Film]. USA: Miramax.
2 Moseley, R.L., et al. (2021). Autistic People's Experiences of Stigma and the Impact on Mental Health. *Autism*, 25(2), pp. 452–463.
3 Martino, D.C., Brantley, A. & Scarpa, A. (2025). The Role of Self-advocacy and Self-determination in Positive Adjustment for Autistic Adolescents and Young Adults: A Mini-review. *Frontiers in Child and Adolescent Psychiatry*, 4, p. 1542543. https://doi.org/10.3389/frcha.2025.1542543.
4 Cooper, K., et al. (2020). Self-Concept in Youth with Autism Spectrum Disorder. *Journal of Autism and Developmental Disorders*, 50(10), pp. 3662–3674.
5 Botha, M. & Frost, D.M. (2020). Extending the Minority Stress Model to Understand Mental Health Problems Experienced by the Autistic Population. *Society and Mental Health*, 10(1), pp. 20–34.
6 Botha, M. & Frost, D.M. (2020). Extending the Minority Stress Model to Understand Mental Health Problems Experienced by the Autistic Population. *Society and Mental Health*, 10(1), pp. 20–34.

# Chapter 17

# Reassure

*Reassure the child that it is going to be OK.*

My mother had a nervous breakdown when she was 11 and was sent away to a mental institution. We never really spoke about it. All I know is that while in the hospital, she planned and executed a daring escape, and bravely on her own, running through the city of Portsmouth, in the middle of the night, to her aunt's house, where she stayed hidden, thankfully, never to return to the institution she had been locked away in. During the '50s, when she was institutionalised, professionals mostly disagreed on how to support children with mental health issues, mainly because there were health and education services that did not have clear medical or legal rules to follow.[1] I can only imagine how it must have felt for her. How scared and alone she must have been. Still, I like to think of her as a little warrior, standing up for her life, heart-pounding as she escaped the cold hospital walls, running for her freedom, into an unknown future, guided by the hope that it was all somehow *going to be OK.*

This chapter introduces the third foundation: *reassure*, conveying a message of hope and reassurance to autistic children and young people through the affirmation "*It's going to be OK*". The aim here is to further create conditions of safety and trust by drawing on the concept of acceptance, and to continue the message of hope that things will be OK, whatever happens. Reassurance is about showing a child or young person that they can find a way through a difficulty, no matter what happens.

## The Importance of Reassurance

It is well known that autistic children often experience anxiety, and hearing that everything will be OK, regardless of circumstances, is much more comforting than a message implying things *won't* be OK. The Reassure Foundation was developed to help a child feel psychologically safe. No matter what is going on, in a classroom or at home, the idea here is to stop everything and focus completely on calming everything down. When reassuring a child, we ease their worries about school, friendships, expectations, and the fear of failure with a simple message of hope.

DOI: 10.4324/9781003686064-21

Simply by being with them when life feels too much, standing by them when they don't feel supported. Listening to them when they feel like a failure.

## Psychological Safety

In humanistic psychology, reassurance guides a child or young person to experience what Carl Rogers termed *psychological safety.*[2] Rogers said psychological safety for a child is created "*whenever a teacher, parent, therapist, or other person with a facilitating function feels basically that this individual is or worth in his own right and in his own unfolding, no matter what his present condition or behaviour*".[3]

Without psychological safety, children will protect themselves through avoidance, masking, and compliance. However, when a child feels psychologically safe, they are more likely to accept themselves, lower their defences and explore their feelings and issues more openly. We often see a child who does not feel psychologically safe when they are masking.

Reassurance helps reduce the need for masking and establishes psychological safety alongside the other foundations of acceptance. If a parent, educator, or mental health practitioner reassures a child that things will be OK, the child begins to *believe* it and builds their own confidence to be who they are, realising it's OK to tell their parents they can't go to school anymore because it's too much for them. Or to tell the teacher that they are not OK and need some help. Or to have the confidence to speak to their therapist about how they *really* feel. These responses can only happen if a child feels psychologically safe.

### Reflection

It is important to recognise that reassurance does not imply that everything is perfect in the world. The idea of reassurance is to be as honest as possible with the child and to be a consistent adult, conveying the same message, regardless of their feelings and behaviours.

## Reassurance: The Foundation of Safety

Abraham Maslow also recognised the importance of safety. In his *hierarchy of needs*,[4] he showed that when safety is threatened, all other needs are inhibited. In other words, a child needs to feel safe, above everything else. This is seen in autistic children who cannot engage in school. When they feel unsafe, learning cannot happen. All that is going on with these children is that they are in a daily battle, fighting to survive, where education and learning are the last things on their minds.

**Real-Life Experience 17**

During a visit to a secondary mainstream school, I was asked to support an autistic student who was in trouble for swearing at his teacher and leaving class without permission. A staff member told me, "*He has sworn at his teacher again, refusing to take his coat off, and has ended up running out of class. This is totally unacceptable. Can you please speak to him and tell him he must not swear at teachers!*"

We moved into a small meeting room, where I could speak directly to the young person. Immediately, my focus was to get him to a place of *psychological safety*. He knew me because I had been supporting him for a while, which helped. However, on that day in that moment, I could see he was visibly upset. His face was red, and he was breathing fast. To calm him down, I reassured him it was going to be OK and completely *ignored* that he had sworn at his teacher. Choosing not to address this at all, I then reminded him that *it is not his fault* that he is having a tough day. The conversation went something like this.

> *Don't worry about what's just happened. How are you feeling? The teacher must have really annoyed you for you to walk out. Do you want to talk about it?*

Immediately, I saw him calm down. His breathing slowed to a normal pace, and his face was no longer as red. He told me,

> *I was late for class, and I hate going in when I am late. I hate being looked at by everyone.*

He told me he likes to leave his coat on with his hood up when he feels anxious, as it helps him to get through the classroom door and take a seat. Hiding under his hood helps him avoid being *seen*. He continued telling me what happened:

> *The teacher then asked me why I was late and told me to take my coat off. I told him to f——k off. He shouted at me, and I ran out of class.*

Still focusing on creating a safe space for him, I tried to relate to his situation.

> *I am so sorry this happened to you. I can only imagine how you must have felt being spoken to like that.*

As we talked more, I reassured him that I would suggest to the teacher that they rethink how they speak to you when you are late. Here is what my advice was: (1) Leave the boy alone if he is late. Don't speak to him. Let him sit down and settle into the lesson. And (2) let him wear his coat until he feels calmer. This is an essential coping strategy for him.

I was then asked to speak with his parents and to arrange a meeting. Despite his issues in school, he had also not been getting out of bed in the mornings, and they wanted some advice. When in school, he got into fights, skipped lessons, and refused to do his work. He was in a bad place. The school had tried to be supportive and helped the best they could; however, things were not changing or improving. He had been put on report, temporarily excluded, and placed into isolation, but nothing was working. He was still angry and stressed, which caused significant concern for his family and the school.

I met with his parents to get a better picture of what was going on at home. Both Mum and Dad said nothing was working, and that telling him off, taking things away from him as a consequence, and even trying to talk to him about his behaviour only led to more arguing. I advised them to try the following steps at home.

1. First thing was to reassure him when he was upset, to tell him that it was going to be OK and that they understood he was struggling and would do what he needed to help him.
2. In the mornings, when he got upset and frustrated, instead of arguing with him, I advised the parents to give him time to process how he was feeling. I advised them to allow that time, to remove the pressure, and not to worry if he arrived late to school. The school supported this approach and agreed that it was OK for him to arrive late if it helped him feel calmer and less stressed.
3. On the really bad days, he should be told that it's OK if he couldn't go to school. I said to reassure him that he didn't have to go. By doing this, they were taking the stress away when the demands of school were too much for him. I encouraged the parents on these days to call the school and tell them the truth, that they were trying everything to get him in, but he was not able to due to his anxiety and stress levels.
4. I also advised that they give him as much time on his own as he needed when at home, not to expect him to spend time with family he didn't want to, and to allow him to have as much space on his own as he needed.
5. I also talked to them about the importance of reminding him *it was not his fault* he struggled, and to reassure him they were on his side, and they will do whatever he needed them to do.

After a few weeks, I was keen to find out how the advice had gone for them. Despite him still having a few issues with school, his parents told me he now woke up and didn't get as upset in the mornings and was even starting to get up on his own and arrive at school on time. He was also attending more lessons and was not getting into as much trouble as before. His parents had said that by accepting him more at home, he was able to better manage his emotions and was generally happier with himself, especially when given more time on his own and no longer expected to eat with the family. They said these changes really helped him.

A few months after this initial support, I received a phone call from his mother, who was in tears. I was a little concerned at first that something may have happened. But nothing had, in fact, she was crying happy tears and calling me because she wanted me to know he had just hugged her for the first time in 11 years. This boy had *never* hugged his mother before.

## Reassurance as a Human Need

Carl Rogers described psychological safety as an essential part of helping someone drop their guard.[5] When someone feels safe, they no longer act defensively, and in this case, it was clear that this boy was being defensive towards people in his life. Not because he was manipulative or rude, but because he was trying to keep himself safe.

Reassuring an autistic child or young person that it's going to be OK is an important part of basic human need. As Maslow described, safety is key to human development. Without safety, a child cannot learn or explore. When a child feels safe, they stop presuming that bad things will happen and start embracing possibilities.

## Summary

My mother had a lot of mental health issues growing up, and a lot of problems she tried to manage on her own. When she was a child, mental health issues were taboo subjects and not really spoken about. Maybe my mother saw herself in me, and when I struggled as a child, she saw the need to reassure me that it *was going to be OK*. This is why reassurance is one of the Four Foundations of Acceptance. It is so powerful because even as a professional, a teacher, or a parent, when you don't have an answer and your child is crying, or they are scared, you can tell them "*it is going to be OK*" and leave it there and give them a reassuring nod, or play a game with them on the computer, or watch their favourite film for the hundredth time. Sometimes that is all these kids need, to be told it is going to be OK. In the next chapter, we will consider the fourth foundation of acceptance: *reaffirm*.

## Notes

1 Evans, B. (2017). *The Metamorphosis of Autism: A History of Child Development in Britain*. Manchester, UK: Manchester University Press. Chapter 3, Inside the Maudsley Child Psychotic Clinic in the 1950s. https://www.ncbi.nlm.nih.gov/books/NBK436849/
2 Rogers, C.R. (1961). *On Becoming a Person*. Boston: Houghton Mifflin.
3 Rogers, C.R. (1961). *On Becoming a Person*. Boston: Houghton Mifflin, p. 382.
4 Maslow, A.H. (1943). A Theory of Human Motivation. *Psychological Review*, 50(4), pp. 370–396.
5 Rogers, C.R. (1959). A Theory of Therapy, Personality, and Interpersonal Relationships. In S. Koch (Ed.), *Psychology: A Study of a Science*. New York: McGraw Hill.

Chapter 18

# Reaffirm

*Reaffirm that you accept the child unconditionally.*

Standing by an autistic child, when they are struggling, misbehaving, refusing to follow orders, verbally offensive, isolated, not leaving their house, refusing to go to school, running out of lessons, fighting in the playground, ripping up their work, having a meltdown in a shop, or locking themselves in the bathroom, is not easy. Making the decision to unconditionally accept a child or young person, *despite* how they are acting, is even harder. With the fourth foundation of *reaffirm,* you are doing exactly this. You are making an active decision to stand beside a child without judgement or conditions, becoming someone who accepts them *exactly* as they are. When a child knows you stand by them, no matter what, they know that they can be completely themselves around you because you are not going to judge them or place unrealistic expectations on them. In this chapter, we will explore the challenges and significance of acceptance, as well as common misconceptions about what it truly means to accept a child unconditionally.

## Being a Consistent Adult

When you apply the *reaffirm* foundation, you connect with the child by becoming a *consistent adult,* standing by them, unwavering, no matter what is thrown your way. When they are overwhelmed, anxious, angry, or avoiding demands, you are the adult who says, "*It's OK. I am not going anywhere*". A consistent adult does not withdraw support because a child is not engaging. A consistent adult does not put a time constraint on support. A consistent adult knows that communication in whatever form is *not* an act of defiance; it is a desire for safety and the need to belong and to be accepted.

## Unconditional Acceptance

As a consistent adult, you are offering a child unconditional acceptance, communicating that they are OK just as they are, no matter what is happening or has

DOI: 10.4324/9781003686064-22

happened; the child or young person is enough. They don't have to improve or be anyone else. This thinking again aligns with Carl Rogers' idea of *unconditional positive regard.* He believed it is vital to recognise our self-worth regardless of our achievements and imperfections, to embrace ourselves as imperfect beings and begin from there.

The aim of the *reaffirm* foundation, like the other foundations of acceptance, is to accept an autistic child exactly as they are. The Accept Approach emphasises accepting the child and trusting that, through this acceptance, they will find their path, with your support guiding them along the way, *even* if they do something you disagree with. We will now consider a real-life example of how and why I believe we should always accept an autistic child, *especially* when they have done something perceived as *wrong*.

**Real-Life Experience 18**

During a conversation with the father of a teenager we were supporting, he shared openly about his struggles with accepting his daughter's behaviour. There had been an incident in which she had hit out at her mother, and the father was telling me his struggle to *accept* the situation.

> *Our daughter is 14 and recently stopped taking her medication. We don't know why she stopped, because every time we tried to ask her, she would shut down. She would often scream at us to "Get out!" and say we never listen, blaming us for everything. Her anxiety is so bad at the moment that she hardly leaves the house. We feel like prisoners in our own home. We love her dearly and know it's not her fault, but it's just so tough to apply acceptance, especially when she hits us and says horrible things.*

He continued to explain:

> *Last night, she became extremely distressed in the kitchen when making cookies with her mother. A disagreement arose, prompting her to lash out and punch her mother on the arm. As parents, we both knew this was unacceptable behaviour, and my initial instinct was to tell her off. But I chose not to say anything, and instead I left the room. I tried to remind myself that she is having a really tough time and that it isn't her fault. Still, it's just so hard to know how to react when she hits out.*

This reflection is an example of how difficult it can be when applying acceptance in a tough situation. It is extremely exhausting for parents, especially when they feel conflicted and unsure if they are doing the *right* thing. But it is exactly in those moments, I believe, when a child needs acceptance the most. It is in those moments that the foundations of acceptance are effective, as the child is learning that even in the most difficult times, the adult is standing with them. During these moments, they begin to learn that despite what has happened, they are *still* unconditionally accepted.

For context, acceptance here does not mean you are excusing the hitting; it is about staying present in the moment so that the conflict does not escalate. Moments like these are when families feel judged by others, and you hear familiar opinions from family members or even close friends: "*I wouldn't let them get away with that!*" Society's norm is to discipline them by imposing a sanction or removing a privilege until the child reflects on their behaviour and apologises.

Acceptance is the *opposite* of this. In the midst of the behaviour, it is about being aware that they are communicating that something is too much for them to cope with; it is *not* a defiant act that needs punishing. Acceptance in these moments is also *not* about sending the message "*It's OK to hit someone*". It is about the child witnessing the act of acceptance, so that they can still feel safe, no matter what is happening.

The father continued:

> *We know she cannot hit her mother. But telling her off doesn't work. We have tried it many times before! It just makes things worse. With our daughter, we have to think differently, and acceptance really is the best option for us. But it's incredibly tough in those intense moments. The truth is, she knows it was wrong. What does help is to remember when she has shown us how much she loves us.*

He shared some recent moments that reassured him she is not the kind of person who would hit her mother; it was entirely out of character.

> *She struggles to express herself in typical ways, but the other day she sent me a TikTok clip to our WhatsApp family chat, featuring a video saying, "Why my mum is the best!" and another time she shared a video, "My dad is autistic and here is why I love him".*
>
> *I also hold on to those rare moments when she comes into my office, hugs me, and then disappears back to her room. She is a fantastic kid, and we know in those moments when she chooses to express herself, how hard that is for her. It's those moments I see who she really is, a loving, kind, and thoughtful person. When she hit her mother, that was not who she is. It's out of character, and that's why we still try to accept her even in tough times. It's just so difficult.*

We also talked about how the Accept Approach helps in these situations, and he told me that knowing how to remove anxiety and to remind her it's not her fault. He said the one foundation she responds to most is knowing *it's going to be OK*, which turned this situation all around for them.

> *Reassuring her it's going to be OK, when she is in a state of emotion, seems to calm her down a lot more than anything else, and in this instance it worked well. We didn't respond to the hitting and gave it time. After she calmed down, we had*

*a chat, and she admitted that she had been missing her medication and needed help to be reminded to take it.*

In this instance, the family were able to calm things down through applying acceptance. They then were also able to get to the bottom of what the behaviour was telling them: that she needed help being reminded to take her medication, *not* to be told off for hitting out.

## Misconceptions of Acceptance

There are often misconceptions around acceptance-based support and its purpose, which can be confusing because the idea that to accept a child exactly as they are goes against the idea that autistic children need boundaries and to follow rules set for them, so that they can be kept safe. Of course, we all need boundaries and rules to stay safe. I wish to address these now.

### *Misconception 1: "You Can't Just Let Them Do Whatever They Want"*

When supporting autistic children and young people, it is so important to accept that they will experience the world very differently from other children. They will react differently. They will engage in life differently. To think that acceptance is just "*letting them do what they want*" is missing who these children *really* are. By offering unconditional acceptance and giving them space to explore freely what they want to do, you help them find themselves *within* their life experiences, whether that is in education or at home.

When a child has the freedom to do what they want to in life, they begin to move *towards* their interests, and their engagement switches on, and genuine, meaningful learning occurs. What you *don't* see with autistic children and young people who are given the freedom to do what they want, are anxious and overwhelmed children pushed by stress and expectations placed on them by others. In moments of acceptance, you will witness children in a state of flow as they engage in meaningful learning that is important to *them*.

### *Misconception 2: Accepting Unwanted Behaviours Is Dangerous*

Most negative behaviours are labelled as unwanted. For example, I supported an autistic child who was in a primary school for a few years, and every year he would have the same repeated target to reach, which was to put his hand up when responding to a question from the teacher. He never could. His response was always, "*I already know the answer! Why should I raise my hand?*" This made perfect sense to me, but the school never saw it that way.

They wanted conformity in the classroom, and for all the children not to call out when answering questions. The problem was that this caused the child a lot of stress, and as a result of the demand, in lessons, he stopped engaging. He went from a child who was engaged and enthusiastic, and often had the correct answers, but because he couldn't put his hand up, he began to disengage. I recall supporting this child in schools for over four years, and he could never put his hand up.

**Real-Life Experience 19**

I was asked to support another autistic child who was having serious difficulty at school, to the extent that she had started to escape the school building, where, on several occasions, she was found running down the road trying to find her way home. The school and her parents were very concerned, and no one knew how to handle the situation.

I was told that many behaviours occurred during lesson time, with her often becoming upset quickly, especially when she couldn't meet the demands or expectations asked of her. When she was unable to answer a question, she would become visibly distressed and frequently run out of the classroom, into an empty room where she would tip chairs, hit cupboards, and throw things around. When she was upset, staff were worried about her safety and the safety of others. So they would close the door whenever she was throwing things and wouldn't let her out until she stopped. If that didn't help, they would enter and restrain her until she settled, which was also often ineffective. The only reliable method to calm her was to call her mother to pick her up. As soon as she knew her mother was coming to collect her, she would instantly calm down.

After observing her in class, I saw that the main issue was the excessive demands placed on her, and I suggested that a mainstream setting might not be suitable for her. However, the process of exploring whether she needed an education, health, and care plan to determine whether she requires specialised support was lengthy, and the school wanted to help her now.

My advice was as follows:

1. When she enters the empty classroom, do not close the door; leave it open and sit on the floor, away from any objects that might be thrown, to ensure safety for the staff.
2. Don't respond initially; sit there and allow her to express how she is feeling.
3. Tell her you understand she's going through a tough time and reassure her it's OK. Let her know you're here to support her and acknowledge that *it's not her fault* she got upset. Be present in the moment as a consistent, unconditional adult.
4. Do this *before* you opt for the other strategies.

After a few weeks, I checked in and learned that her behaviour had changed significantly. The staff member supporting her mentioned that she still needs to go into the room when upset, but that they no longer close the door. She said, "*I now sit on the floor with her, and she cries or vents her frustrations, but she no longer gets angry. While she still gets upset, the difference is truly remarkable*".

During difficult moments, especially when an autistic child is angry, frustrated, or running out of the classroom, the consistent adult presence is *crucial*. When an adult remains present, no matter what the child says or does, the child will begin to feel *psychologically safe*. This sense of safety helps reduce the child's internal anxieties, making it easier to support them more effectively.

Conversely, reacting with crossed arms or standing firm at the door often worsens the situation, as it did with this child. The key takeaway is that she simply needed time to vent and someone dependable to lean on. As a result, she never tried to escape school that year, and no other chairs were thrown.

### *Misconception 3: A Child Will Learn Nothing About Life If All You Do Is Accept Them*

For me, this is one of the most frustrating misconceptions about acceptance. I believe autistic children and young people learn more about life when they are shown that they can be in control of their lives and their learning. Allowing an autistic child to find their *own* way is vital. Naturally, they will encounter situations outside their control, as everyone does. However, embracing acceptance-based principles offers a more optimistic outlook. When autistic children are given complete autonomy, reassured that they can manage their lives, and provided with support, guidance, and unconditional acceptance, they tend to become more balanced and grounded. This approach is so much more effective than pressuring them to learn things they resist just to conform to societal expectations.

## Natural Consequence

Another issue I want to address here is that when an autistic child or young person does something wrong, there are different ways to apply consequences. A behavioural consequence would be to tell them off, to correct them for their wrongdoing. The naughty step comes to mind here. Behavioural consequences treat the situation as a problem in which the child is to blame, and the child must feel bad about what they did and fix it. This type of consequence focuses on teaching the child a lesson. You have done wrong, so you must face the consequences of your actions. For an autistic child in distress, such as the young girl who hit out at her mother, these consequences only add further threats to an already overloaded nervous system and can often make a situation worse, not better. This approach does not help a young person understand what has happened; it only conveys the message that their behaviour is unacceptable and that their sense of safety is removed as a result of the adult placing conditions and expectations on them.

There is another consequence that is much more effective for helping autistic children understand when they do something wrong: *natural consequence*. The most important process of natural consequence is that it does not remove safety. The adult continues to offer unconditional positive regard, accepting the child *no matter* what has happened. You are not focusing here on any expectation to be better or to improve behaviour. When you are applying a natural consequence, you simply explain to the young person that they hit their mother, and that is why she is upset. That is why she is crying. When conveying this, you are also reaffirming that you still completely accept them. With a natural consequence, you are explaining what is happening while still offering unconditional acceptance. You explain, "*Your mum will be upset for a while, but then she will be OK. It's all right, we still accept, we all make mistakes. It's OK*". There are no sanctions, nor removal of privilege. Nothing else needs to happen. The situation is over. Let's move on. By applying natural consequences, you help a child or young person understand that actions do affect others and that they are still and always accepted unconditionally, regardless of what happens. In turn, the child is learning to be responsible for their actions, remaining free from shame or blame.

## Summary

In this chapter, I have attempted to show that, when an overwhelmed child seeks psychological safety, what matters most is that they know they are *accepted unconditionally*. This is also one of the hardest things to do. It is never easy to reaffirm that you accept them unconditionally when they swear at you, withdraw into their rooms, not wash for weeks, shout in your face that they "*hate you*," or hit you. Acceptance when faced with challenging behaviours can be one of the loneliest places to be sometimes, especially when an autistic child is struggling in *their* life, with issues that begin to impact on *yours*.

When considering the daughter who hit her mother, acceptance is *not* about remaining silent, of course; it's OK to say, "*Please don't hit me*". But actually, what is more powerful is to move away and *not* react in the moment. The most important thing to do in those situations is to always find a way to calm the child and to still make them feel safe, loved, and accepted, no matter what has happened. In this case, his daughter knew she shouldn't have hit her mother, and it was out of place for her. She did say sorry, in her own way – not by saying sorry, but by giving her mother a hug. One of those big, rare hugs that mattered the most.

When you apply the foundation of *reaffirm*, you are making a stance that you accept the child unconditionally no matter what has happened. You accept them completely, remembering they are autistic, and knowing that it is *not their fault*. You look *past* the behaviour and at the whole child in front of you. Instead of thinking you have to teach them through consequences, you instead learn to stand beside them as a consistent adult, striving to show them that, even in their darkest moments, they do not have to change or improve to be accepted by you.

Chapter 19

# The Acceptance-Based Curriculum™

## What Is the National Curriculum?

I think it is crucial to discuss the need to develop a new curriculum for autistic children and young people. This begins with first looking at who the National Curriculum was initially created for. Most will be aware of what a curriculum is: a guide for teaching particular subjects, supporting a child's learning, setting content, and providing resources related to specific subjects. Ofsted defines a curriculum as

> *the substance of what is taught. It is the specific plan of what learners need to know and should be able to do. The curriculum shapes and determines what learners of all ages will get out of their educational experience.*[1]

In the UK we have a specific National Curriculum, defined by the UK Government as:

> *a set of subjects and standards used by primary and secondary schools so that children learn the same things. It covers what subjects are taught and the standards children should reach in each subject.*[2]

The National Curriculum is effective for many children and young people, but *only* if they can cope with the demands and pace of the learning. In my experience, it often fails to support autistic children with specific needs, such as those with anxiety and demand avoidance issues. These children and young people require a curriculum that aligns with their unique learning styles and focuses solely on their interests.

## Developing a New Curriculum

In 2023, I asked a question: *Is the National Curriculum working for autistic children and young people?* In an attempt to find an answer, I created a survey to gather

DOI: 10.4324/9781003686064-23

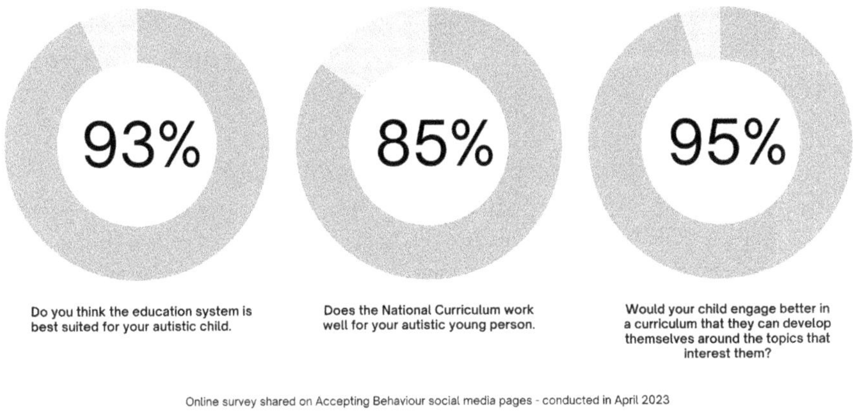


*Figure 19.1* Online Survey

parents' views on the impact of the National Curriculum on their autistic children and young people. The survey was posted on our Accepting Behaviour social media pages and received 600 responses from parents. Of those respondents, 56% reported that their autistic child had an EHCP, while 45% reported that they did not. The age distribution reflected the education system, with 35% attending primary school, 55% in secondary school, and 8% in post-16 education.

Families were initially asked whether the education system as a whole is most suitable for their autistic children, with 93% responding "*no*". When asked if the National Curriculum was effective for their children, 85% said "*no*". Conversely, when asked if their autistic children would be more engaged with a curriculum tailored to their interests, 95% responded "*yes*". Expressed here in Figure 19.1.

What this survey revealed to me is that many autistic children and young people are not disengaged from learning itself; they are disengaged from a curriculum that was never really developed for them. Even with a small sample of 600 families, the message was compelling. There are so many autistic children with the inability to cope with rigid lesson structures, constant instructions, academic targets, and sustained pressure, and they need something different because it is clear that the National Curriculum *fails* to meet the educational needs of many autistic children and young people.

Therefore, I developed the Acceptance-Based Curriculum[3] to address these issues. Inspired by the humanistic principles of psychological safety, unconditional positive regard, interest-led learning, and intrinsic motivation, the ABC focuses on a single area of learning: *doing what captures the child's interest, then using this as the basis for their education.* The central principle of the ABC is that the curriculum naturally forms as learning occurs. It grows from the child's interests and from what is meaningful to them, going at their pace, focused on their emotional capacity and motivations, all within environments where they are in control and feel safe to learn.

## The Three Components of the ABC

When I created the ABC, my goal was to go beyond teaching a set of predetermined subjects. The children I worked with at the time couldn't follow that way of learning; even with reasonable adjustments and additional support, they all struggled with the concept of being told what to learn. Instead, they needed a curriculum that allowed them to take charge of their own learning.

To achieve this, the ABC is built around three main components (*see Figure 19.2*). The first component, *the student is in control of their learning*, positions themselves as the decision-maker, the one who decides what they do. They then choose what, when, and how they want to learn. The second component, *adult-suggested learning,* places the role of the adult as a supporter of their learning, suggesting ideas rather than leading or directing. The adult's role is to offer support, resources, and ideas, only as suggestions, ultimately with the student as the final decision-maker. The third component, *purposeful aims*, is the aims the student chooses to work towards, emerging from collaboration, either chosen by the student or supported by the adult. Together, these three components make up a curriculum that is accessible for autistic children and young people, built on autonomy, acceptance, and interest-led learning.

## The Acceptance-Based Curriculum

### *1. Purposeful Aims*

Purposeful aims are not targets. They are not predicted outcomes written in advance. They are naturally identified *themes* that develop during the learning process, as the child or young person begins to show interest, curiosity, or engagement in a given subject or topic of their choosing. Purposeful aims are written as you move through the learning process, and are formed from informal conversations with the student, observations of their interests, and collaborative discussions with parents. When a child chooses a purposeful aim, they are motivated to pursue it because it aligns with their interests.

Purposeful aims become the building blocks of a child's learning developed through adopting humanistic approaches to supporting the Four Areas of SEND (*see Figure 19.3*), which are:

1. Preferred learning way (*cognition and learning*)
2. Natural communication *(communication and interaction)*
3. Sensory differences (*sensory and physical*)
4. Self-acceptance reached (*social, emotional, and mental health*)

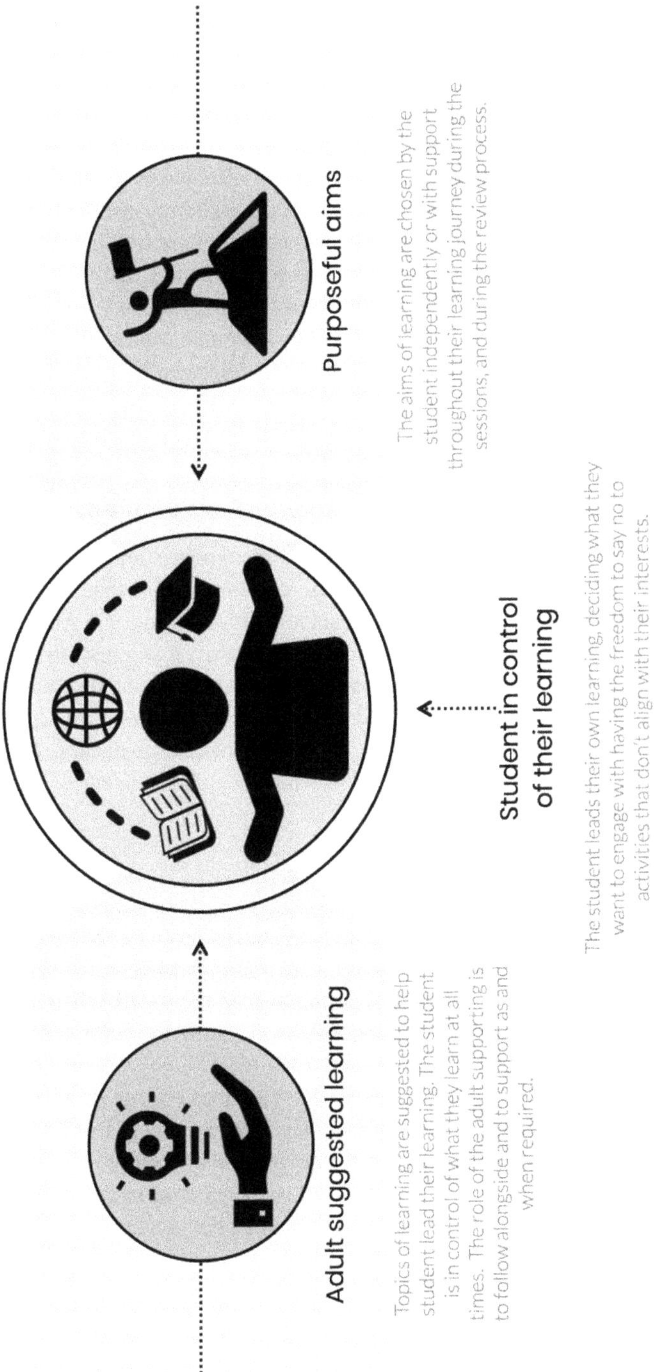


*Figure 19.2* The Three Components of the ABC

## *Purposeful Aims: Four Areas of SEND*

### 1. PREFERRED LEARNING WAY (*COGNITION AND LEARNING*)

The first purposeful aim asks, "*How does the child prefer to learn?*" and is designed to support the child's cognitive development. This can be identified through simply asking them, or something you will naturally discover after working with a child. As the ABC works alongside the Accept Approach, you are already removing anything that causes anxiety and reminding them that their struggles are not their fault.

In the learning environment, you may, for example, identify that the young person prefers to learn quietly or likes to talk nonstop. Maybe they want to be in their pyjamas or wear their favourite hoodie. They may also prefer afternoons over mornings. They may prefer short bursts of learning followed by playing their favourite game. As you move through the process, you will begin to form a picture of how they *prefer to learn*, and these preferences guide how you teach/support them.

### 2. NATURAL COMMUNICATION (*COMMUNICATION AND INTERACTION*)

The second purposeful aim emphasises the need to recognise a child's natural communication and interaction style. Instead of the common belief that autistic children have "social skill deficits" and require social skills training, the ABC centres on understanding how each child *naturally* communicates. It suggests that autistic children *already* possess the ability to share their preferences socially; we simply need to observe and support their preferred methods. When we focus on their natural ways of communicating and interacting, a significant change occurs. The child begins to feel accepted for who they are, knowing they can connect with you on their own terms and in their unique way.

### 3. SENSORY DIFFERENCES (*SENSORY AND PHYSICAL*)

Sensory needs, like social skills, are sometimes treated as problems to be fixed. For example, a child who needs to pace around the classroom is often viewed as disruptive and placed on a red spot or a wobble cushion to *keep them still*, when in fact all they need is the freedom to move. With the ABC, you do precisely that: give them the sensory freedom they need to learn.

For example, a child may prefer to learn with their shoes off, not to speak during a session, or to wear ear defenders. They may need to learn away from other children or to have short breaks during sessions. They may also prefer to start their day after 10 a.m., giving them time to wake up. Whatever they need to feel comfortable enough to communicate and interact with you, that is what we do.

### 4. SELF-ACCEPTANCE REACHED (*SOCIAL, EMOTIONAL, MENTAL HEALTH*)

The final purposeful aim focuses on a child's well-being. As the adult, you are the one offering unconditional positive regard to help a child feel safe, throughout the

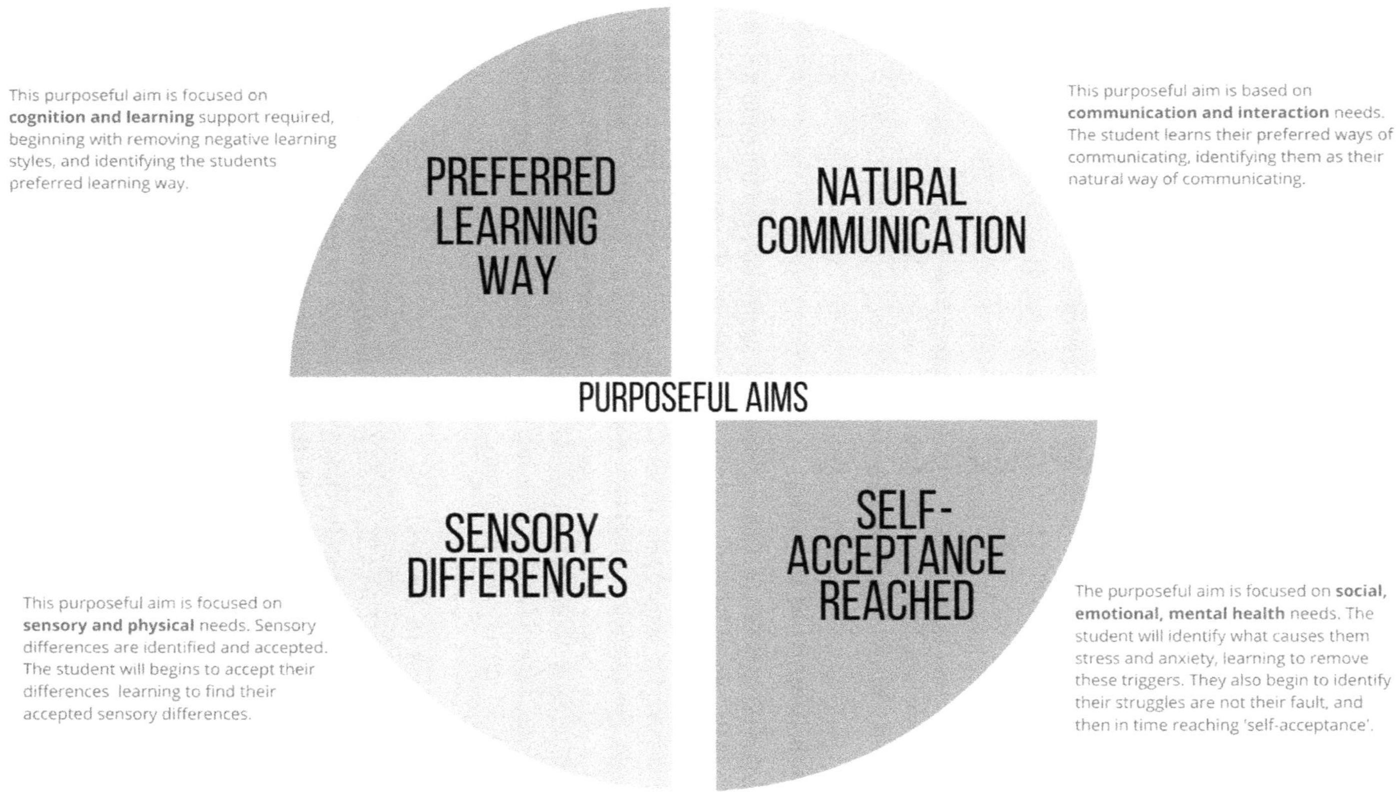


*Figure 19.3* Purposeful Aims

whole learning process, teaching them that they can say no if they don't want to do something and that they can be in complete control of their learning. This, in turn, helps a child to develop self-acceptance, knowing that it is OK to be exactly who they are.

The most effective way to do this is to follow the Two Rules of Learning during our sessions, which were developed while supporting the Pyjama Kid, in Chapter 14. When I noticed how positively he responded to being told he was the boss, I decided to see how other children and young people would respond, which we have found that it too helps so many of our students to begin to find their way and build confidence, knowing they are ultimately in control of their learning. Our role is to guide them through the process and offer advice and support as needed.

The two rules are as follows:

1. The child is the boss of their learning.
   *Direction comes from the child; guidance comes from the adult.*
2. They do not have to do anything they do not want to do.
   *The child's interests set the agenda; the adults' support brings it to life.*

### 2. *Adult-Suggested Learning*

The traditional approach to teaching is that the adult leads, and the child follows. With the ABC, the child leads, and the adult supports, if required. The role is to offer guidance when the child needs it or to suggest ways to build on their interests. The adult provides suggestions, if, for example, a child does not know what they want to do. For example, a child may want to become a "YouTuber" but does not know how. As an adult, you can suggest online tutorials, creative tasks, or sign up for coding projects. With adult-suggested learning, you are in a supporting role, not a leading one, aligned with the principle that learners build their own knowledge through special interests and preferred choices.

### 3. *The Student in Control*

The final component of the ABC naturally occurs during the learning process, with the student taking control and directing all learning. As purposeful aims are developed and the adult settles into the role, the student will naturally begin to lead their learning. They will choose the activities and the pace at which they learn. They choose when to have a break and how to communicate their preferences.

When students have control over their learning, the impact can be significant. This is evident in real cases: one student, who was completely housebound and unable to participate in any education, is now learning to fly and has joined the Air Cadets. Another student, who couldn't access any learning, now leaves her house, participates in community groups, and confidently manages her own education. Other students who could barely leave the safety of their home are now studying nature photography, working toward diplomas, and developing impressive technical and creative skills behind the camera independently. These examples demonstrate that removing pressure, respecting autonomy, and allowing learning to happen naturally can lead to remarkable outcomes. More importantly, all these cases are of autistic children who had all the traditional support, had attended mainstream and specialist settings, all of which did not work for them. Acceptance-based support has been the one approach that has transformed their engagement and learning.

## Applying the Acceptance-Based Curriculum

I am now going to share a real-life experience of how we have applied the acceptance-based curriculum with children and young people we have supported, to give you a clearer idea of how to implement it effectively.

**Real-Life Experience 20**

We were asked to support two autistic twins, both aged 15, who were struggling to engage in their school and had not attended for over two years. They were unable to engage in learning at home with tutors and could only complete some work with their mother on their home computers. They also found it challenging to speak to people and would only talk to their mother briefly during their favourite TV shows. They both struggled with extreme anxiety and demand avoidance and would only leave their house to walk the family dog.

When we began supporting them, the staff were only allowed in the home because their dog accepted the adults, and as a result, the twins were OK with us being there. However, they did not speak or engage with anyone for the first few months, and all they could manage was to sit silently in their living room, staring at the wall.

Both twins needed to feel safe before any learning could take place. As I was the first supporting adult during the first few months, I took on the role of a consistent adult, sharing the rules of acceptance with them, and following the four foundations. Each week, I would relay the message that they did not have to do anything that made them anxious, that it was not their fault they were struggling, and that it would be OK, and together we would help them find a way.

There were no expectations, no demands, and no pressure to engage in any activities. All I did was show up consistently, and they would welcome me into their world, willingly, and they knew that there was no expectation to see me if they could not cope. Fortunately, the message they gave their mother was that they were OK with me visiting each week.

As the months went by, I gradually offered suggested activities and any interests they might want to pursue. At no time did I lead learning or expect them to follow a module or complete a worksheet. I bought books to read, and suggested watching their favourite shows, in the hope we could create something from there. I also offered to join their dog walks in the mornings. Nothing changed. They were just happy to sit there during my weekly visits until I left.

Until one session, I had decided to bring some camera equipment to explore, because their parents said they liked to spot different birds on their dog walk. I brought my bird-watching lens to show them, as this was a hobby of mine. We talked about all the different birds I have spotted over the years, and they seemed to like seeing some of my photos.

This interest in photography sparked an almost overnight interest. Their parents brought them some cameras with their own lenses, and they were off, walking and taking photos of as many birds as they could. They spent hours on tutorials outside our sessions, learning about bird photography. They began extending their walks to lakes, forests, and nature reserves.

This was a turning point for us. We had not given up on them, staying consistent for those first few months, believing that they would find their way, in their own time, which they did. Learning was now something *they* had chosen to do, and they started requesting that our staff take them out independently of their parents, which had never happened before. As their interest grew, we made sure they knew they were in control of their learning and that we would facilitate and support them however they needed. They took to this and we soon went from 20 minutes a week to full sessions going out most days exploring anywhere we could go to find the best places to photograph.

Their interest in bird photography led them to set up their own Instagram pages, enter competitions, and talk to staff daily. They would talk to us all, and even at home, they spoke to more family members. It was clear they were finding their safety and purpose in life again. They set out to find rare birds around the West Midlands, and we took them to places they had never been before. One highlight trip for us was setting off at 6:30 a.m. one morning to find a rare bird at Cannock Chase, a great grey shrike. We found the bird, and it was such an achievement for them. They were so proud of themselves.

This interest-led approach quickly inspired the twins to independently seek out community groups and volunteer at nearby nature reserves. Their photography and editing skills grew, and their talent and sharp eye for bird photography are outstanding. When they turned 18, we began discussing their plans, and the idea of pursuing a photography diploma emerged. Currently, at the time of writing, they are pursuing that path. None of this would have been possible without first finding and then following *their* interests. The acceptance-based curriculum provided a structured way to support their growth, emphasising safety, autonomy, and personal interest, all driven by the twins, with staff supporting all they do.

Recently, a moment that showed the impact of acceptance was when staff received a message from their mother with a photo of them sitting on a plane. Both smiling away, bursting with excitement. This was their first ever trip on a plane, as they headed for Sweden. With their camera bags packed, they were off on a trip of a lifetime. Something their parents thought would never happen.

This real-life experience demonstrates just one situation in which the acceptance-based curriculum has been effective in helping these students find purpose. By following the process, we were able to engage with two boys who had previously been housebound, unable to engage in any meaningful learning, and were without purpose. They now have a future ahead of them full of possibilities that finally feel like something they have created themselves, guided by their interests and by our unconditional acceptance.

## Summary

Although a newly developed model, the Acceptance-Based Curriculum is transformative, continuing to provide an alternative to the National Curriculum for autistic children and young people who struggle with traditional learning methods. I believe that this curriculum could be considered in schools and education settings as an alternative approach to supporting autistic children and young people. It centres on acceptance, interest-led learning, and autonomy, allowing students to learn at their own pace and in their own style. The curriculum, alongside the Accept Approach, encourages educators to explore learning alongside the child rather than impose it upon them, giving autistic children a sense of being understood, respected, and in control of their learning experience.

## Notes

1 Description of the Curriculum. https://www.gov.uk/government/consultations/education-inspection-framework-2019-inspecting-the-substance-of-education/education-inspection-framework-2019-inspecting-the-substance-of-education#:~:text=The%20curriculum%20is%20the%20substance,out%20of%20their%20educational%20experience
2 National Curriculum. https://www.gov.uk/national-curriculum
3 Yorke, A. (2023). Using an Acceptance-Based Curriculum to Support Autistic Students Who Have Not Engaged in the National Curriculum. *Good Autism Practice*, 24(2).

Chapter 20

# The SEED Plan

## Social Emotional Educational Development

Throughout the book, I have shared real-life experiences of autistic children and young people who do not fit the current education system. The Pyjama Kid, in Chapter 14, was one such example. The main issue for me was how to *show* that acceptance worked for him. Until we began supporting him, the focus had been only on managing his issues, rather than on understanding his personal experience and what he was *truly* going through, and on beginning support from there. The problem I found was that there were not many effective ways to record and document in real time what was happening, so I could return to the school and other professionals involved to show the realities this boy and his family faced.

In this chapter, I introduce the SEED Plan (Social Emotional Educational Development Plan).[1] This plan, which I created, is a way to record a child's journey more effectively when applying the Accept Approach[2] and the Acceptance-Based Curriculum.[3] The SEED Plan differs from conventional approaches to documenting progress and predicting outcomes. The idea of the SEED Plan is to capture a *realistic* picture of a child's experiences and to build appropriate support aligned with their values and interests, with the process beginning by addressing social and emotional barriers *before* supporting educational/learning aims.

## Why I Developed the SEED Plan

I always had issues with paperwork as a teacher. It never seemed relevant to the children I was supporting or to what I was trying to do, especially when recording the children's progress or predicting outcomes. Most of my teaching was in special schools, where I was always asked to *show* progress. The methods of recording were about showing that a child has gone from A to B, and how they can then move to C, which was fine for those who could do that, but not for the ones who were either never interested in *doing* the lesson content, or had completely different ways of learning that never matched the paperwork.

When developing the Accept Approach, I wanted to create a different way to record, one that placed the child at the forefront of everything while also

DOI: 10.4324/9781003686064-24

allowing me to apply acceptance to support them. I am fully aware that we need to record a child's education journey and to effectively record what we are doing to show how they are doing. However, throughout my years as a teacher and then as a local authority autism advisor, I was never satisfied with the paperwork we were required to complete. For me, it was never tailored to individual children or their specific needs. Instead, it focused solely on setting targets and tracking progress.

Take, for example, the idea of SMART targets. They are everywhere, within education systems to measure children's progress and in health systems to improve mental health.[4] Standing for *specific, measurable, assignable, realistic,* and *time-related*, SMART targets for me have one major flaw: they were *not* developed for autistic children; George T. Doran created them as a method for writing practical management goals.[5]

Let me explain further: when using a SMART target with an autistic child, it presumes they can meet a specific set of targets or outcomes that can be easily measured in a time-bound way. For example, expecting an autistic child to engage in an activity for 15 minutes, three times a week, can only work if the child is emotionally stable and consistent enough to do so. Some may, however, many children and young people I have supported often fall short in achieving targets set in this way.

SMART targets also assume an autistic child can cope with anxiety at the exact moment the target expects them to; for example, Child A will stay in the classroom for 30 minutes, and engage in an activity they have not chosen for 10 minutes, or Child B will use two strategies to cope with their feelings of anxiety before having a time-out. I do not see that SMART targets are effective for autistic children and young people, especially if they do not feel safe or are struggling to engage due to high levels of anxiety. In my opinion, SMART targets can fail autistic children if they are not emotionally able to do what is expected of them.

The key difference with the SEED Plan is that it is not designed to record achievements or track progress toward predetermined targets; its focus is on three key elements: (a) developing purposeful aims for the specific areas of support, (b) applying the Four Foundations of Acceptance to support the aims, and then (c) reviewing the support, through a RAG (red, amber, green) rating system taken from the summaries of written *session notes*. Before we discuss this process in more detail, I want to discuss the reasoning behind the areas of support.

## Areas of Support

The areas of support are focused on what is essential to the child and young person on their learning journey, and within each area is where you write *the purposeful aims* to guide them through their learning. There are four areas of focus: the social focus, the emotional focus, the educational focus, and the development focus, which we will now discuss.

### 1. *Social Focus*

This focus supports the child's social engagement during learning. The aim here is to respect the child's *natural* way of communicating. You are not looking to write a purposeful aim on how to improve their social skills or to identify any deficits. The key here is to identify *their* preferences, not what we think we should focus on. We are identifying how the child wants to learn through a social lens. For example, they may prefer to learn alone, away from other children, or to play a game before doing their work. They may want to talk first or not talk at all. Our role here is to record a purposeful aim that matches the child's social preferences.

Here are some examples of purposeful aims with a social focus.

*Child A prefers to learn without other children present. Sessions will remain one-to-one, with no expectation of peer interaction.*

*Child B appears cautious at the start of our sessions. Time will be prioritised for informal connection with the adult before any learning begins, allowing trust to develop naturally.*

*Child C prefers less verbal interaction during learning. Support will be offered with no expectation to talk, allowing the child to engage in their own preferred way.*

### 2. *Emotional Focus*

This is where you focus on writing purposeful aims that centre on children's emotional responses to learning, helping them feel safe and engaged in the process. You are not looking to change emotions; instead, the aim is to support them in accepting and acknowledging how they feel. For example, you may recognise that a young person is too anxious to begin sessions early, so you schedule the learning for later in the day. You may notice that when a child is engaged in a session, they get frustrated. The aim here is to help them accept that it's OK to feel anxiety and stress, by responding with positive unconditional positive regard. With the emotional focus, it is crucial to recognise that the purposeful aims written here are based on acceptance rather than on building resilience or learning to cope. When a child feels emotionally safe, learning will happen more effectively.

Here are some examples of purposeful aims with an emotional focus.

*Child A finds early mornings emotionally overwhelming. I will acknowledge this is totally OK, and sessions will begin after 10:30 a.m. to support emotional regulation and readiness.*

*Child B sometimes feels frustrated when tasks feel difficult. Unconditional positive regard will be offered, as we accept the feelings of frustration, without challenging, instead reassuring that this is totally fine and we can pause or adapt as needed.*

*Child C prefers to know there is no pressure to complete a task if they can't. Sessions will be guided by their feelings of emotional safety, by working at their pace.*

### 3. *Educational Focus*

This focus is where we write purposeful aims around what the child or young person wants to learn. We are looking to identify their interests and build learning around them. This may entail a mix of traditional subjects alongside gaming, drawing, or other interests. This could include fixing a bike, talking about their favourite animals, or solving maths problems. The aim here is to focus on what *they* want to do, not what *we* think they should be learning. This is where the Acceptance-Based Curriculum is at the core of all we do, where we follow their preferences for how they want to learn and what they want to learn.

Here are some examples of purposeful aims with an education focus.

*Child A has a special interest in Minecraft. Learning will be centred around building, planning, and problem-solving within Minecraft, following their lead.*

*Child B enjoys drawing on paper and the iPad. Educational engagement will focus on art-based activities chosen by them, with no requirement to link to core subjects unless the child chooses to.*

*Child C has shown curiosity about numbers through playing problem-solving games. Mathematical learning will be explored when initiated by the child and embedded within preferred activities.*

> **Reflection**
>
> The idea of the SEED Plan, and writing purposeful aims, is not about creating outcomes. You are not setting objectives for what must be achieved. You are observing, responding, and following the child's lead as their learning *unfolds*. Over time, you will see that purposeful aims build a clearer picture of a child's learning journey.

### 4. *Development Focus*

The final focus area is allowing the child or young person to write or say how they are feeling about the sessions. It is also a place for adults to comment on how they feel things are going and if there is anything we can adapt or change. Often, here the parents will comment on how they have noticed differences in their children away from the sessions. They report feeling less anxious, eager to start the session, and excited for the teacher to arrive. Sometimes, a parent may write that their child is worried about the session before it begins, so we can prepare to support them when we arrive.

It may also be that you input feedback from emails or conversations you have had with the child or their parents. All you do is record, in general, what was said in the development box, e.g. Child A said he *really enjoyed today's session!*

## Developing Purposeful Aims

Purposeful aims, as discussed in the previous chapter, are what we use instead of predicted outcomes. These are created with the child during informal conversations during sessions. The idea is for the child to lead in choosing what they want to do.

I use the term *aims* here because it moves you away from the more traditional process of writing predicted *outcomes*. As discussed, I am critical of writing outcomes, as I do not believe they work effectively for many of the young people I have supported over the years. I have come to see that there is so much more benefit in recording a child's learning journey and documenting its progress rather than predicting it.

## Applying the Four Foundations of Acceptance

As discussed in detail in Chapters 14–18, these foundations are the fundamental approaches that underpin the acceptance-based support process. *Remove* what makes a child anxious, *remind* them it is not their fault, *reassure* them that it is going to be OK, and *reaffirm* you accept them unconditionally.

## Review of Support

The idea of using a RAG rating system is to keep the recording process as simple as possible. In the **session notes**, as the adult supporting, you would write a summary of what happens during each session. The focus here is to be as open and honest as possible, then revisit the notes and read through them, looking for any patterns within the text. You then take these and RAG rate them, placing them in the review section of the plan.

The RAG rating system here stands for:

Red – Not able to do it
Amber – Almost there
Green – Acceptance achieved

## An Example of the SEED Plan

We will look at an example of how to do this by comparing sessions 1, 2, and 4 of the Pyjama Kids SEED Plan. His real-life experience can be found Chapter 14.

### Session 1 Notes

**He was anxious at first and refused to come downstairs as he thought I was going to tell him to go to school**. Instead, I spoke in length to the parents, and we created a plan of action, and I discussed a way forward focusing on the foundations. I called up to him on my way out and told him it's OK. I am on his side, and he doesn't have to go to school if he does not want to.

*The section highlighted would be RAG rated as red; he was too anxious (not able to do it yet).*

### Session 2

**He came downstairs to talk with me. We talked about things and he told me how he was feeling**. I focused on telling him he does not have to go back to school and that it is not his fault that he is finding things difficult. We talked about his favourite things and discussed superheroes in great detail. Good session: he was happy to know he was the boss. He really embraced this strategy.

*We can see how he responded to session 1. I RAG rate this as amber (almost there).*

### Session 4

He was talking about school and what makes him happy. His mum told me he has even expressed an interest in **going to school during dinner times to see his friends**. Amazing turnaround. His anxiety is less and he wants to try to go back to school. Mum said he is saying it's fine because *he is the boss and knows he does not have to go if he does not want to.* Here we can see he is requesting to go back to school, to see his friends, which was an amazing turnaround from not being able to leave his house to go to school.

*This would be RAG rated as green (acceptance achieved).*

As we can see in these session notes, the young person began by being too anxious to come to the session, then responded with a message of acceptance, and was able to sit with me during the sessions, which led him to want to go back to school to see his friends.

When reading his real-life experience, you can see the journey he was on from being completely in distress, not able to engage in any learning, to then going back to school and eventually finding the right setting for him, where he returned full-time with no more anxiety. This was due to his positive response to the Accept Approach, which I was able to record effectively step by step in his SEED Plan. *The following is a version of one of his SEED Plans for you to read through in more detail.*

## Summary

The SEED Plan sits at the heart of the Aceept approach, giving you a clear picture of what is really happening for the child or young person during the support process. It consolidates social, emotional, educational, and developmental insights into a single, evolving document that captures the child/young person's journey.

Instead of focusing solely on outcomes or targets, the SEED Plan helps you observe how they respond in *real time*. It reveals how the child reacts when pressure is eased and acceptance is shown. This understanding enables you to tailor support intentionally, rather than based on assumptions. The SEED Plan doesn't prescribe who the child should become; it reveals who they already are and how they learn best when they feel truly understood.

This document can be used by parents, teachers, and mental health practitioners at anytime, anywhere. It is designed to be easy, less word-focused, and more child-focused, moving us away from predicted outcomes toward real-life experiences that document successes and achievements as they happen.

### SEED Plan Example

| 1. Areas of Support | 2. The Four Foundations of Acceptance | 3. Review of Support |
|---|---|---|
| *To achieve the aim identified within the EHCP, we identify FOUR areas of need where issues exist and agree on what we will be supporting.* | *How We Will Support*<br>*We apply acceptance-based approaches to support the identified areas of need by implementing the four foundations taken from the Accept Approach (Yorke, 2021). These are the key areas we use to engage with the learner.* | *We use the RAG rating to assess the purposeful aims of measuring the impact of the Four Foundations of Acceptance alongside EHCP targets.* |

*(Continued)*

(Continued)

| | | |
|---|---|---|
| SOCIAL<br>Struggling with school and is anxious about going. Choosing to stay at home. Not wanting to get dressed. Staying in pyjamas all day and night. Spending most of his day in his room on his gaming. Has not engaged with professionals and is refusing to speak with me.<br><br>EMOTIONAL<br>He is very anxious at the moment, and we need to focus on raising his self-value and helping him to feel worthy again.<br>EDUCATIONAL<br>Leave this until he is ready to talk about school. No pressure.<br>Follow his lead. | REMOVE<br>I have advised Mum and Dad that we need to take away the pressure of him thinking he must go to school. For the next few weeks, we are going to tell him that he does not have to go to school if he doesn't want to. School will stop calling and parents will ring to keep them informed of how things are going. I will visit one session per week and inform school of sessions.<br><br>REMIND<br>During our sessions we will talk about autism and what it is. I will remind him that it is not his fault if he does not want to go to school. I told him he cannot help how he feels and I want to help him find out why he is anxious. *Also remind him he is the boss of the sessions, and we will only do what he wants to do.*<br><br>REASSURE<br>Self-esteem is low so all activities will be focused on raising his self-esteem. Reassure him it is going to be OK. We will find a way to help him feel less anxious. I suggested he wear his pyjamas all day and to not get dressed if he does not want to. It is OK. | **Session 1**<br>He was anxious at first and refused to come downstairs as he thought I was going to tell him to go to school. Instead, I spoke in length to the parents, and we created a plan of action, and I discussed a way forward focusing on the foundations. I called up on my way out and told him it's OK. I am on his side, and he doesn't have to go to school if he does not want to.<br><br>**Session 2**<br>He came downstairs to talk with me! We talked about things and he told me how he was feeling. I focused on telling him he does not have to go back to school and that it is not his fault that he is finding things difficult. We talked about his favourite things and discussed superheroes in great detail. Good session – he was happy to know he was the boss. He really embraced this strategy.<br><br>**Session 3**<br>Mum told me he was talking a lot about being the boss and making the decisions. He was calmer and less anxious. We had another low demand session. No mention of school and the conversation was all on his terms and we only spoke about things he was interested in. Good session. I feel he is less anxious than in session 1. |

*(Continued)*

*(Continued)*

| | | |
|---|---|---|
| | REAFFIRM<br>Show him that we are on his side and will go with what he wants to do. We will focus and adapt sessions to support what he wants to do.<br><br>ACTIVITIES<br>Low demand, motivated by what he wants to do. Eg talking about superheroes, creating Lego, walking around in the garden, watching him play a game. | **Session 4**<br>He was talking about school and what makes him Mum told me he has even expressed an interest in going to school during dinner times to see his friends. Amazing turn around! His anxiety is less and he wants to try to go back to school. Mum said he is saying it's fine because he is the boss, and he does not have to go if he does not want to.<br><br>**Session 5**<br>First session in school for dinner. He was quiet, but happy and smiling again. First discussion about a different placement with parents, as a consideration for the next steps. Continue with sessions. |
| DEVELOPMENT<br>Conversations with Mum and Dad on a weekly basis. Feedback how he feels about the sessions and if he is responding positively to them | "He is responding really well, and was even smiling the other day, which we have not seen in a while", Mother commented.<br>"He really likes the idea of knowing he is the boss! It is helping him to take control of his day", Mother commented. | |

*The Pyjama Kid SEED Plan Example*[6]

## Notes

1 Yorke, A. (2021). A Case Study of Two Autistic Children Supported by the ACCEPT Approach: A New Acceptance-Based Strategy. *Good Autism Practice*, 22(2), pp. 58–72.

2 Yorke, A. (2021). A Case Study of Two Autistic Children Supported by the ACCEPT Approach: A New Acceptance-Based Strategy. *Good Autism Practice*, 22(2), pp. 58–72.

3 Yorke, A. (2021). A Case Study of Two Autistic Children Supported by the ACCEPT Approach: A New Acceptance-Based Strategy. *Good Autism Practice*, 22(2), pp. 58–72.

4 https://www.psychiatrycentre.co.uk/blog/goal-setting-a-practical-way-to-improve-your-mental-health/
5 Doran, G.T. (1981). There's a S.M.A.R.T. Way to Write Management's Goals and Objectives. *Management Review*, 70(11), pp. 35–36.
6 Yorke, A. (2021). A Case Study of Two Autistic Children Supported by the ACCEPT Approach: A New Acceptance-Based Strategy. *Good Autism Practice*, 22(2), pp. 58–72.

Chapter 21

# Without Conditions

What would happen if a group of autistic children who had previously struggled to fit into traditional education settings were introduced to a new learning environment where they were free to learn whatever they wanted, could arrive and leave whenever they wished, and would be completely accepted by the adults supporting them, who, instead of instructing, would follow the children's interests and develop learning based on their ideas *without conditions*. This chapter explores such a group of children who were invited to attend *the Accepting Behaviour Learning Centre*, a place grounded in the humanistic principles of psychological safety, unconditional positive regard, self-acceptance, and interest-led learning.

From the moment a child enters an educational setting, whether mainstream or specialist, they are subjected to conditions in the form of *expectations*. For example, children are expected to arrive on time, be school-ready, follow rules, participate in lessons, and engage with predetermined core curriculum content such as maths, English, and science. They are told when to have a break, when they can eat, when they can rest, and when they must ask permission to leave their seats, have a drink, or use the toilet. In traditional educational settings, expectations are rooted in one ultimate condition: *the adults lead, and the children follow.*

What would happen if the roles were reversed: *the children lead, and the adults follow*? How would an autistic child with demand avoidance and high levels of anxiety respond if conditions were *completely* removed and replaced with the freedom to learn, without demands or expectations, in an environment where they could learn what they want, in any way they chose to? The Accepting Behaviour Learning Centre was designed to do just that. To offer something new and fundamentally different, grounded in acceptance-based support, following the Accept Approach[1] and the Acceptance-Based Curriculum.[2]

## The Accepting Behaviour Learning Centre

The idea for the setting was born in response to the consistent failure of traditional education settings to support a specific group of autistic children and young people. As demand for our acceptance-based support grew, we decided to set up the centre alongside the home education support we were providing for local authorities within

DOI: 10.4324/9781003686064-25

the West Midlands. Based in Worcestershire, the Centre was set up to help children and young people access more learning opportunities within the community. All children involved required an education, health, and care plan due to their complex autism needs, which included additional needs such as anxiety and demand-avoidance.

Initially, we operated on a part-time schedule with open morning and afternoon sessions, tailoring activities to each child's needs. Some children also attended with parents, which was fully supported, with pickup and drop-off arrangements set up for the more independent children. We scheduled one-to-one time for vulnerable children who preferred solitude, and for other children who enjoyed more spontaneous, lively interactions, we organised small group activities, where they could be free to learn, whether that was trying their hand at cooking their favourite food, conduct science experiments, art, going for a walk, reading a book, learning an instrument, and so much more.

### *Creating a Psychologically Safe Space*

All staff involved at the centre were aware that the children attending needed to first feel psychologically safe *before* any learning could occur. To achieve this, all staff were trained in acceptance-based support, specifically in humanistic principles, holding onto the notion that all *children need to feel safe before engaging in any kind of learning.*

The idea of psychological safety in the context of the centre was to ensure that whenever a child walked through the door, they knew the adults greeting them unconditionally accepted them and were there to support whatever they wanted to do during the session.

The centre comprised three main rooms: a small room, a large kitchen, and a large hall. In the small room, we set up sensory games, bean bags, and cushions. The large hall was set up with a mix of tables with activities, such as building blocks, books to read, instruments to play, and art and crafts. The kitchen was set up for cooking, so we would ask the children the week before what they would like to make and provide the ingredients. The centre was also surrounded by fields and a playground where other children could go with support to explore the countryside, do some bird watching, take some photographs, or try the obstacle course built into the playground.

#### Reflection

Whatever a child needed to feel safe, that was what we did. If they needed their parents by their side, then their parents attended. If a child could only engage at a certain time of the day, then that was when their sessions began. If they wanted to talk, or sit and be quiet, then we did that. If they chose to not do any learning on a particular day, and instead have a hot chocolate, that's what we did. There were no conditions placed on them, *all learning* was led by the child or young person.

### *Following Their Interests*

All staff knew to follow interest-led learning, much the same as we do during home sessions, beginning with the child's interests as the starting point for learning. For example, an autistic child, can have a passion for anything, gaming, dinosaurs, graphic design, gardening, knitting, walking, reading, history, or numbers; the list is endless, and this is where interest-led learning can thrive: *you tap into the child's interests*, without the barrier of anxiety, demands, or expectations being place on them to learn something they are not interested in.

Interest-led learning encourages children's confidence and fosters their autonomy. It can also spark ideas that can be very ambitious, which we encourage. One young person, having been assured he was the boss of his learning, suddenly announced during one session that he would like to drive to Scotland. He said to me, "*If I am the boss, I want to go now to Scotland for the day and visit the Highlands!*" This raises an important question about acceptance: if a child expresses a wish, are we always obliged to fulfil it? Here we learn that with acceptance and following the child's lead, we will never be able to provide everything, but we can come very close, using impossible requests to create other opportunities to explore their imagination.

Regarding the request to travel to Scotland, I mentioned it would be nice but explained we couldn't manage the trip there and back in time. I then proposed choosing an alternative location that they enjoy. He selected the skate park, which he was more than happy with. Ultimately, the key factor of interest-led learning is that the child is the one who, even after some discussion, decides what we do during our session, which is the most important message.

## Examples From Practice

Although still in the early stages, the learning centre is now set up and is running well. We are learning as we go along and dealing with issues as they arise. I will now share some experiences that have stood out to us in our review of the centre's impact and how children have responded. It is important to note that I am not trying to claim any outcomes here or to evaluate their effects; I am merely describing what happened through practical observations, based on both staff and parent feedback, and reflecting on early-stage engagement, which does not represent a formal evaluation of the centre.

At the time of setting up the centre, we were supporting 48 children and young people, of whom 15 had expressed interest in attending. We had nine at primary school age, three at secondary school age, and three at post-16 age. They all arrived at different times, with flexible attendance. Engagement was completely on their terms, and we followed their interests as much as we possibly could. Here are some of their experiences.

**Real-Life Experience 21**

We were supporting a 7-year-old autistic boy whose experiences in a specialist school setting had become too much for him to cope with, and he could no longer attend. He was even having regular nightmares about school, and when we began our support, we were explicitly told not by his mother to avoid using the word "school" because it caused him extreme distress.

Our early sessions focused entirely on relationship building and safety, guided by the Four Foundations of Acceptance. We sometimes went for short walks to his favourite shop, sat in his living room, and talked about games and YouTube channels. During the first few sessions, we noticed he responded positively to the Two Rules of Learning, particularly the idea that he was the boss. His mother later said that was the turning point for him. Those simple words, "You are the boss", helped him feel safe and in control, which I am confident led him to want to come and visit the centre. While there was no obligation for him to attend, everyone understood that if he did, it would be a huge milestone for him, as this would be his first time stepping into an educational setting in nearly two years.

He did manage to make his first visit; however, he chose to stay in the car and asked if I could come and sit with him, which I did. I reminded him of the rules, that he was in control and didn't have to do anything he wasn't comfortable with. Eventually, he decided to come in briefly, get a drink, and return to the safety of the car. He stayed for an hour and then left. The important thing we all noticed was that he remained calm and said he wanted to return for another session, which he did. This time, stepping out of the car and spending more time in the centre. Within just a few weeks, he was engaging well, making friends, and choosing his own learning activities.

The feedback was that he loved the centre. His mother would tell us that when he is not there, he asks when his next session is and how many days are left before he can go again. He never missed a session. Some days, he hesitated. Other days, he ran straight in. What made engagement possible was not pressure or structure, but knowing he has the control. The centre became a place he wanted to attend, without being told he had to. For a child who had previously been unable to tolerate the idea of school, attending the centre and being happy to engage in learning again has been transformative, not just for him but also for his mother.

**Real-Life Experience 22**

The moment Harold the Duck waddled into our centre, I knew we were making a positive impact on the children and young people we were supporting. You see, Harold was no *ordinary* duck; he had been rescued from the fate of the local farm shop, only to be saved by the inquisitory mind of Milly an autistic teenager who had an idea: "*If I brought a duck egg and put it into an incubator, would it hatch?*" After 28 days of care and attention, she got her answer, as something started to move inside the incubator. Her experiment had been a complete success, and suddenly, Harold emerged into the world, instantly imprinting himself on Milly and becoming her best friend.

Just seeing the young person in the group was enough for us, because the staff who had been supporting her in the home had known for many months how difficult it was for her to leave her house. Previously, she had been very anxious and struggled to engage in any kind of learning. Most of her sessions had to be in the home and could only happen in the afternoons due to her unsettled sleep pattern.

Prior to our support, nothing had worked in the education setting she had been in. She just could not engage and never felt safe in the school. Her mother told us that when she did manage to attend for a few hours, she would hide under the stairs, frozen with anxiety, unable to access any kind of learning or engagement. Initially, when she started support with us, she was reluctant to have anyone in her house. However, after a few sessions, she began to respond well to the staff and engage with us. Sometimes, just showing her face around the door at first, until engagement slowly started to increase.

One of the turning points for Milly was accepting us, and knowing that we would follow her interests, and never try to get her to do anything she didn't want to do in her sessions. Everything was led by Milly, and over time, she began to embrace this newfound way of learning. I also think she accepted us because we accepted Harold.

When we invited Milly to the centre, we were unsure whether she would be able to attend. She had begun attending some community clubs in the evening and was beginning to feel safe enough with us to walk to the shops with a member of staff, and of course with Harold in his pram. To our surprise, one morning we received a message from her mother saying she would like to come and visit, on one condition: that she bring Harold. Of course, we accepted.

When Harold the duck entered the hall, we were witnessing first-hand the transformative power of acceptance, a young person choosing to engage on their terms, knowing that both in the home and the centre she is unconditionally accepted, and so was Harold. Her mother was in complete shock because this had never happened before. This was the first time in years that Milly had been able to engage in any kind of educational learning outside of her home. Here is some feedback her mother shared with us.

> *She didn't leave the house to engage in anything social. Since the demands and expectations have been taken away, she now wants to do certain things. If she had been made to, it would have resulted in a meltdown or a step backwards, halting any progress. I don't know where we would be if this support hadn't been an option.*

## Summary

Although at the time of writing, the centre is in its early days, and if it grows, we will have to consider moving to different premises. What we have seen so far is that children are happy to attend, and parents report that they want to come and that they have seen their children happier and less anxious. Although some children attend in brief moments, and some attend for the whole session, this was expected and accepted. Some children have happily left their parents, while others still need them by their side. This, too, was expected and accepted.

What we have been able to develop within the centre, alongside home support, is what I discussed in Chapter 6, showing that square pegs need square holes. These children *do not* need to be made to fit into the education models and systems that don't work for them. They *do not* need reasonable adjustments to fit in either. What they need are *new* ways of learning. Acceptance-based support is one such model that shows promise as an effective approach for children and young people who have not been able to engage in traditional education. For these children, acceptance seems to work, and, without conditions, we have noticed that they engage so much more with learning.

Here is some feedback from the parent evaluations of children attending our sessions.[3]

> *Our child was unable to engage in anything they deemed educational or "school-type" work. Giving our child autonomy has enabled him to re-engage with education at his own pace, his choice of themes, and no pressure.*
>
> *They are like a different person. I wouldn't have anticipated their life would change so much for the better three years ago.*
>
> *My child now feels people understand and has stopped blaming herself. It is a long road to recovery but there has definitely been progress and she feels understood.*
>
> *Seeing definite improvement in the want and willingness to engage and spend time with others, even in situations where previously she wouldn't have even entertained it.*
>
> *This support has changed our lives.*

The Accepting Behaviour Learning Centre is the start of something *new*. It shows what can happen when children learn *without conditions:* engagement happens. Without conditions, these children do more. They want to show up. So what does this mean for our understanding of education? Could it be that we have got it completely wrong for these children? Do these children need complete control of their learning, embraced by unconditional acceptance, removed completely from conditions and expectations? I believe they do.

## Notes

1 Yorke, A. (2021). A Case Study of Two Autistic Children Supported by the Accept Approach: A New Acceptance-Based Strategy. *Good Autism Practice*, 22(2).

2 Yorke, A. (2023). Using an Acceptance Based Curriculum to Support Autistic Students Who Have Not Engaged in the National Curriculum. *Good Autism Practice*, 24(2), pp. 45, 54.

3 Parental feedback referenced in this book is drawn from anonymised termly and yearly evaluations collected via SurveyMonkey. Forty-two parents completed the forms. Participation is voluntary, and surveys are configured so that no identifying information or email addresses are visible to us, allowing parents to share honest feedback about what is working, what is not, and how support could be improved.

** The responses provide an overview of parental perceptions of their child's well-being, engagement, and progress within acceptance-based support and are used to inform practice, improve provision, and contribute anonymised evidence to training and publications. In some cases, to further protect children's identities, names, ages, and genders have been changed without altering the substance or meaning of the feedback shared.

Chapter 22

# Developing the Accept Approach

As we approach the end of the book, I want to discuss the ongoing development of the models mentioned in Part Three. The Accept Approach and Acceptance-Based Curriculum were never designed to be complete or fixed models, but rather as evolving frameworks developed in response to the ever-growing demand for this kind of support. The autistic children and young people for whom these frameworks were developed are the ones who have not been able to engage with traditional educational provision, needing something new, something different, and the type of support that is always developing and growing alongside them.

It is my hope that this book, grounded in real-life experiences and reflective practice, will contribute to the advancement of autism support by offering new approaches rooted in humanistic principles and acceptance. By sharing real-life experiences and the impact of the support through qualitative methods, I aim to position the Accept Approach and the Acceptance-Based Curriculum as effective frameworks for autistic children and young people who have not been adequately supported by existing models.

## Qualitative Feedback

As I continue to develop the models, it is important for me to receive regular feedback from those most involved in the support. This includes the children and young people, professionals delivering the sessions, and parents. To gather feedback, we send out regular surveys to staff and also have training sessions and ongoing conversations. We also hold parent groups throughout the year and send out anonymous surveys, giving people the chance to share how they feel and comment honestly. We also run regular webinars where people ask questions and can engage during the session. I have received regular feedback from parents, families, educators, and professionals across the UK who also share their independent experiences of applying the models.

What stands out in the feedback so far is that children respond positively to the Four Foundations of Acceptance, with *remove* and *remind* as the most effective. The *reassure* foundation has also been shown to help teenagers who feel they are missing out or comparing themselves to peers. Lastly, the *reaffirm* foundation is

DOI: 10.4324/9781003686064-26

shared as a whole, something parents say is effective through sessions and staff engagement. Here are some parent feedback responses from surveys and evaluations.[1]

> *For our daughter to be heard and for her to be treated with respect was a game-changer for her. She has been supported and has received regular reminders* ***that things are not her fault, which has been important for her to know****. Anxiety is difficult to combat, but by removing pressures around schooling and going out shopping, etc.,* ***we have managed to alleviate the levels of her anxiety****. She now knows why she presents how she is. Her diagnosis has answered a lot of questions she had herself.* ***Reaffirmation that she is unconditionally accepted and knowledge that she will be supported has given our child confidence in her abilities****.*
>
> ***The Accept Approach has worked so well****. He has never looked forward to a teacher coming as he does now. Every session is positive. He loves engaging with his tutor.*
>
> *He has now learnt more about his autism and knows that* ***it is not always his fault*** *and that people will be there for him no matter what.*
>
> ***Removing the anxiety*** *takes away the fear of trying new things when she feels the safety and autonomy that this approach brings.*
>
> *When he has needed to end his sessions, which he does by walking away or by telling me, the tutor* ***has not drawn attention to this, which has helped him feel comfortable****. In the past, his way has not been understood or listened to, meaning he would be pushed beyond his capacity.*
>
> *Absolutely everything the team do with my son ensures that the four foundations are utilised to their fullest.* ***This has such an impact on my son's mental health and well-being, and is giving him confidence to be himself****.*
>
> ***Reassuring my son*** *that he can choose when sessions end. This helps a lot to reduce his anxiety.*
>
> ***Removing the pressure to come downstairs to see the tutors is huge****. She knows when they are there and knows if she can't come down, then that is OK, and everyone is accepting and understands* ***it's not her fault****. The removal of that pressure has enabled her to come down when she can.*

Here is some feedback received from specialist tutors, who are applying the principles firsthand and how they are seeing the impact of support for the children and young people they are working with. This is a survey our staff complete anonymously, which allows them to give honest and authentic feedback.

> *The accept approach is benefitting my students because they reassured that they are enough and that they can be authentically themselves. This helps them gain confidence, which in turn improves engagement. Students report feeling more regulated because they're not being forced to engage in things that do not interest them or mask to fit into an environment not beneficial to them. Building a relationship of trust through acceptance, has helped my students feel safe with me, also improving engagement.*

*The accept approach is hugely beneficial. R is becoming really confident in talking to me and the sense of ownership allows him to engage in our activities fully. Students at the group are really enjoying engaging in science activities, having 1:1 support helps keep them safe and helps with regulation but the group setting allows for collaboration with other students in a low-demand way.*

*Students that have not been able to engage in any other school or alternative provision are engaging well in sessions. Students feel heard and respected which means they want to participate.*

*All of the students I see have gained a sense of safety – they know that we will show up for them no matter what each week and understand that they are in control and can decide what we do. The students have opened up about things that worry them because they know that they are in a safe space. Two students have recently suggested going out together, despite have anxieties about leaving the house. Engagement levels have generally increased within just a few visits to all of my students and they all seem more confident now.*

*I'm grateful to be part of such an amazing team. Staff are very supportive of each other and are always happy to offer advice/share ideas. I've learnt so much in the past year and the job is really rewarding. Families are also very appreciative and value the Accept approach.*

*Just that I'm more convinced than ever that the approach has improved the lives of many students and their families, and it's a joy to see this first hand.*

We also gather ongoing feedback from our students, whenever we can, which, in itself, is a challenge because they often find it difficult to express how they feel, and there is never any pressure for them to give us feedback. We often go by the fact that they are turning up to sessions and are visibly relaxed, not anxious or stressed, as evidence that the provision is working. As one young person told me when asked for some feedback, *If I didn't like the sessions, I wouldn't be here!* However, brief and to the point, here are some responses from students who were asked the question: *Can we improve the sessions in any way?*

*More volcanoes and marshmallows.*

*You are doing a great job!*

*You can be yourself, and I feel accepted and embraced just for being me. You incorporate my interests into learning, which helps it to make sense, and so I want to learn more.*

*I'm happy with how my teacher runs the sessions.*

*I like to choose what to do, and it reduces my anxiety being in control.*

*No.*

We have found through the feedback that although many children and young people like to have control over everything they do, some will initially struggle to know how to begin this process. For example, some children are still stuck in the idea that they have to apply themselves or learn subjects they don't want to. It can take time for these children to accept that they can choose to learn freely. Once they do, these issues fade away. Here are some views we received that helped us develop the support for children in finding what they would like to learn through *adult suggestions.*

> ***My child does not know what they want to learn****. They can't deal with choices, but also struggle to suggest things, so learning has not really happened yet. However, she is still in burnout, so not yet ready to learn.*
>
> ***Even though she has the choice of learning and is the boss, at the moment I'm finding she isn't suggesting anything that is educational as such****, but even so seen massive improvement in her willingness and wants to engage with others, leave the house more, etc., so am very happy.*

This type of feedback is invaluable to us as a team because we can work directly with the parents behind the scenes to explore ways to support these children, to find out what they would like to learn. Sometimes this is a longer process, and other times immediate, much like this young person, who needs to be in total control in order to engage in learning:

> *He likes* ***to have full control****. If he picked something to do that was not within safety limits, he would not take this well.*

I am aware that there must be an ongoing process of critical examination of these models. This is especially important where a child, for example, may not initially let staff into their house, or will let them in but not come out of their room. The first step in these situations is to be a *consistent adult* and to continue offering support. The idea of being a consistent adult is to keep showing up, in the hope that a child will eventually, in their time, begin to engage. Where this often works well as they begin to develop trust in us, I have had some occasions when a young person has not wanted to engage at all. No matter how many times support was offered. Here are some examples of this and how we responded.

**Real-Life Experience 23**

One example of this was a young person who had said "no" to any support from the start, but his parents and school still wanted to try. He was at a post-16 college but had never shown interest in learning and had only attended for a couple of days during the two years he had been on their roll. The college commissioned us to help because nothing was working, and he just kept repeating the same message: whenever anyone tried to help, "*I do not want an education*".

I was commissioned to offer support for six weeks. Each session, I would arrive and sit with his parents to talk about how the week had been and offer any advice and guidance. Their son was not interested in anything other than gaming and occasionally spending time downstairs watching TV with his family. Generally, he was happy and had no mental health issues, apart from whenever the pressure for him to attend college or to engage in any kind of provision.

I never did see this young person. The acceptance-based support helped the family somewhat to accept their young person for who they were. Ultimately, however, the young person kept repeating the same message: *they did not want to pursue education.* As they were almost 18, my advice was to remove what was causing the anxiety, which in this instance was the pressure to engage with college and us. Although difficult for me personally, I had to step back and realise that all along this young person had been saying what they wanted: no education of any kind. The approach, therefore, was to *value* their decision and to *listen* to them. Sadly, the funding ended, so I was not able to see whether the person would have changed their mind later.

In cases like this, which do occur, listening completely and unconditionally to the young person is what is needed. Even if they say no to support, that needs to be respected and acted upon because that is what they are saying. The most important thing is not to add any stress or pressure to these young people, especially when it comes from others who want them to learn, but they don't. My advice in these instances is to always follow the young person's voice, even if it is not what people want to hear.

**Real-Life Experience 24**

Another difficult situation occurred when we were supporting a young adult in her early 20s. Acceptance was something she had struggled with; there were moments she embraced the idea of accepting herself, then other times her mental health issues would often make sessions too hard to cope with. There were times when she slept through the day and stayed awake all night, which affected her ability to engage in our sessions. As we could not offer evening support, our focus shifted to helping her parents and to sharing ideas and guidance during those times.

Another issue we came up against was that funding from her local authority was sometimes delayed, and at other times we were only allowed to provide support for a few hours a week. We were working with what was possible, but this proved difficult for us to maintain consistency, as we could not offer support without funding in place. It was particularly challenging for staff, especially when, after being housebound for over two years, she finally felt safe enough to go out with a member of staff and spend time in the community, only for the provision to stop for several months until we could secure further funding. This happened a few times, and it was difficult to keep starting again.

There were also times when she was very low and needed a lot of mental health support, because she could only manage being in her room or the living room. Answering the door and speaking on the phone were also impossible things for her, even receiving parcels she had ordered. She was also not able to visit the doctors, and a lot of support was not possible because she couldn't leave her house.

Then we would see moments when she really engaged with acceptance, and her mother said she would answer the door, and even spoke to her doctor on the phone, went to the dentist, visited her family, and spent time at their house, which she could not do before. These moments, although not education-based, were far more important to her.

Sadly, the time came when her EHCP was ceased, and funding was cut. This was difficult for us all as a team because we could no longer continue supporting her. Her mother applies the Accept Approach as much as she can, but she still struggles with helping her daughter with her life. This experience is difficult for me as a practitioner. How can we help when the provision ends? Who supports these families when the system no longer offers funding? These questions are not all on me, I understand that. This is why I am more passionate about sharing our work. We offer free resources on our website and a free YouTube channel with information videos for all families and educators. It is my hope that the information on there is at least something people can tap into and use independently. We still stay in contact with her mother, and she shares how her daughter is doing. Some weeks are good, some not so good. Here is some feedback she gave when we were supporting her daughter.

> *She is more social at home, and we understand each other better. I think you are doing all you can at this moment. She still doesn't go out much, but converses well with staff and misses your support when it's taken away. Acceptance helps her feel in control; she knows it's OK to say no to something and people won't be angry.*

## Adapting for Need

I am always eager to grow and improve the Accept Approach to meet the needs of the children and young people we support, especially given the complexities of their needs. Many are demand-avoidant, with anxiety affecting their day-to-day lives. It is always encouraging when parents tell us that their child no longer feels this way and that acceptance-based support has been the very thing that has helped. Take, for example, recent feedback we received from Charlie's parents in Chapter 2:

> *We would never have anticipated the amount of progress our child has made. He accepts himself for who he is, knows his worth, and develops confidence not only in himself but to say no if he finds something too much. He volunteers with air cadets, bag packing in supermarkets, stands in our local village selling Poppies, has completed a remembrance parade with his squadron, and wants to travel to different destinations as a family for holidays.*

Acceptance-based support also needs time and consistency to work. We always strive to develop strategies to accommodate needs, like meeting children in their cars or adjusting session times. Sometimes, we hire staff for later hours to help where they can. We are always looking to offer more flexibility, such as evening programs, understanding that not all solutions fit everyone. However, we find that some commissioning bodies will only fund during school and term-time hours, which is something else we have to consider.

## Summary

Acceptance-based support discussed here is best understood as a developing model and not a finished solution. Life is complex for so many autistic children and young people, and I can't see it getting any easier anytime soon. The challenge of moving forward in these times is how to grow the models *without* compromising acceptance. For me, that is the biggest concern, which is why I have written this book and why I continue to stand strong in my beliefs. Acceptance-based support is working for the children and young people we support. I can't say whether it will work for every child, but I hope I have provided enough evidence to give you the confidence to try it and see for yourself.

When looking at the principles of humanistic psychology that underpin the work I do, Maslow described self-actualisation as an ongoing process rather than a fixed state, which is how I see the models I have developed. They will continue to grow into something else, something better, shaped by the voices of the children and families we support. I would like to end this chapter with some feedback from a parent of children we support, as evidence that unconditional acceptance is transformative and *life-changing*.

> *This support has been one of the few support services that has made a difference in our son's life. He is more confident within the community and is even learning how to cook. He has been able to push himself to do activities he wouldn't normally have been able to do. Before this support, he was shut away in his room, scared of life. You have helped us, as parents, understand him better, accept him for who he is, and build a better life for us. Our son was challenging, and our life was miserable before your support. You did everything in your power to help. You were calm, approachable, and patient. Your approach is perfect for our son. He has come a long way, and we hope to keep moving forward.*

## Note

1 Parental feedback referenced in this book is drawn from anonymised termly and yearly evaluations collected via SurveyMonkey. Forty-two parents completed the forms. Participation was voluntary, and surveys are configured so that no identifying information or email addresses are visible to us, allowing parents to share honest feedback about what is working, what is not, and how support could be improved.

# Conclusion

Completing this book and writing my final thoughts has not been easy. Especially when the submission deadline drew closer, my confidence began to waver, and self-doubt crept in. Who am I to write a book? What gives me the credibility to develop a model? Who am I to challenge systems that are more established than I am? Then I reminded myself of the children and young people I have supported over the years. The ones who have been through it all. The ones labelled “complex”, “demand-avoidant”, “resistant”, and “unreachable”. The ones rejected by schools, because they could not meet their needs, and turned away from mental health support, *because* they were autistic. These are the children that this book speaks for.

I am reminded of the real-life responses from children and their families who have been impacted by acceptance-based support. Where children are not rejected but accepted unconditionally, for who they are. Where the children labelled demand avoidant and resistant can learn to be in control of their lives.

I thought about Charlie in Chapter 2, who, three and a half years ago, went from being wrapped in his grey blanket, hiding from the world, and blaming himself for everything that had gone wrong, to now achieving the impossible. He had a dream, but anxiety left him helpless. This dream was formed through his obsession with a game he played day and night. This game was a flying simulator. We would often visit and sit with him as he “flew” us to different places around the world, learning independently all the settings needed to fly, master landing, and become a natural at handling the virtual pressures of flying a plane. His anxiety left him housebound, but as acceptance grew, he learned to be OK with what he could and couldn’t do.

One day, his mother called after sending me a video of a plane flying in the distance at an airfield. Bursting with pride, she told me, “*Aaron, he is flying a plane! He is completely on his own flying a plane!*” Step by step, at his own pace and in his own time, Charlie made the decision to join the air cadets, going to classes when he could. Taking exams when he felt ready. After receiving his first examination certificate, he decided to start having flying lessons, and as time went by, he felt safe and ready. Helping him take his first solo flight. This is what acceptance makes possible: breaking down boundaries not by facing anxiety, but by accepting it; not by putting in effort, but by knowing limits. On that day, Charlie went from housebound to airborne.

DOI: 10.4324/9781003686064-27

The Accept Approach completely *removes* expectations and conditions. It does not try to motivate children to step outside their comfort zones or confront their anxieties. It does not encourage children to push through their limits and *rejects* the assumption of emotional resilience, and *refutes* the implicit conformity, where children are often told "*We all have to do things we don't want to*", "*You have to push through in life, or nothing will change*", and "*If you don't apply yourself, you will fail*". These are all untrue.

With acceptance, children can be exactly who they are, without conditions. Where safety and belonging come *before* learning or engagement. Where they are accepted as *whole humans*, knowing they are free to try things they want to, in their time, and in their way. With acceptance, development emerges when anxiety and pressure are no longer the drivers of achievement. Acceptance is what happens when you stop asking children to endure and start showing them that they are *already* enough.

It's time now to act. To make a difference before another generation of autistic children and young people are failed and left behind. Autistic children and young people are not failing in education; education is failing them, and autism strategies and interventions often don't focus on offering new ways for children to learn and to engage; instead, they focus on trying to fit them into that round hole, when all they need is a square one.

I do not claim that acceptance-based support will work for everyone. That is impossible to say about any support model. I do not believe in universal solutions because they can never exist. People are just too complex for that. However, what acceptance does show in the real-life experiences and stories shared throughout the book is that children who once experienced extreme anxiety, unable to cope with the challenges and expectations placed on them, when these anxieties and pressures were "removed", significant changes began to occur.

The autistic children and young people we support are less anxious and engage more, not less. When the pressure of attending school is removed, they begin to learn again, in their own way. When responsibilities for engagement are transferred to the child, they tend to engage more with what matters to them. Knowing they are the boss of their learning and that adults support them unconditionally, they realise they no longer have to mask because they know they are accepted completely.

With acceptance, when a child is having a tough day, we remind them it's not their fault. With this simple affirmation, we have seen so many changes for many of our children. They learn to know when they are having a bad day, it's OK. They can start again tomorrow. Telling a child "*It's not your fault*" is transformative and life-changing. Just like reassuring them that it's going to be OK. Children learn this through adults supporting them, telling them, "*Don't worry, we will work this out together. It's going to be OK*". Again, a simple affirmation that is impactful and important. The message of hope allows for a child to believe in purpose, and to know that their life has meaning, even if in the moment they don't think it has.

As a parent, I am worried about my children's future. As a professional, I am concerned about doing the right thing. The decision to create new models of support was not to say, "*Here is the answer*" but rather "*I have seen enough to decide that acceptance-based support, when applied to these specific children and young people, is transformative*".

Many families describe acceptance-based support as *life-changing*, telling us it has given them their child back. Parents tell us they finally feel listened to after years of being dismissed and feeling like failures. I often hear stories of how life at home has improved dramatically, with their children calmer and happier, showing more confidence and joy that once seemed an impossibility. Professionals also share positive experiences with me, with teachers, social workers, and health practitioners saying the approach has helped them recognise other ways to support autistic children when nothing else has worked, and that they have seen positive changes in the children they support.

This book has been an invitation to stand with the thousands of autistic children and young people who have been left behind, and to *do something about it*, to stop repeating the same mistakes, and to break the cycles of failure by doing something *different.* To some, the ideas in the book may not be suitable for every setting or child, and that is how it should be. Mental health and education systems can only move forward through open inquiry, and advancement of any kind can only occur by acknowledging successes and limitations, allowing others to build upon the findings identified in my research and practice.

I wish to end this book as I began, acknowledging that acceptance-based support may not be for everyone, much like Marmite. Some of you may embrace the ideas shared; others may decide to give them a try and see what happens, and some may dismiss them altogether. I just hope you at least try it, taste it, and decide for yourself. Remember, though, that just because you may not like Marmite doesn't mean others have to stop eating it.

# Resources

# The Four Foundations of Acceptance

THE ACCEPT APPROACH

1 **REMOVE**

**Must happen first.** *Remove* whatever is making a child anxious or stressed.

**REMOVE** What can we remove to help you?

2 **REMIND**

*Remind* that 'It is not their fault" they are struggling in this moment

3 **REASSURE**

*Reassure* it is going to be ok, and you will work through this together.

4 **REAFFIRM**

*Reaffirm* that you accept them unconditionally, 100%, without conditions

*The Power of Acceptance*

THE ACCEPT APPROACH

# THE TWO RULES OF LEARNING

**During a session these are the rules to follow.**

## 1 YOU ARE THE BOSS OF YOUR LEARNING

**Direction comes from you,
Guidance comes from us.**

## 2 YOU DON'T HAVE TO DO ANYTHING YOU DON'T WANT TO DO

**Your interest sets the agenda,
our support brings it to life.**



SUPPORT MATERIAL

SUPPORT MATERIAL

THE ACCEPT APPROACH

# REMOVE YOUR ANXIETY

## 1 HOW ARE YOU FEELING NOW?

## 2 WHAT'S UP?

## 3 DRAW IT

## 4 WHAT'S CAUSING IT?

# REMOVE YOUR ANXIETY

## 5 HOW CAN WE REMOVE YOUR ANXIETY?

## 6 LET'S GET THIS SORTED

## 7 HOW ARE YOU FEELING NOW?

BETTER | OK | STILL SAD | STILL HAD ENOUGH

SUPPORT MATERIAL

THE ACCEPT APPROACH

CUT THIS OUT AND REMEMBER IT!

# REMOVE WHAT MAKES YOU ANXIOUS

*This Worksheet helps to undo internalised blame.*
***Ask yourself how many young people you support believe they are broken?***

THE ACCEPT APPROACH

# "Its Not Your Fault"

## What's up?

I am finding things difficult to understand

Tasks are hard to do

I can't cope with these demands

I am upset because.....

**Write your thoughts here**

______________________

______________________

______________________

______________________

## Reasons why <u>it is not your fault</u>

My brain works differently

I have different ideas

I don't think the same way and thats ok

I am autistic

I can't sit still, I need to move,

I have a noisy brain

I am not broken and I don't need to be fixed

I have ADHD

**Write your thoughts here**

______________________

______________________

______________________

______________________



SUPPORT MATERIAL

SUPPORT MATERIAL

THE ACCEPT APPROACH

# IS IT YOUR FAULT?

1 HOW ARE YOU FEELING NOW?

2 DO YOU THINK SOME THINGS ARE YOUR FAULT?

3 WHY DO YOU THINK THESE THINGS ARE YOUR FAULT?

THE ACCEPT APPROACH

# IS IT YOUR FAULT?

# 4 DO YOU KNOW THE FACTS ABOUT AUTISM?

FEELING OVERWHELMED

FINDING IT DIFFICULT TO CONCENTRATE

NEEDED MORE TIME TO PROCESS THINS

**NONE OF THESE ARE YOUR FAULT**

FINDING IT HARD TO SOCALISE

NOT LIKING LOUD NOISES

COPING WITH CHANGE

## AUTISM IS A NEURODEVELOPMENTAL CONDITION



SUPPORT MATERIAL

SUPPORT MATERIAL

THE ACCEPT APPROACH

# IS IT YOUR FAULT?

5 LETS SEE IF ANY OF THESE ARE YOUR FAULT?

FIND PEOPLE DIFFICULT

MAKING NOISES

FINDING IT HARD TO SOCALISE

CAN'T KEEP STILL

STAYING IN MY ROOM

NOT SLEEPING

WALKING OUT OF A LESSON/SESSION

NOT LISTENING

FEELING SAD

NOT GIVING EYE CONTACT

ANYTHING ELSE?

## NOT MY FAULT

## MY FAULT

5 HOW ARE YOU FEELING NOW?

CUT THIS OUT AND REMEMBER IT!

THE ACCEPT APPROACH

# IT IS NOT MY FAULT!



SUPPORT MATERIAL

# IT IS GOING TO BE OK

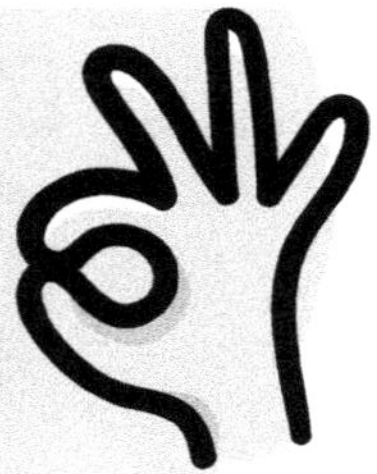

1 HOW ARE YOU FEELING NOW?

FINE | OK I GUESS | SAD | I'VE HAD ENOUGH

2 IS THERE ANYTHING YOU ARE WORRIED ABOUT?

# IT IS GOING TO BE OK

THE ACCEPT APPROACH

## 3 WHAT IS HOPE? - GOOGLE IT

## 4 HOW COULD WE APPLY HOPE TO YOUR WORRY/S?

## 5 HOW ARE YOU FEELING NOW?

BETTER | STILL OK | STILL SAD | STILL HAD ENOUGH



SUPPORT MATERIAL

SUPPORT MATERIAL

THE ACCEPT APPROACH

## CUT THIS OUT AND REMEMBER IT!

# IT IS GOING TO BE OK

*This Worksheet helps to identify what helps a child feel safe.*

# Psychological Safety Check In

**What helps you feel Safe?**

**Do you feel safe today?**

**Any examples?**

**What can we do to help you when you don't feel safe?**

*This Worksheet allows for the child to open up honestly about how they feel about the adult.*
***There is space for honesty without consequence.***

# Trusting Adults Check In

**What helps you trust an adult?**

**What would break trust?**

**Is there anything I can do to?**

*This worksheet focuses only on the present moment.*
*You sit alongside the young person and explore what feels too much right now in the moment, without judgment.*
***Remember No conditions, no expectations, just unconditional acceptance of how they feel.***

THE ACCEPT APPROACH

# What Is Too Much Right Now?

What is too much right now?

Is there anything we can do together to help?



SUPPORT MATERIAL

SUPPORT MATERIAL

*This worksheet focuses on one clear principle: nothing else happens until anxiety is removed.*
*This reinforces the foundation that removing anxiety is what is needed before anything else can happen.*
***You are not offering solutions. Your role is to remove whatever is causing anxiety/stress and by doing anything a child needs for them to feel psychologically safe.***

THE ACCEPT APPROACH

# "What needs to be *removed* for you to feel safe?"

# WHAT'S UP?

## 1 WHAT'S UP?

## 2 WHAT WOULD YOU DO TO SORT THIS OUT?

## 3 WHAT CAN I DO?

THE ACCEPT APPROACH

SUPPORT MATERIAL

SUPPORT MATERIAL

*This Worksheet is to be used to identify purposeful aims which can be placed into a child's SEED plan.*

THE ACCEPT APPROACH

# SOCIAL FOCUS

Use this document to *reflect* on the child's preferred ways of being social.

You are not focusing on what *you* think they need to learn to be social, you are trying to understanding their *natural* ways of communicating/socialising. Without condition.

## What is *their* social?

Ask the child - What are your preferred ways to be with others?

## YOUR SOCIAL WAY

SEED PLAN FOCUS

What below best describes their way of being social?
Don't forget to add anything that may be missed in the 'other' box.

| | |
|---|---|
| I like to be alone | I like being near other people but not talking to them. |
| I prefer not to talk to other people | I feel safer in quiet spaces. |
| I prefer to work on my own | I like to choose when I talk. |
| I enjoy being around others | I prefer adults to come and speak to me quietly. |
| I like to control what I am learning | I communicate better when I feel calm. |
| I like to talk about my favourite subjects | I do not like putting my hand up in class. |
| I need time to think before I respond. | I listen better when I am not expected to look at you. |
| Other | |

SEED PLAN FOCUS *e.g. Prefers to be alone, so looking for more moments in the day they can have this. Remove expectations to work with others.*

THE ACCEPT APPROACH

# EMOTION FOCUS

- Use this document to *reflect* on their view of how they feel emotionally.
- How do they use emotions to cope with issues?

## What is *your* emotional response?

- Ask the child - If you were in total control how would you prefer to react to issues/problems/situations?

## YOUR EMOTIONAL RESPONSE

SEED PLAN FOCUS

Pick the suggestions here that most support who you are. Don't forget to add anything that may be missed in the 'other' box.

| | |
|---|---|
| I can easily become angry | I notice emotions in my body before my thoughts. |
| I can go quiet when I am upset | I find emotions confusing. |
| I will walk out of rooms when upset | I am anxious most of the time |
| My emotions change quickly. | I need time to work out my feelings |
| I like to pace up and down when stressed | I hide my emotions from others |
| It takes me a long time to calm down | I get low a lot of the time. |
| I shut down when things feel too much. | I feel safe when adults are calm. |
| Other | |

SEED PLAN FOCUS *e.g. Easily upset and needs longer periods of time to process emotions. Whaty cna we do to reduce demand and strssors that triggeryour emotional response? How can we set up a way of you being able to go and calm down that helps you the best way?.*

SUPPORT MATERIAL

SUPPORT MATERIAL

THE ACCEPT APPROACH

# EDUCATION FOCUS

Use this document to *reflect* on how they want to learn and what education support they feel they need.

How do they feel about learning, e.g. what do they like, what don't they like.

## What are your Education goals?

Ask the child- If you were in total control, what would you like to learn? What would you not want to learn?

## YOUR EDUCATION GOALS

SEED PLAN FOCUS

Pick the suggestions here that most support who you are. Don't forget to add anything that may be missed in the 'other' box.

| | |
|---|---|
| I do not like school/college | I can only do work for short periods of time |
| I like some school but not all lessons | If I don't like a topic I find it hard to learn about it |
| I tend to walk out of lessons and classrooms when stressed/anxious | I can feel anxious in school |
| I am happier if I am doing what I want to do | I tend to shut down a lot during lessons |
| I do not not like writing | I find it hard to concentrate and listen in class |
| I like to work with computers, laptops, iPads | I don't like to be here all of the time |

Other

SEED PLAN FOCUS *e.g. Hates some lessons. Look at ways of removing the lessons. Can we set up something else for them to do instead? Focus on their favourite subjects more than the ones they do not engage with.*

# DEVELOPMENT FOCUS

- Use this document to discuss how the support is going.
- Discuss ways we can improve anything, or continue with what is working well.
- Ask the child - How do you feel our sessions are going?

## YOUR DEVELOPMENT FOCUS

SEED PLAN FOCUS

Pick the suggestions here that most support who you are. Don't forget to add anything that may be missed in the 'other' box.

| | |
|---|---|
| It is going great | I feel you accept me. |
| You understand me | I am getting more confident |
| I think you need to listen a bit more | I am learning to like myself more |
| I am fine, it is going ok. | You don't listen to me |
| I want you to focus on other things a bit more. | I see things are going to be ok |
| I still don't feel accepted by you | I am still finding things difficult |
| Other | |

SEED PLAN FOCUS *Development focus - how are things going, what are we going to improve on, or carry on doing.*

# Index

Note: page numbers in *italics* indicate figures and page numbers in **bold** indicate tables on the corresponding page.

For Product Safety Concerns and Information please contact our EU
representative GPSR@taylorandfrancis.com
Taylor & Francis Verlag GmbH, Kaufingerstraße 24, 80331 München, Germany

www.ingramcontent.com/pod-product-compliance
Ingram Content Group UK Ltd.
Pitfield, Milton Keynes, MK11 3LW, UK
UKHW022021180926
475701UK00005B/971
* 9 7 8 1 0 4 1 1 6 7 1 3 6 *